Virtually Free Marketing

Virtually Free Marketing

Harnessing the power of the Web for your small business

Philip R Holden

A & C Black • London

First published in Great Britain 2008

A&C Black Publishers Ltd
38 Soho Square, London W1D 3HB
www.acblack.com

Copyright © Philip R Holden, 2008

A CIP record for this book is available from the British Library.

ISBN: 9-781-4081-0072-1

This book is produced using paper that is made from wood grown
in managed, sustainable forests. It is natural, renewable and
recyclable. The logging and manufacturing processes conform to the
environmental regulations of the country of origin.

Design by Fiona Pike, Pike Design, Winchester
Typeset by RefineCatch Ltd, Bungay, Suffolk
Printed and bound in Great Britain by CPI Cox & Wyman, Reading,
RG1 8EX

CONTENTS

328540

ACKNOWLEDGEMENTS

I'd like to thank all the people who have contributed directly and indirectly to this book. As far as possible, I've tried to name-check them in the text and to put a link to their own work online.

I urge you to visit all of the links in the book as you go along because whilst I'm presenting a snapshot of what is happening in the Web world, the real chroniclers of new developments are out there writing every day and night and, in some cases, actually making it happen.

The following lovely people wrote useful things for me from their own experiences or as a result of research, responded to my stupid questions or have otherwise been useful in what they wrote or discussed online:

Julia Kosela, of Infrared Group and herself an accomplished entrepreneurial marketer, contributed much of Chapter 11. Chris Rojas of Crux Photography gave me a glimpse into his business and flickr.com. Dave McClure allowed me to reproduce his insightful map in Chapter 2. Kulveer Taggar of boso.com and auctomatic.com (see Chapter 6) shared his thoughts on promotion, especially on Facebook for Chapters 7 and 8. John Unger of HeatSeeker Technology Partners and David Mullings of realvibezmedia.com gave me some insight into their use of social media too. Nataliya Yakushev of Webmill pointed me in the direction of some useful promotional techniques. Ina Stanley of Virtual Sidekick showed me how realising the benefits of new Web tools can reshape a business. David Fireman discussed and listened to ideas about marketing his lovely company Mr Humbug – see Chapter 4. Paul Harrison made me jealous by describing his relaxed approach to his eBay business for Chapter 6. Also David House of Banquet Records and Ina Steiner of auctionbytes. com shared their experiences of social networking.

The following are referred to in the text and also well worth a visit:

Hugh MacLeod of gapingvoid.com, king of blog marketing and

cartooning, and Guy Kawasaki (guykawasaki.com) author of *Art of the Start,* influential blogger and e-entrepreneur; both inspirational. Kfir Pravda (pravdam.com) is a bit of a Facebook guru, as is Justin Smith of insidefacebook.com whilst Mari Smith of facebookcoach.com gives great 'podclasses'.

Thanks also to Nick Wilde – 'brother' at www.pleasewalkonthegrass. com and Greenwich – for urging me to take on this book and promoting it to anyone who would listen and to Lisa Carden at A&C Black for being enthusiastic, insistent . . . and patient.

Of course any mistakes in the following chapters are entirely mine – as is the responsibility for the omission of anyone from these acknowledgements.

Finally, but most of all, I'd like to thank Annie and the boys; the best social network ever!

Note

All the prices, Web addresses and other information presented in *Virtually Free* were correct at the time of going to press.

INTRODUCTION

Facebook – the social networking website (see Chapter 8) was recently conservatively valued at around £15 million. eBay, itself worth billions, paid £14 billion for a company offering phone calls over the Internet. Bebo – which I guess you may have heard of but never visited – sold for $850 million.

It all sounds like a gold rush or a bubble, and some commentators have suggested that a few of the websites currently grabbing the headlines won't be around very long. But this book isn't about being the next Jeff Bezos (the founder of Amazon) or Mark Zuckerberg (the founder of Facebook). Instead, this book is for the owner or manager of any small business, club, non-profit or social enterprise; it's for you, whether you run a one-person concern or a 500-employee business. It's for anyone who thinks that there is something in Amazon or Facebook or any one of hundreds of other sites and products that might just work for them.

There is; and it can.

What this book does – and what you have to do

Many of the ideas and insights here are gleaned from the Web itself. So I think it's only fair, along the way, to give you the links to the sources of much of this wisdom and to the products and services themselves. That way you can check for yourself what we're talking about, and the originators get some credit too. There's an awful lot of genius out there and I wouldn't want to steal their thunder.

Of course that means that you need to read and surf to get a complete introduction to online marketing. You can read this in bed if you like, but don't forget to scribble notes and follow things up on your computer.

To be honest, this isn't a *complete* guide. There's no shortage of advice online, some of it extremely detailed, but this book is more like a road atlas to help you get an idea of where you are going and the route you might take.

This book is, of course, about marketing. But it's also inevitably about software that you have to install or access online. Believe me, I'm not a geek (despite what some colleagues may say). So I'm actually not concerned too much about *how* the websites and tools here work: more interesting is *why* they might work for *you* and your business. To get even more specific, we're exploring how they work for *marketing* you and your business.

I try to give you an insight into how you make some of the software and websites work – sometimes that's a step-by-step guide – so that you can then explore for yourself. Where it's been possible, I've included examples drawn from real people's experiences making (or sometimes saving) money at *virtually* no cost. At other times I've set up examples online myself; indeed, for almost every product or site explored here I've signed up and tested it myself – and checked out some alternatives.

You also have the opportunity to speak to me and my colleagues and to write about your own experience by visiting www.pleasewalkonthegrass. com. Naturally there's a blog (see Chapter 3) and a forum (see Chapter 12), so plenty of opportunity for you to tell us your experience or to question us further on what we're talking about. We welcome all comments.

And what is marketing?

If you don't already have a firm idea of what marketing really is for a small business (and why it's different to the marketing done by Heinz and Unilever), read Chapter 2 closely. Even if you think you know what marketing is, Chapter 2 is still worth a look because it introduces a strategic approach to marketing. What you get out of the Web depends partly on what you put in, and partly on what you aim for. Just in case you need reminding, marketing is not just promotion or selling, it's everything about your business that relates to customers, so in a small business that's pretty much everything.

If your concern is to get more customers, keep hold of the customers you have, and to sell more (more profitably), then you should find something of use in the following chapters. If your aim is to compete head-to-head with Microsoft or News International, then possibly you won't.

One final warning. Things are changing, rapidly. This book presents my opinions regarding online marketing, and I may be wrong – if not today, then tomorrow, when a new website or application bursts onto the scene and changes everything. However, I believe that if you want to catch the next big wave to your advantage, you need to be out there now. This book should get you started.

CHAPTER 1

MARKETING AND THE 'NEW' WEB

The world is changing.

It's not just that the World Wide Web happened: the fact is 'it' is still happening – evolving. It will have changed by the time you finish reading this chapter. We're not so much feeling the aftershock of a revolution as still living through it. The revolution hasn't just affected how we communicate, but it has had an impact on our definition of what we consider to be a business, a product or a market.

But it's so difficult to say anything new about the Web. And it's difficult not to sound like those snake-oil merchants you read in the business press every week.

One problem is that for many of us, as *customers*, it's all become too familiar. E-mail, shopping, surfing, downloading music and watching online videos are pretty much everyday experiences in the developed world – we just don't notice it as new. The other reason is that there is just too much 'newness' to take in.

As *business people*, no sooner have we come to terms with the necessity of using e-mail and having a website (and not everyone has) than we're perplexed by the buzz about social networking. Other people have swish websites, make money on eBay, know how e-commerce works and 'microblog' their daily life from their BlackBerry®.

Unfortunately, if you thought you could just be left alone to sell cars or flower arrangements or photography services or houses or garden design or antiques (or *almost* anything), recruit members or raise funds, your business has already been affected by the Web.

So what's changed?

Well, clearly there has been a massive increase in the uptake of Web access (especially broadband) so there are just more people connecting more easily (that is, more quickly, more often and more capable of handling big chunks of data) than ever before. Access to the Web is increasingly available through mobile devices and TVs – or TV is being watched online and on mobiles. It all points to the necessity of a Web presence; you cannot afford for your business to be difficult to find.

Secondly, the step-change of what is known as Web 2.0 – like the latest release of a software product – has been to increasingly *involve* people (like you *and* your customers) in deciding for themselves what goes on the Web – what's called 'user-generated content' or the 'read-write Web'. This second change is crucial to marketing.

Social networking sites such as Facebook and Bebo are examples of Web 2.0. But this is not primarily about a new technology (although developments like Ajax allow for improvements in usability), it is about entrepreneurs trying to make the technology do new things . . . just because they can.

O'Reilly, a leading technology consultancy (www.oreilly.com), pointed out the scale of change in their 2004 Web 2.0 conference – in fact 'Web 2.0' was a phrase they invented – and since then changes have been accelerating. In late 2006 they described the growth of blogs, user-generated content, podcasts and wikis as 'user-driven, intelligent Web'. They are already arguing over the definition of Web 3.0.

What will work?

For some, it's tempting to bury their head in the sand and try to ignore what's happening. In any case, the big success stories are high-tech products and services, aren't they?

Not necessarily. As we'll see in later chapters, a large number of small companies and organisations – some very small – are making use of Web 2.0 to change the way they run their business, even the way they think about their business. They could be in almost any sector – food retailers, plumbers, engineers, builders, musicians, artists: literally anything.

Way, way back in the 1990s (the Palaeolithic era as far as the Web is concerned), some very astute people – Joseph Pine, Don Peppers and Martha Rogers[1] – were far-sighted enough to predict the kinds of business that could benefit from technological advances still then in their infancy.

Pine and co identified that the ubiquity of information technology – the *World Wide* Web – had led to a shift in emphasis from markets and products to customers and service, and in particular that technology allowed customers to interrogate information and required businesses to provide it. This in itself, they argue, becomes the market. Instead of vying for each purchase by a customer we could, in effect, be competing for their information needs. Instead of having a share of a market, we could have a dominant share of a number of customers.

If this sounds a little esoteric, don't despair. As you read through the rest of this book you'll find plenty of examples that demonstrate that online marketing *is* about interaction and engagement and getting genuinely involved with customers, and we'll clarify this in Chapter 2. As much as you might be an expert in *supplying* cars or flower arrangements or photography services or houses or garden design or antiques, you now also need to be proficient in *communicating* that expertise.

Why? Well simply because customers are not out there waiting patiently for you to sell to them: they are online looking for what they want . . . at the right price . . . delivered tomorrow. In other words, customers are becoming far more active partners in the process of marketing.

Let's look at how Pine and Co categorised the products and services of this new economy.

Complex products or services. Those which can be made to order – when a supplier can advise the customer online and remember the

---

[1] Pine II, B J, D Peppers, et al. (1995). 'Do you want to keep your customers for ever?' *Harvard Business Review* (March/April): 103–114.

information for the future and when, perhaps, the customer can play with different specifications, finishes, delivery terms etc. Here the product isn't just the box that's delivered at the end of the process, it's the support in making a decision.

> *Who thought you could get a fitted kitchen online or a bespoke conservatory? You can, and increasingly customers want to see what their kitchen or conservatory might look like and, though they may visit a store, like to be able to 'play' with the design (see Ikea's room design applications at http://tinyurl.com/2pnhdf)*

'Big ticket' items. Expensive purchases where hunting around can make a huge difference in purchase price.

> *As we'll see in the next chapter, 'expensive' is all relative, and for many consumers means infrequent purchases such as their car or holiday. How many people don't now look on the Web to compare options, itineraries, hotels and prices?*

Digitisable products and services. Anything that can be 'delivered' online is now, inevitably, online.

> *Nearly 25 years ago, when Joseph Pine and pals were writing, NetBank[2] was just about to launch. Interestingly, it went bust in 1997, but every mainstream financial organisation is now online to some extent. If you offer a service, some or all of it could be online – not to save you money but to make the service more useful for some clients.*

Luxury and speciality products. Products that aren't easy to find and for which you might have very specific requirements.

---

[2] For the history of NetBank, see http://en.wikipedia.org/wiki/NetBank.

Luxury foods, clothing and even jewellery for your pet can be bought online. Indeed, it wouldn't be worthwhile to open a physical store for 'Sparkly Stuff' in your local high street, but it's well worth them having a website and an eBay store (www.sparkly-stuff.co.uk).

Retailing services. Shopping that is seen as a drag because you don't really want to schlep around the stores, or you would like to be able to go from store to store comparing prices and features.

Last Christmas in the UK, 25 per cent of all electrical goods were sold online. Search all the stores you know, and some you don't, for the best price and you'll be tempted to buy online just to secure the best deal. Even if you buy in the real world, your choice of store will be influenced by your online search.

Pine, Peppers and Rogers therefore suggested that businesses needed to develop:

- *an* information *strategy – knowing what information your customer needs, and providing it*
- *a* production/delivery *strategy – knowing how the product or service (including information) can get to the customer, despite their dealing with you at a distance*
- *an* organisational *strategy – what needs to happen in your business to enable everything else to happen for the customer, and*
- *an* assessment *strategy – a way of monitoring success (and failure)*

to which we should add a **marketing** strategy (focusing on customers) to steer all the above in the direction your company needs to follow in order to achieve its aims. We'll come back to this in the next chapter, but for now it's worth bearing in mind that if you are to take advantage of this new marketing world, your business *will* change – inside and out.

In this environment, where some products can be digitised but where information is key, there is the possibility for endless subtle variations and a mass of data instantly accessible, globally.

More recently, Chris Anderson (http://tinyurl.com/2okqbk) has coined the phrase 'freeconomics' to describe the revolution of digitisation which leads to an inversion of the normal rules of business. It enables companies to give away significant products (which cost relatively little to reproduce) in anticipation of relatively small future revenues. That income can come as a small amount from many people or it can be a recognisably fair amount for a fairly conventional job – like fixing your wiring.

However, if you need to find an electrical engineer in your area with experience in fitting out factories, a *mass* of digitised data isn't what you need. You really just need to be able to *search* a directory, quickly, for exactly the half-dozen or so you want, to get a recommendation and some reassurance about their skills or reliability. And you might even pay to have those results quickly.

It's worth thinking about this for a moment. In searching for that engineer, it's not just information you want, it's the ability to *get the right bit* of information – including some insight into how they work, their reliability and so on. Providing that is a service that could be developed and tailored to your needs by someone with access to the whole directory. It could be automated.

That directory is, in effect, the Web. And that someone needn't be a big company; they just need to be there when they're needed.

Of course your business is different, isn't it?

Well, yes and no. The challenge in developing your business using the tools of the new Web is to be able to see the information needs of your customers and respond to them – sometimes before they have realised their need themselves. This is *in addition* to buying and selling cars, arranging bouquets, taking photographs, selling houses, recruiting supporters and so on.

The crucial point is that your understanding of those particular needs of a particular group of customers – or maybe just one or two individuals – can be your distinguishing feature. If it means that those customers don't need to go elsewhere, then it's what marketing calls a 'sustainable competitive advantage': the holy grail of business.

Some of the ideas in this book

In the next chapter we'll go on to think about developing a marketing plan that will work in this new environment. First, though, I'd like to offer some ideas of this new marketing that have arisen in the course of writing this book.

Some of these come from discussions with colleagues, including Nick Wilde (co-author of *Marketing & PR on a Shoestring*, published by A & C Black in 2007), whilst others come via some online and real-world contacts, some of whom are even closer to the coalface. There is probably a whole other book in examining the impact of these new business principles on companies, but (fortunately perhaps) we don't have the time or the space to explore them. Instead we'll just summarise them. As you read the rest of this book, bear them in mind and be thankful that yours is a small business or organisation – these principles are a thousand times more difficult for big organisations to accept.

Truth and honesty. When we come on to talk about a brand for a small business, this is what we mean. You may not be the best (or cheapest) plumbers in the world but . . . what's the 'but'? You're the quickest, the most reliable, the friendliest? If there isn't something that you're proud to be truthful about, then you're in trouble.

Be *part* of the market. Don't think of the market as 'out there': be in amongst it. If you don't use your product every day, you don't know as much as your customers. If it's not a product you can use every day, then play with it, test it to destruction, update and improve it regularly.

Never dismiss people who are 'just looking'. They are 'just looking' because that's what you do before you buy, and the more you look, the easier it is to make a buying decision. People who search for information related to your product or service are actually trying to fulfil their information needs – it has a real value for them. By helping them 'just look' you can be there when they make a decision to buy.

Don't be afraid to sell, but only sell to people who want to buy. Selling involves going on and on . . . until you close a deal. Marketing involves finding people who want to buy and helping them. Just occasionally, the help becomes a more important product than the product itself.

Don't let technology create distance. The technology is central – if customers are already using it, then *you* can. But don't ignore the value of face-to-face contact, or by telephone or the occasional handwritten thank-you note.

Give people tools to complain. What do people do when they don't like you or your service? They probably tell other people. You need to hear their complaints and respond.

If you want people to enthuse about you, enthuse with them. What do people do when they do like you? Probably nothing. Just enjoy talking about your product and give your best customers the ability to broadcast their joy. You can even enthuse about something that goes wrong and the pleasure of putting it right!

For every strength your product has, admit a weakness. This seems like more of a character-building exercise than anything. However, if you're being honest you will want to tell customers what it is that you *can't* do. That way neither of you wastes time.

Don't pretend you know what people want. Just ask them – all the time. Oh, and give it to them.

You don't have to be good at marketing to be good at what you do. Don't get distracted by what big businesses call 'marketing'. Finding and looking after customers is one of the things you do, because you're a small business and you have to. If there are other things you can't do (like actually making the product), outsource it.

Being connected is more important than advertising. Connections are for your support and growth as well as getting customers. In fact, the two are very often the same. Really enthusiastic customers are priceless for your business – consider them partners. Likewise cherish the really great colleagues who can get enthusiastic about your business: the one who rescues your computer when it crashes, the one who designs your ads, the one who sorts out your accounts each month, the one who drives the delivery van – they are all assets. Never begrudge them their share.

Remember that your success may contain the seeds of your industry's destruction. Doing things a little better than the next firm won't get you very far. Doing things differently and ten times better might, but it might also do you out of a job. Are you ready for that?

Imagine you were a plumber and you developed a clip-on device that instantly stopped the flow of water in a pipe? What a great idea. If you were really successful your plumbing work would dry up (!). So what – you'd get rich?

Now suppose someone else invents it instead, and starts marketing it. What do you do? Hold on until you can plumb no more? No, pick up the phone, get some supplies and start selling it (or giving it) to your best customers because they need and deserve it. You're making their life better and you're positioning yourself as the person who cared enough to bring this revolutionary device to their attention.

You can't please everyone (so don't try). But make sure you *really* please the ones you can. Don't forget, in the end you want people to voluntarily give you money and to believe with all their heart that they've done the right thing in doing so. So be nice, since everything you do has an effect on the customer's sense of justice, fairness, their happiness and their wealth.

Swimming against the tide is tiring: try surfing. Don't expect to get everything right or even to be in the same kind of business a year later. When you discover customers whose needs are unmet, then you've found a seam of gold, even if you struggle to know what you can do for them. When you *do* meet their needs, they become *your* customers and you can choose to follow them or let them drift away.

Can you do all this 'virtually free'?

Well, yes. Small businesses usually survive on the commitment and time of a few important people, and that's how you'll begin to exploit the possibilities of some of the sites and technologies in this book.

If you really are starting from scratch then look at pp. 246–250 which tell you about some of the equipment and software that can be useful. Even here some of it is free or virtually so.

Beyond the basic equipment, however, you may spend a little money here and there following the ideas in the following chapters. But you should do so only when you've established that the benefits to your customers, and therefore your business, outweigh the costs. The biggest investment you will be making in your business is your time and talent.

CHAPTER 2

WHAT KIND OF MARKETING ARE YOU DOING?

By now you should have an idea of the approach taken in this book, and you may want to fast-forward to start putting some of the later chapters to practical use. That's fine, but I'd just advise you to take a moment to think about what you want to achieve.

Most of all, you need to think about where your business is now and where you would (realistically) like it to be over the next few months and years. I hate to use the word this early on, but you need to have a 'strategy' – which is to say, you need to have a sense of direction pointing towards your objectives.

To make it even simpler: if you want to get something out of your business, you have to have customers putting something in. So your business strategy is, in fact, a customer strategy. Let me clarify this further. Of course your business has to be efficient; the product or service needs to be looked at again and again to make sure you're not wasting time or money in its production. You probably need some technical ability to do what you do, you may need for employees, and you obviously don't want costs to get out of hand. You also need a firm grasp of the money coming in and going out of the company, and it's absolutely essential to keep the tax authorities happy. So, yes, you need production, personnel and finance skills.

Unfortunately, making any of these aspects of running a business more efficient won't help unless you have, keep and continue to recruit customers. I'm not saying the other things aren't important, but I am saying this book is about *marketing*, which is a central function of any business – getting and keeping customers.

Now for some people, this is like saying 'go out there and sell, sell, sell!', but I'm suggesting a rather different view. Think about all the reasons why your customers should come to you time and time again. Take a piece of paper and draw a vertical line down it; all the reasons why people would buy things from you (and not from others) can go down the left-hand side, and all the reasons they'll go to someone else go down on the other – pros and cons.

You see, customers *always* have a choice. Increasingly, however, this choice is not simply between one supplier and another, but between a whole range of alternatives. Products or services like new cars, TVs, holidays, haircuts, meals out and music CDs or downloads are not necessities, but are so-called 'discretionary' purchases. Even supposedly mundane things like clothing, plumbing, car maintenance and opticians can fall into this category. How long can you put up with that dripping tap while you're saving up for a holiday?

Many people look at such purchases as things that can be put off, and the money that otherwise would have been used goes elsewhere. In a recession, it's even clearer that consumers look closely at alternatives, and one alternative is not spending at all. As a small business, almost everything and everyone is in competition with you.

This view doesn't mean, however, that you should give up. If you really want to focus on what your company is about and what you want to achieve, then I can do no better than recommend you read *Marketing & PR*, which is especially for small businesses. It takes you through the simple but effective process of developing a marketing strategy.

Rather than go into a long discussion of what strategy is, I want to set out some basic principles of a customer-based strategy which you can explore further in *Marketing & PR* if you choose to.

What is marketing?

For the moment, let's stick with the simple truths about marketing. Your aims are one of the following:

a) to get more customers

b) to get more business from your existing customers

or both a) and b).

It sounds simple but there are, of course, some complexities. First and foremost, existing customers are, generally speaking, more profitable than new ones. To put it another way, it costs more to get a new customer than it does to hold on to an existing one.

Many companies seem to forget this and spend much of their marketing budget (however small it may be) on prospecting and selling to new customers while neglecting the people who are actually paying the bills – loyal, quiet, uncomplaining customers.

Without going into great detail, this means that existing customers can start wandering, looking for someone who *will* look after them. And there are plenty of competitors out there (and on the Web) to find.

So, if you are already in business, you should probably start by asking yourself how you can get your customers to stay with you and, ideally, give you more business.

Some of the tools described later in this book help you to do that. But a word of warning. You can't *force* your customers to use Web-based tools or to carry out their transactions online, they have to *want* to. In fact, they should be using these tools already – Trip Advisor (www.tripadvisor.co.uk) or Last Minute (www.lastminute.com) for holidays, Autotrader (www.autotrader.co.uk) for cars, PrimeLocation (www.primelocation.com) for houses and eBay (www.ebay.co.uk) for . . . well, almost anything. There are some obvious places where a mass of customers are, now, ready to buy – so why spend time and money trying to get them to go elsewhere?

Your first action point could be to find the sites where your kind of customer goes and see how you could be a part of that. Some of these are mentioned in later chapters.

A sense of purpose

There are two ways of understanding your business. Most small businesses are very good at looking at what they do day to day. After all, no one has quite the understanding you do of your floristry business, or your knowledge of industrial weighing machines . . . do they?

The inside-out view is very good for thinking about what you want to achieve. Indeed, it is often the first and only strategic thinking small businesses' founders do. When they start, they have ambition – perhaps about getting away from a job in a big company; perhaps about realising a dream. In fact, according to some research, the majority of entrepreneurs start up because they anticipate the enjoyment of creating something – like amazing flower arrangements or incredibly accurate weighing machines. You should hold on to this feeling.

As your business develops, it is this unique view of the business that you need to express. Your dreams and beliefs are central to what customers come to see as your brand, and will help to distinguish you from the competition.

Guy Kawasaki (author of *Art of the Start* and e-entrepreneur – www.guykawasaki.com) says the most successful businesses aren't out to make money, primarily: they are out to make meaning, to improve quality of life, to right wrongs and to prevent the end of something good.

That may sound a little way-out for your business, but if you stop and think for a while, you'll probably admit that your motivation is more complex than simply making money. We don't need to spend too much time thinking about this but you'll see in later chapters that this approach – which I'd argue is more familiar to small businesses – is absolutely in tune with the Web 2.0 philosophy.

You need to think about what your unique position in the market could be. This is your brand. You could be, for example, a plumber who also plays in a rock band or a computer engineer who goes morris dancing. You could be a florist who's very keen on the traditional meaning of flowers or you could be a motor mechanic who is a coffee connoisseur.

Now, if you have this unique – maybe slightly odd – mix of interests and skills then you should give full expression to them. The florist could, and should, make a big thing about 'translating' bouquets (for example, yellow carnations stand for rejection or disappointment!) and could offer guidance in selecting flowers and share resources on folklore. The motor mechanic had better get a great coffee machine for his or her waiting customers!

The point here is that whatever you are known for (over and above the basic service or product you offer) will help you stand out: it gives your brand another dimension.

Like others, Guy Kawasaki also argues that your organisation needs a mantra – three or four words, not a mission statement – to sum up your 'purpose': what makes you get up every day and do the best job. Again, we discuss this in *Marketing & PR*, suggesting an exercise that might make clear what it is you want to achieve.

However, your sense of purpose is only one half of the equation. On the other side you need insight into the needs and wants of a number of customers[1].

Outside in

The outside-in view is really about looking at your customers. Or, rather, it's putting yourself in the customer's shoes to see what it is they want and need, how they go about searching for it, and how they buy and use it.

Now normally it's next to impossible to see exactly what customers are looking for; you really only get to know customers who come into close contact with your business. Actually, that first point isn't quite true. We won't go into detail here but, if you're online, you *do* have an opportunity to find out what people are looking for – because it's easier to ask and easier to monitor. We'll deal with this a little more in different ways in Chapters 5, 6 and 7, and when we come to talk about social networking in Chapters 8 and 9.

One of the great things about being online is the amount of customer and market information you can access without leaving your desk. But

---

[1] The classic discussion of this approach can be found in Andrew Campbell and Marcus Alexander's important paper in *Harvard Business Review* Nov/Dec 1997, 'What's wrong with strategy?'.

you should also talk to customers, directly or online. We touch on these opportunities in most chapters. This aspect of the outside-in view is what customers expect to see when they look at your business.

For the moment you should think back to those principles mentioned in Chapter 1. What is the one thing you're known for? What can you say about your business that few (perhaps no one else) can say?

By the way, there are some things you don't have to say – *reliable* aircraft engines, *safe* toys – because these are the things that customers *expect*. According to Frederick Herzberg (you can see an account at http://tinyurl.com/429slw), these kinds of expected features are 'hygiene' factors. As far as customers are concerned, if they're not there, they won't buy . . . but their presence isn't enough on its own.

Incidentally, if you want to reassure your customers that you do adhere to certain minimum standards, then you need to look at all the quality assurance schemes which many industries have. You could also look at the Office of Fair Trading (http://tinyurl.com/2th9yl) which has recently developed a scheme to approve of codes of practice from various trades.

Nevertheless, the presence of these 'hygiene' factors alone isn't enough to make the sale. For that you need 'motivators'.

As far as marketing is concerned, motivation – the thing that makes a customer buy – is the holy grail (another one!?). It's fairly clear that it isn't just one thing anyway: more likely it's a whole cluster of things that are often alluded to as the 'marketing mix' (also covered in more depth in *Marketing & PR*). Here's a quick checklist to help you consider these questions from your customers' point of view:

- ***What are the customers' needs?***
- ***What is the cost to the customers of meeting those needs?***
- ***How can meeting their needs be made more convenient for them?***
- ***What are their communication needs?***

By answering each of these for all the various customers you may serve, you can develop a checklist that at the very least avoids you making simple mistakes. As we see in Chapter 6, for example, even the way you label an article for sale has a direct impact on the number of customers who will look at it or consider buying it – and therefore try to buy it.

If, for example, your customer is looking for a new 'Head' brand tennis racquet as cheaply as possible, you could simply list a 'cheap tennis racquet' and wait for people to show interest.

You could, however, list it as new: include the brand name, include photos that show the racquet in full and in close up (to show the branding and the size) and maybe even a picture of the appropriate tennis star in action with the same racquet. You'd also say something about how quickly you dispatch it and how well it's packed and insured. You'd also make sure you respond to enquiries immediately and helpfully *and* make sure you follow up the sale to be sure the purchaser is happy.

Beyond all the very tangible needs you can identify in this relatively simple sale (cheap branded tennis racquet), the 'hygiene factor' most likely to be missing online is a sense of security. How does the buyer know that you are going to honour the deal? How do you meet their most basic need of reassurance?

A sense of direction

A successful small business also has to have a good sense of where their customers already are and therefore what they have to do to get close to them.

In the case of a start-up business, that of course means knowing where the most immediate sales can be gained, and you may be in the position of needing to sell products as quickly as possible. Depending on the type of product or service, online markets may be the right place to start – Chapter 6, for example, looks at the ready-made markets eBay and Amazon – but we'd advise you not to get *too* focused on quick one-off transactions.

So that you can stabilise your business and build it for the future, you will also want to look for sustainable 'streams' of customers. The customers that will come back to you time and again (simply because they are frequent purchasers of your product or service, and you look after them) are vitally important to you. Beyond your first sale, you need to start looking to the longer-term goals such as looking after the customers you have and finding more like them.

Over and above simply selling, a marketing strategy involves looking around for concentrations of customers and potential customers to see where future profits and growth might come from. The good news is that the Web is a great help in finding these.

Mapping *your* market

To help you develop your strategy, in *Marketing & PR* we introduced the impressive-sounding 'Holden-Wilde matrix' (opposite) which is nothing more than a way of visualising the size, accessibility and (potential) profitability of groups of customers – what you might call markets or segments.

Looking at the top axis, you could place your business on a scale going left to right according to whether there are few customers in the world (and/or purchases are made infrequently) or there are many customers (and/or purchases are made more frequently).

On the left-hand axis, a similar scale shows whether customers look upon these purchases as relatively large or small. In a sense, this scale indicates how involved customers are in making purchase decisions.

Of course, as you can see, this 'map' is oversimplified. But it actually functions at several levels. Initially you can look at your business and compare it with others – for example, direct competitors. You can go on to compare various types of customers buying, perhaps, different products and services from you. With a little more application, you can also use it to identify areas of growth.

The crucial lesson from applying the Holden-Wilde matrix is that each of the 'clusters' of customers, represented by their different relative positions on the grid, demand different marketing plans – different marketing actions to be taken.

RELATIVELY	Few customers Infrequent purchase	Many customers More frequent purchase
Large transactions (from the point of view of the customer)	1 There are few customers who buy what we make and they generally spend a lot. They're highly involved.	2 There are many customers (and therefore competitors) and the product is still expensive. They're less involved because it's pretty accessible.
Small transactions (from the point of view of the customer)	3 This is an infrequent purchase, but people don't see it as high value. However they're involved because it's not routine.	4 A lot of people buy this frequently and it's not valued highly. They're not involved because it's routine.

Figure 1 *A simple explanation of the 'quadrants' of the Holden-Wilde matrix*[2]*.*

In the context of online marketing, you are unlikely to identify a group of customers who are currently not served by someone. Online or not, there are very few customers waiting with bated breath for you to find them.

If you're involved in an online market for such products as cars, houses or electronics – categories where people hunt around for the 'right' item and are relatively unconcerned about the supplier – then over and above selling, you have to do more to keep the customers who contact you coming back a second time.

Going through the kind of analysis suggested by the matrix above – for an established company, or one with a very good feel for the market (for example, if you're working for someone who will end up being a competitor of your new business venture!) – is a matter of looking at customers close at hand and making a judgement about how and why they buy. Some of this can be done through direct conversation with clients; a lot can be discovered online.

---

[2] I know this looks over-simplified. That's because it is, and I really would urge you to read *Marketing & PR* for a lengthier explanation. Suffice to say you should try out the matrix with different data and different levels of magnification to see if anything interesting leaps out – if it does, then it's been useful.

Crucially, and usefully, clusters of the customers you identify above often make themselves known online by either searching for particular products (so search-based marketing in Chapters 5 and 7 is important) or by visiting certain sites or, increasingly, by joining forums or networks related to their interest (see Chapters 8 and 9).

Making marketing strategy real

By way of example, towards the end of *Marketing & PR* we showed the Holden-Wilde matrix applied to an outdoor clothing company – Goose Loose Ltd – and its development of a marketing strategy.

The company is based at a single store in a medium-sized market town in the South East of England. The ground floor is mostly taken up with outdoor clothing and equipment, and the upstairs recently became a small coffee and book shop. Upstairs is also where they run occasional evening events such as talks from travel writers.

The company had a clear desire to expand, but was frustrated by the limited 'footfall' through the store and their inability to get customers visiting (and spending) more frequently. The development of the upper floor was partly to make the store more of a destination, and the company

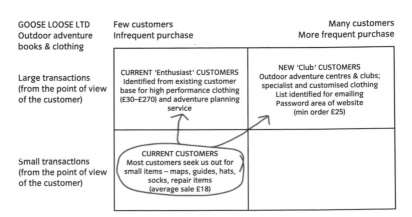

Figure 2 *A strategy 'snapshot' using the Holden-Wilde matrix*

did a lot of work identifying groups of different customers within their existing customer base.

Without going through the planning process in great detail, it's hard to fully explain how a company such as Goose Loose would develop their marketing. But it is easy to see from Figure 2 that they have at least three groups of customers – individuals and groups – and that each of these requires something a little different.

It is worth pointing out that their strategy is, as all marketing strategies should be:

- **about customers**
- **about maintaining or improving profitability, and**
- **dependent on accurate targeting of known customer needs**

None of which is rocket science. The diagram above shows that the company had to develop new marketing activities, including products, services and ways of communicating and pricing to suit these new customers and their newly recognised needs.

They did this by building on what they already know not just of their products but crucially of their existing customers. Their priorities (you could call them marketing objectives) are broadly about:

- **selling more to (identified) existing customers**
- **finding more customers like them**
- **doing all this more profitably**

. . . just as we said at the beginning of this chapter.

So, in short, much of marketing isn't about selling. At least, it's not just about selling what you have and desperately seeking new customers. Marketing is actually using the best information you can get about customers to ensure that you meet their needs now and in the foreseeable future to build a sustainable business. It can be put more succinctly: it's the whole business seen from the point of view of the customer.

With that in mind, Goose Loose can now begin to approach the Web with at least some requirements in mind. They want to cultivate their existing customers, getting them to visit more often and spend more, but they also want to acquire more new customers who are similar to their existing ones. The Web can play a part in achieving both these objectives, profitably.

If *you* want to grow quickly and profitably then, depending on your business, it's possible that the Web on its own can make this happen for you. It's more likely that you will need to use techniques that are 'blended' – they are on- and offline. If you want to establish a business that will grow organically and steadily (according to how much time and money you put in), then some of the following chapters will help you do that.

A little knowledge is a dangerous thing

For many commentators, Web 2.0 is about engagement and participation, which can be translated by those who know marketing jargon as 'relationship marketing' or even 'promoting to' and 'getting sales from' customers. Both of these are wrong.

When you participate online on sites like MySpace or Bebo, you cannot behave as a business out hunting for customers; most online communities just won't accept this. Instead you have to be genuine and transparent. Put simply, it's sticking to the truth.

With an online marketplace, if you fail to deliver the promised product or service to a customer, they'll tell other people. In some cases, they'll give instant online feedback in a place where all future customers may look, to imply that you are unreliable (see Chapter 6 for the eBay example). Imagine that in the offline world. Imagine a disgruntled customer writing to every other customer – and every potential customer too – to say what they think of you!

Part of the challenge, then, is to stick to the truth about your product, your service, your approach, your terms, your delivery, your motivation, your pricing . . . in fact, pretty much everything: to be consistent. The further challenge is to try and make your truth compelling.

If you're selling travel services online, is it better to sell everything – tickets from every airline, package holidays from every supplier (like a high street travel agent) – or to specialise in just the products and places you know intimately, because you've travelled there? Which is likely to be the most compelling (true) story?

Again, Goose Loose choose the latter because their vision for the business is partly inspired by their own experience of travelling and of using the Web – it simply doesn't make sense for them to sell package coach tours to Spain.

As we go through the various websites and technology available, we'll be referring back to our Goose Loose friends and their use of the Web occasionally, but we'll also look at other examples of small and very small businesses that have found their niche online.

This *isn't* marketing

Incidentally, getting the emphasis wrong between keeping and gaining customers is one reason why you, and other business people, might fall prey to some of the online con artists. There are literally thousands and maybe millions of websites with headlines like '$50,000 a week' or 'Make millions without moving from your home'.

Most of these get-rich-quick sites are easy to spot. They give you a long story to read about the success enjoyed by the author and signally fail to tell you what they do. It's often a 'system', or it refers to a 'technique', that eBay, Google or others 'don't want you to know'.

Almost without exception, these sites rely on you giving them a fairly small amount of money to receive a book (often an e-book), or sometimes a CD or access to a site or an online seminar. Sometimes these sites suggest you use search engine optimisation tools (SEO) to find out what people are searching for and then somehow, magically, produce a website full of links and, probably, an e-book that purports to meet the need. Sometimes you'll have to recruit other people to the system in order to earn some kind of commission. In other words, these are pyramid or multi-level marketing schemes.

Many of these sites will probably end up suggesting that you too set up a site with a headline like '$50,000 a week' or 'Make millions without moving from your home' and sell a 'system' or 'technique'. There, I just told you for free![3]

Mostly this is all hot air, and the moment you've parted with your $50 (discounted from $350 'for this week only'), the game is over. You've just covered the overheads of one of the many sites offering the same kind of snake-oil. Of course, if you understand marketing, you won't be fooled. So start from the premise that you want customers to want to come back to you time and time again. That means treating them well and not trying to make a fast buck.

So what else can you do online, virtually free?

Implicit in much of what follows is the use of the Web for *research*. Never has it been so easy to check out the competition, from websites to accounts (at Companies House) or online credit checks. You can, if you need to, order 'real' market research online to download and view immediately, and there are an increasing number of agencies offering bespoke online research.

At the same time, it's also easier to get your own information about customers. As we see in Chapter 8, you can easily get a profile of members of a social networking site showing age, sex, location and even level of education. More than that, you can engage customers in a discussion in which they can tell you what they want and even what they are prepared to pay. You may not think of it as research, but simply being in amongst your potential customers and listening and observing (as in Chapter 3) will pay dividends. And you don't have to commission market research.

If you need formal, quantitative research, then it's easy to set up an online questionnaire on a stand-alone site (such as http://free-online-surveys. co.uk or www.smart-survey.co.uk), or a petition (www.petitiononline.com or www.ipetitions.com) on your own website or within a discussion group or a Facebook group. They are all virtually free.

---

[3] But, please, *don't* do it.

Most of the following chapters deal with small companies selling things. So, in effect, websites of various types become a storefront for them. It's easy to forget how much of an impact this has had on retailing in particular. It's now possible for you to set up your business selling only pink luggage (www.pink-luggage.co.uk) in Sevenoaks and reach right around to Sydney, Australia without ever paying rent on a shop. You may not even need to keep any stock, but if you do, it's increasingly easy to use free online tools to keep track of sales, costs, stock and invoicing so that you don't even need to leave home. We'll touch on some of these tools in Chapters 4, 5 and 6.

As soon as you recognise the possibilities of having numerous shop windows online, you begin to see business in a different light. These virtual shops or channels are the doorways through which certain customers come to you – but you'd like to them to come back time and again.

The Web is making it easier to keep in touch with your existing customers without ever having to send a letter or make a phone call. You may still write letters (Chapter 7), but social networking and other tools (Chapters 8, 9 and 12) make online collaboration a reality for even the smallest business and, crucially, this enables you to deal with different customers in different ways.

As we've said, your participation online in communities of potential customers is research, but it can also be promotion. It's an opportunity to network like no other. If you're selling a new boat or a drink or a new float valve for the paint industry you can probably plug into a forum somewhere online where people are discussing buying a boat, mixing the perfect martini or streamlining paint manufacturing. So what are you waiting for?

Being surrounded by customers day to day doesn't just give you sales leads, but can also suggest to you ways in which the market might be changing. Not only might you find out what people want tomorrow, but you may also find out that people won't even need your industry the day after. Any telecoms companies mooching around online could only be struck by the efforts going into online (and preferably free) telephony. It's the same with the music industry and, increasingly, the movie industry. Looking ahead is essential for the sustainability of your business.

And as long as you are ahead of the curve and well-connected in your industry, you should be well-positioned too. Positioning is a curious marketing concept because so many large companies spend a lot of time and money trying to project their position through their advertising and promotion. In some cases, this can be pretty effective, but it can also lead to a false sense of the potency of marketing communications.

Customers get their (outside-in) view of your business from all kinds of places. For a small business this is mostly from direct dealings – how well do you handle the sale, how promptly did you respond? In other words, what you do every day with customers influences your positioning, and as you follow up the ideas in this book you will, I hope, engage with many *potential* customers who will form an opinion about your trustworthiness, your knowledge and your approach to business. You could do all this without spending a penny on advertising; just by engaging with the customers who are already out there ready and able to buy your product.

Your brand, your transparent honesty, your appearance online are the foundations for your success – your inside-out company. What you do, how consistently you perform, how you interact with customers, both current and potential, and what type of impact you have on them is your positioning – your outside-in company.

What does the online market look like?

Like real-world markets, online markets only exist as a cluster of customers and potential customers. A market*place* is where you find lots of customers gathered together. Any picture of a market is simply an indication of how or where you could contact consumers and how many there are.

So, to give you a picture of what the virtual marketplace is like I was going to draw a complicated diagram of all the connections between websites and applications you could make to support your business. Fortunately someone's already done something very similar for me. Dave McClure (http://500hats.com) is an acknowledged expert in social networking and is a good source on trends in the social networking industry.

The picture he draws is an analogy with the battle between the forces of darkness and light in the *Star Wars* movies, a reference to the competing interests in Web 2.0 – itself a market opportunity for Microsoft, Google and others offering consumers and you their services.

Social Graph Platform Wars

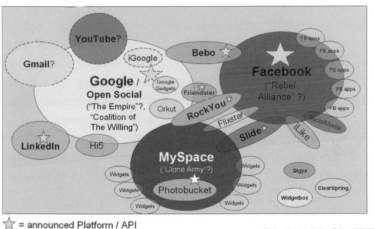

☆ = announced Platform / API
☆ = unannounced Platform / API

Platform Wars Insanity: Dave McClure, 12/12/07
http://500hats.typepad.com | http://500hats.com

Figure 3 *Dave McClure's 'Platform Wars'* © *2007 Dave McClure, reproduced with permission*

As you can see from Figure 3, there is a confusion of sites and services ('API' means Application Programming Interface – an environment for running applications and utilities), only some of which will be familiar to everyone. No one can possibly know the details of every site shown, and I certainly do not claim to be able to guide you through them in the following chapters. However, with a few examples and dealing with the main or most promising sites, I hope to get you started.

What Dave is also pointing out in his map and accompanying presentation is not only the separate factions in the war for subscribers (and therefore the potential market sizes for you and other companies targeting them) but also the increasingly 'leaky' boundaries between these sites.

Apart from the imperial ambitions of Google–taking over YouTube, for example—there is a growing movement to build bridges between these platforms. Technologically this is happening now as small developers build applications to share content and functions between various sites and users. What may happen in the future is the development of an agreed standard that will enable all of these to talk a common language. There's more on this in Chapter 8.

Until that day, there is still a bewildering range of sites, products and terminologies out there, so I recommend you explore them and play with them (as we do in the following chapters) but keep one acid test in mind: does it help me approach and keep in touch with a worthwhile number of customers? You may not be able to answer this until you've already committed some time to the sites and platforms in this book, but if you ask the question at regular intervals, you'll soon know if your investment is worthwhile.

The good news and the bad news about online marketing

The good news is that there are very simple things you can do to start promoting yourself to the millions of potential customers out there. The bad news is that there are almost too many options. Oh, and the other bad news is that even the simple things can get quite complicated! So in what follows, excuse me if I oversimplify or if I don't explain every website and every option there is out there. What I will do, however, is take you from no Web marketing to involved, aware and reasonably professional Web marketing in, roughly, twelve and a half chapters.

But keep in mind that it's *your* company and *your* brand you want to build and promote. Check your strategy, pin your objectives up above your desk and tighten up your seatbelt.

We'll start with a visit to the blog.

CHAPTER 3

START A BLOG NOW

The title of this chapter is entirely serious. Without doing very much at all in the way of preparation, it's now possible for you to go online and set up a blog. You could do it today. In fact, I think you should.

Of course, for those of you of a more cautious disposition, you might well ask 'why?' Well firstly, writing a blog is arguably the easiest way of getting an online presence.

'Blog' is a contraction of 'Web log', and there are probably 150 million them in existence and around 175,000 being created every day[1]. You can, if you want, read the history of the idea of blogging on Wikipedia but, for our purposes, it's sufficient just to know how easy it is to have a fairly polished Web presence by blogging – and to start a dialogue that is accessible to around a billion people worldwide (38 million in the UK)[2].

Essentially, all blogs offer commentary on something seen (if only by a very specialised group) as being of current interest, but some are now disproportionately powerful[3]. The size of the so-called 'blogosphere' is not the only important aspect. It's the essence of blogging that those who read often also write. Those same people are instrumental in directing other people who are interested in the same things to other sources of useful information and insight, and all of these can connect on a more or less permanent basis. In other words, blogs represent virtual meeting points for people with similar interests – clusters of customers – feeding

---

[1] According to www.technorati.com

[2] For world Internet usage statistics, see www.internetworldstats.com

[3] See http://tinyurl.com/yr2up2 for *The Guardian's* list of the most powerful, from the genuinely useful to the frankly bizarre.

information to those people who are already likely to be buying. The question is, though: if you start writing about your interest will you attract other people, customers even?

Well no, not at first. And no, not if Holden's first law of DIY applies: 'Nothing is ever as simple as it seems'. Just being on the Web doesn't bring you customers: it's those connections between bloggers that are important – more so than the blogs themselves. We'll come to promotion later (in Chapter 7); for the moment, think about *your* blog as the hub of your new Web network, and let's do some online research for the competition and for possible collaborators – people with whom you might link.

Research what other people are doing

Let's suppose you have a business restoring old chairs. You'd like to know what is already out there for your customers and for you. By visiting Google, you could search for a string of keywords. Keying in 'blog antique restoration' doesn't seem to generate much of interest. You might consider this to be good news! Typing 'blog expert antique restoration' doesn't do much better. Instead, try 'antique restoration' in Google Blog Search (http://blogsearch.google.co.uk) which will search primarily amongst the thousands of blogs out there.

A crucial fact of Google searches (which we'll return to in later chapters) is that the results are, in part, ranked according to the number of links they support. In other words, the more people refer to a site, the more that site is rated as popular. The blog search is actually finding blog entries – individual messages posted onto blogs – and as these are date-stamped will also give you a way of sorting blogs according to how recent they are.

What you find depends on what's most active and what's useful to others searching for similar things.

Of course, there is quite a lot that's useless, and it will take a while to find blogs that are genuinely interesting and look to be alive – that is, they are updated fairly frequently. You will also need to experiment with different search terms: 'antique chairs restored' will get you a different set of results from 'restoring antique furniture'.

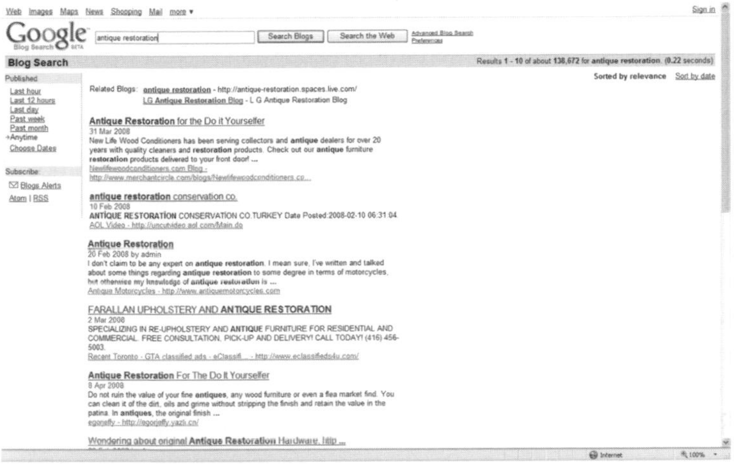

Figure 1 *The first results of our blog search*

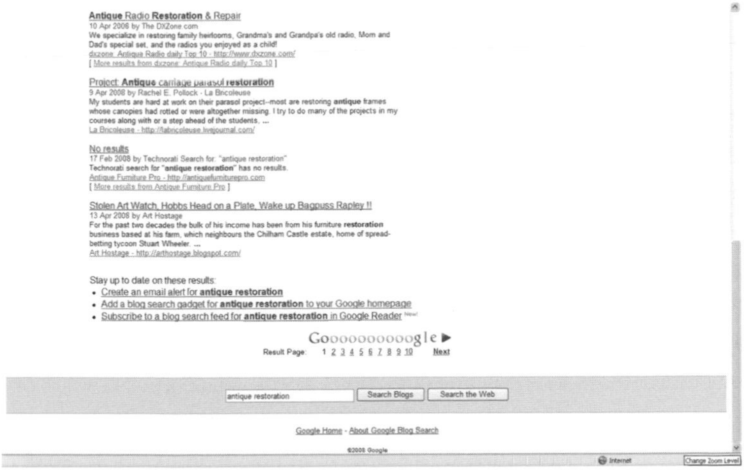

Figure 2 *The bottom of the first screen of our blog search*

Towards the bottom of the page of results (Figure 2), you'll see a link headed 'No results' that comes from the Technorati website – Google searches that too – a good place to discover which blogs are attracting attention. You could also look for lists of the best blogs at places such as Blogflux (www.blogflux.com). There's no substitute for hunting around and generally acting like a customer in search of information.

At the bottom of the page you'll also see three options to help you keep up to date with 'antique restoration'. It's a good idea to use one or more of these 'feeds' to keep track, and it's easy if you've already signed up to Google and use your personalised iGoogle set-up as your default home page in your browser. At this stage you need to feel you are collecting information from every possible source; you can reject some of them later.

Once you start exploring blogs, you'll see how much they vary. Some blogs are well organised, and so it's easy to see how you get to the latest entry or to an index of entries. Some are personal and range over a vast range of subjects. Some seem to be derivative of other blogs and websites, whilst some really do seem to be the font of knowledge in their area.

At the foot of each post, you will generally see a line of text that shows if other readers have commented, and this is a good indication of the audience of a blog. However, you can't read too much into the number of comments – only very few blogs get comments numbering into the hundreds. Ten comments is pretty good going; many posts get no response at all.

If you are tempted to respond to other people's blogs, stop to think about your approach. As we've said elsewhere, the Net is big on transparency. If you post in one place, it's quite likely that someone somewhere will link this to subsequent posts or online appearances elsewhere. I'm not for a moment suggesting that you shouldn't comment: quite the reverse, you should get engaged in as many conversations as you feel you can handle. This is how your name will get known – and all this will lead back to your business, both online and in the real world.

One thing is clear, though: posing as a customer or posting favourable comments about your own site, product or service without making clear your affiliation is unacceptable, and may soon be illegal. At the time of writing, the Unfair Trading Regulations 2007 were coming into force, which have a far-reaching effect on such practices known as 'astroturfing' and 'flogging'.[4]

You can spend a long time refining your search only to conclude that there probably isn't a blog quite like one you would like to set up. It still amazes me that, apart from those discussing the technology of the Internet itself, no two blogs ever deal with quite the same content. There very often is a gap for your interest and your perspective and, if nothing else, for your brand.

What should go into your blog?

Keeping in mind your primary concern – your marketing objectives – it's sometimes easy to invest a lot of time in a personal blog without actually selling anything. Nevertheless, you have to start with an idea – perhaps a list pinned above your desk – of the things you will and will not write about.

Perhaps the easiest way to think about your blog in the short term is as initiating a conversation with customers. Ask yourself what you are interested in and why you are in the business you are in – the values and motivation you may have considered in the last two chapters.

What is the most important thing to your business? It could be the way you manufacture what you do, or your relationship with suppliers. Just explaining these things can do a lot to reassure a potential visitor. It's a truism to say that 'people buy from people', and a blog gives customers an indication of the person – you – behind the business.

As you start, it may seem that you are writing a newsletter or diary, but the aim isn't just to tell the world what you think (though many blogs do this) but also to invite comment and interaction. You can be provocative, within the bounds of decency and legality and in a way that is relevant to your area of expertise and your customers' interests. Just keep asking yourself 'If I was a customer for X, what would I be asking?'

---

[4] Thanks to Melody Bartlett in *The Marketer* (www.themarketer.co.uk) for introducing me to these terms – essentially, they mean acting as if you are giving a disinterested recommendation of a brand or product when you have a personal interest in promoting it.

At its best, a blog gives the reader an insight into your business and how you run it. It also builds up a picture of your aims and values (even as they evolve) which customers don't normally see, but which they get to know as they deal with you.

Your blog can, we hope, also generate business for you. However, it's unlikely that it will do so entirely on its own. The 'connectedness' your blog has will bring you to the attention of other people – slowly – but you will also want to attract readers and visitors, perhaps to a website.

Perhaps the best way of imagining what you could achieve is to look at a cause célèbre in the world of blogging – Stormhoek Wine and Hugh MacLeod (www.stormhoek.com and www.gapingvoid.com respectively).

We'll come back to the issue of selling in the following chapters as we talk about setting up a site or selling through others, but for the moment let's just get started . . . and practise writing.

Blogger

Probably the easiest way to set up a blog is to visit www.blogger.com and sign up. To do that, just follow the first page: create an account, name your blog and then choose a template.

Figure 3 *The Blogger home page*

You'll see straight away that if you already have a Google account you just need to sign in and then create your Blogger account. Either way, you'll end up with a Google ID you can use for other services too.

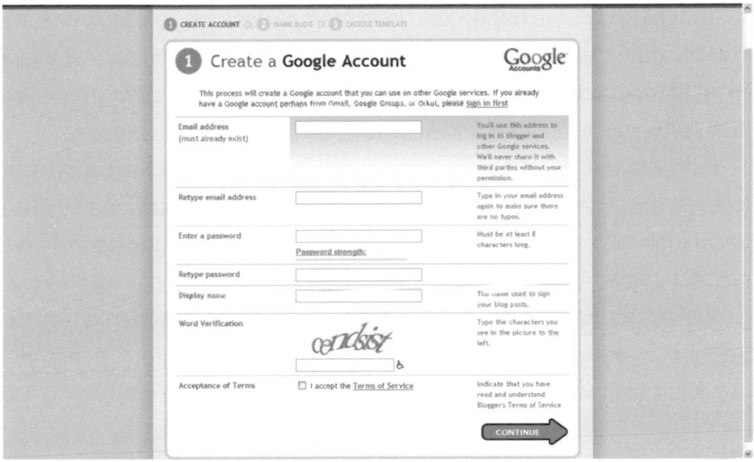

Figure 4 *Blogger's (and Google's) easy sign-up page*

One of the things you do is decide on a 'display name' – the name that will appear with your blog posts (and can therefore be shown when you respond to others' blogs). This is quite important since you will be identified through this in many different contexts. It's worth sticking to a single, recognisable name – your own or one that is related to your company or your brand. Look back at Chapter 2.

On the next screen you will choose a title for your blog. This doesn't have to be the same as the URL (the address) but it makes sense. Helpfully, Blogger addresses are fairly easy – 'yourname' followed by '.blogspot. com' so you can usually have your brand name here. However, if you are starting out by experimenting with a personal blog – not a bad idea – just put your name in here. Blogger will tell you if the name is already used so have in mind some alternatives. You may have to settle for a variant on your name or brand such as 'JoeBloggsPlumber' instead of 'JoeBloggs'.

As you will see in Figure 5 below, you can also use the Blogger set-up to create a blog to be hosted elsewhere – if for example, you already have a website with storage space available. For now, we'll stick to the free Blogger version.

Once through this stage you can start to change the look of your blog. Usefully, the templates for your blog are interchangeable, so even if you come back later wanting to change the look of your blog you can, without losing any of the posts you have written in the interim.

However, as you get more accomplished at tweaking the look and feel of your blog, you will be personalising your template. As you do so, you get a chance to save your template locally (on your own PC) so that if you need to restore it (for example, a new add-on doesn't work or something gets corrupted), you can. Get into the habit of saving the template every few weeks.

After a few clicks, you can start to compose posts for your blog. The best way is simply to try it. As the administrator of the blog, you can always edit posts (even after they have been made public) or delete them altogether.

Figure 5 *You start your design with a Blogger template*

Figure 6 *You're very quickly ready to post your first thoughts*

You'll see a standard text entry field in which you can create a new post. There are tabs for editing posts and moderating comments that others may post on your blog.

The form allows you some control over the look of your text, but the basic parameters are determined by the template you have chosen. It's generally not worth changing type too much, certainly not until you have successfully posted a number of times.

You are able to embolden and italicise text, add bulleted or numbered lists, or change the colour of text – just like a conventional word processor – and a simple eraser button removes this formatting. You can easily add photos or video files too.

There's more about photos and video in Chapter 10, but for the moment it's a simple matter to click on the appropriate button and follow the instructions. Generally speaking, the file needs to be uploaded to Blogger before you then embed it in your post, and you need to be careful about copyright – read the guidance by clicking on the 'Learn more' link. Large files may take a long time to upload and are resized automatically. In any case you are limited to 8Mb for photos and 100Mb for video files.

Your first post can be live in a matter of seconds. From logging into Google and seeing the first post on the GooseLoose blog took me around ten minutes – including time spent mulling over what to write!

Viewing your own blog, as in Figure 8, you will see a number of features such as dates, and the count of responses is automatic. You'll have a blog archive which will, of course, build up as you post more.

Figure 7 *Your confirmation that your post is 'live'*

The little screwdriver and spanner icon may or may not show (depending on settings, which we'll look at in a moment) but these are clickable links which show only to you when you're logged in and enable you to adjust the various elements to which they are attached. In the same way, the pencil icon next to the blog post allows you to edit it. Going back into the post after you have finished enables you to refine the layout or add other content.

The great thing to remember here is that you are working on live Web pages. So if you notice a mistake or you need to rephrase something, you can change it there and then.

Probably the most important things to add to your post are 'tags' or keywords; a list of single words that describe the content of what you've just written. You can see a box for this at the foot of the text entry box.

Having these keywords enables other Web users to search for and sort your blog posts, so they are essential for maximising the chances of you being found . . . and read. If you've just written about installing a new 'NordicTrack' ski machine in your health club then you might include *'nordictrack, nordic, track, ski, skiing, machine, exercise, health, club'* and any other words that someone might use to search. You should probably also include your club's name and location.

We'll discuss keywords more in Chapters 5 and 7 in the context of search optimisation, so you might end up coming back to edit your keywords in your blog – you can, any time. In the case of GooseLoose's first post (in Figure 8), there would be various keywords and phrases relating to the BOC orienteering event that those who follow the sport might be looking for. At this stage it's probably enough to ask yourself

GOOSE LOOSE - EVERYTHING
OUTDOOR

FRIDAY, MAY 9, 2008

Welcome

Hi, and welcome to the forst GooseLoose blog.

My name is Pip and I'm one of the two owners of GooseLoose. I'm
hoping that we can use this blog to let you know what were
planning in the store and online and to pass on to you news about
the sports and activities we love.

It all starts off in the next couple of weeks with the BOC
Orienteering Championships in the Culbin Forest, Moray in
Scotland. We'll be represented by Tony who - as some of you
know - is so keen on running through wilderness that he spent last
Autumn in Canada. He'll be manning our stand and reporting back.

POSTED BY GOOSE LOOSE AT 5:54 AM 0 COMMENTS

BLOG ARCHIVE

▼ 2008 (1)
  ▼ May (1)
    Welcome

ABOUT ME

GOOSE LOOSE

VIEW MY COMPLETE PROFILE

Subscribe to: Posts (Atom)

Figure 8 *A default template applied to the GooseLoose blog*

again what *you* would look for if you were the customer; what kind of
search terms you'd use. You can use as many as you like, so don't
forget to include variants of words, like 'running' and 'run' as well as
perhaps 'marathon', 'cross-country' and so on.

Also on your blog page you'll notice a reference to your profile. All
blogs are associated with an individual Google user, and so interested
visitors are quite likely to click through to find out more about you. As
noted in earlier chapters, the truth is the recommended option. Of
course your profile will be tailored to your reason for being online, but
misleading statements or suggestions can (and will) get you into trouble.
Keep checking this to see it's up to date.

Bear in mind also that you can have several blogs for different parts
of your business or hobbies, and that anyone who looks at your profile
will be able then to go to your other blogs – assuming you've made
them public.

Basic options for your blog

If you now click on the 'Settings' tab, you will see there are a number
of controls you can place on your blog. The default values tend to give

the maximum accessibility to your blog, and for most purposes this is okay.

Your blog will be listed and searchable by search engines, which is essential if you want to be found. You may want to include an e-mailable link for each post so that visitors can pass on your posts to their friends – it probably encourages more rapid word of mouth than visitors having to find your URL and send it in an e-mail. Of course, a private blog can be used for communication between a select group of people; we'll say more about this kind of collaboration in Chapter 12.

Further down the 'Settings' page, you are able to switch on and off the 'WYSIWYG' editor for posts – this 'what you see is what you get' function is pretty much essential for most of us so that we can see what we're posting. Only if you really need to see the code underneath what you're typing is it necessary to change this.

Finally, and useful for some, there is a 'transliteration' feature which supports the use of some, mainly Asian, languages. It cleverly reads any words typed phonetically and renders them in the chosen language. It is not a translation device – so don't depend on it unless you know the language already – but it could be very useful if wanted your blog available in several languages.

The layout of your blog

The 'Layout' tab naturally leads you to a screen that lets you change the way your blog is laid out, within the limits of the template.

At some stage you might want to change the default heading to include your company logo or brand. By clicking on the 'Edit' link next to the title block, you can upload an image which can run behind the title or instead of the title. If you keep the title as given, you will have to experiment with the graphics to make sure the title is readable. The alternative – uploading a graphic that has the title and any pictorial element included in a single file – is, in many ways, preferable, but still technically challenging. The file will come out about 600 to 700 pixels wide (depending on the template), so your image should be tested at

Figure 9 *The GooseLoose blog – complete with logo . . . and typographic errors!*

this size before you upload it to make sure it is still readable. There is more about handling images in Chapter 10.

You can see in Figure 9 that the GooseLoose 'banner' doesn't quite fit on the right and will need to be adjusted. Remember, nothing is set in stone . . . I can change that typo in the 'forst' line!

Perhaps the most interesting next step is to look at the range of page elements you can add to your blog. As standard you'll have the 'blog archive' and 'about me' elements mentioned earlier. These appear as blocks which can be picked up and moved around the page (again, within the constraints of the template you are using).

The link list is particularly useful as it enables you to have a simple menu, which can go towards the top of your page, giving quick links to other pages on the Web – it could be your brochure pages, your store, a discussion forum or contact details. It's just a question of typing some descriptive text (e.g. 'Click here to see our current stock') and a URL – the Web address of the appropriate page.

By now you should have a functioning blog. There are many things you can add as you become familiar with blogging and new add-ons appear. If you see a useful addition on someone else's blog, you can probably have it on yours. And if you don't know how, you can ask the authors of the blog themselves. Blogger also has a pretty good support system in place – managed by its owners Google, of course.

Figure 10 *Some of the elements you can add to your blog*

Wordpress and other alternatives

Wordpress does all that Blogger does and possibly more. At Wordpress. com you can sign up for a free blog just like Blogger. There are more free templates, but other things you may find you have to pay for. Unlike Blogger, for example, if you want to have your own domain name point to the blog, you have to pay; however, addresses are as simple as Blogger (www.yourname.wordpress.com) so you may not feel the need for this. You can buy extra storage and allow an unlimited number of users to a 'private' blog (where users have to be approved and sign in), although you can have a group of up to 35 in a private blog free of charge.

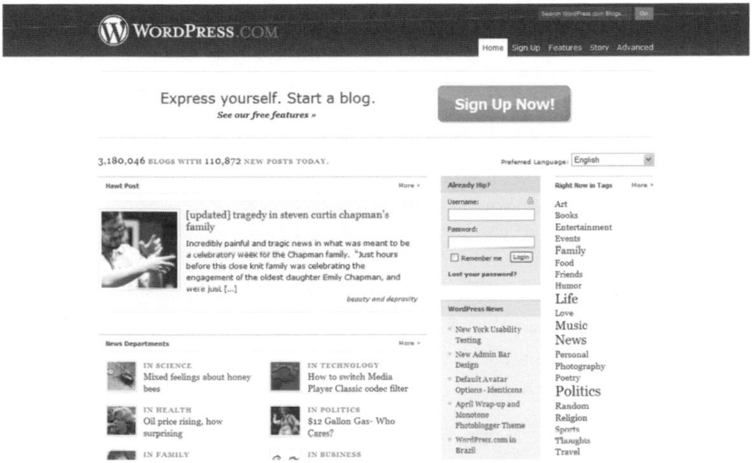

Figure 11 *The Wordpress front page*

At Wordpress.org (note the changed suffix) it is possible to download the Wordpress publishing platform (software) to run your blog on your own Web server. You'd simply rent space on a computer connected to the Net – a 'hosting' service you can buy for a few pounds a year (see Chapters 4 and 5). The download itself is free and opens up the possibility of doing much more than a conventional diary-type blog.

Wordpress also has links to a number of hosts that are set up to help you install the latest version of their platform, for which the going rate seems to be about $7 a month – not bad for all your Web storage including e-mail addresses, but of course you should shop around. Make sure that you can use the latest version of Wordpress on a server before you commit yourself to it.

Setting up Wordpress in this way is more technically challenging, but worth considering. The key difference from off-the-shelf blogs is the ability to set up other kinds of Web content and to manage a more sophisticated site. You can have static information pages – like a regular website – and manage different areas of your site in different ways. For example, you could decide that colleagues can access one area for internal communications, clients can access others and prospective customers can see your most public brochure pages.

Wordpress – hosted on your own server – enables you to set up and control a fully functioning website relatively easily. There is well-developed online support and a network of people who may even code more complex things should they become necessary.

If you start with a Blogger account, it's possible in the future to export your entire blog to a Wordpress account; Wordpress positively encourages this! As you get more proficient in managing your blog plus other pages, you might find the need for a product like K2 (http://getk2. com) which aims to simplify the customisation of pages and templates. Perhaps confusingly at this point, K2 is a piece of software that fits 'on top' of Wordpress and helps you manage the look and feel of your Web pages.

In the interests of giving you choice, you might also look at Typepad (www.typepad.com), which again aims to handle pretty much everything you might need from your Web space. This one isn't free, but offers a free trial, so when you have gained some experience and you want to do something more complex than a basic free blog allows, have a look.

Is it worth learning HTML?

HTML is 'hypertext mark-up language', a computer code used to build and develop Web pages, and knowing some of it is extremely useful. Some blogging sites and software allow you to add emphasis (bold and italics) and may even give you simple buttons on screen for modifying text in this way. Others allow HTML, for example, in text entry boxes, but may not tell you. If you know some basic codes, you can try them out.

It's also useful to be able to recognise HTML codes and have some idea of what they do, since you might have need to put a link from another source into a document that you didn't create. Unfortunately, HTML is dangerously close to being a geek-only computer language – and as for Perl, Java and Ajax . . . they are way, way beyond this book (and this author).

The real problem is that HTML was designed originally to be a universal language that all PCs could read. It is cut down to the bare minimum for ease of transfer across the Web and so uses very brief, generic coding. For example, instead of specifying every typeface to be used, HTML simply indicates that a certain line of text should be in the largest heading size (using a code like <H1>) or that a typeface should be used if it is already resident on the computer being used to view the page, otherwise defaulting to one of the universal typefaces, usually Times or Arial. The main DIY websites (See Chapter 4) use only a few default fonts, which is why they tend to look very similar.

In the same way, type size and paragraphs are specified in the simplest way so that pages will still display on different size of PC screen. This means that headings will always look more prominent than the main body text, but actual sizes on screen will differ and lines will break or wrap around at different points in a sentence.

Things are further complicated by including graphic files, which *are* reproduced at a fixed size. For example, if you upload a graphic file that is 300 × 90 pixels, it will remain that size even if the browser program (like Internet Explorer or Firefox) changes the type size. The graphic will sometimes appear at the top of a line of text, sometimes below, sometimes on the far right and at other times with text wrapped around it. Frustrating for the enthusiastic amateur! The ready-made templates for blogs and those for websites (in the next chapter) get around this by giving you easier tools, but fewer choices.

So, some HTML knowledge is useful. There are still some add-ons that involve you looking at the raw code of your pages or templates and cutting and pasting a few lines in the right place. With a bit of common sense it's reasonably easy and strangely satisfying when it works. As you get accustomed to what HTML code looks like, you might be able to cope with more advanced tools and customisation. However, the user-friendly tools below (and more are available every week) do all that you need to get online virtually free.

Give your customers a tweet

A further development of the connected Web is 'microblogging' in which, rather than fully formed articles about a clearly defined subject, short and informal updates are posted more regularly. If you are a consultant working for a number of clients, this kind of regular information may offer reassurance about where you are and what you're doing. Microblogging is of particular use in keeping your Web presence updated and demonstrating that it is alive, or that you are active in a particular field.

The most original is probably Twitter (www.twitter.com), which allows messages of just 140 characters to be sent to anyone who chooses to receive them. You can have Twitter updates ('tweets') sent to your blog or Facebook pages (see Chapter 8), and you can do this from your mobile phone so you don't have to be sitting in front of a PC.

Jaiku (www.jaiku.com and another part of the Google empire) and Pownce (http://pownce.com) are alternatives that have different approaches and slightly different functions, but it's likely all will converge to some extent. Jaiku is based in Helsinki, which may have implications for accessibility should you be using a mobile phone to blog, whilst Pownce is a lighter-weight product that gives you storage space, but less accessibility through mobile phone, for example.

If updating photos is important to your blog, you can use a combination of sites and technologies to send photos and automatically have them posted. See SnapTweet (http://snaptweet.com) and Chapter 10.

Twitter and similar sites enable interested people to 'follow' you and your updates and be informed through feeds, their mobiles or instant messaging services. In some cases you can specify groups of recipients, which means you could inform certain customers of offers – for example, if you were house-hunting for clients or suddenly had availability of stock.

Getting connected

As you build up your knowledge of what's going on in your industry or market, your blog can start to be the information hub for like-minded people. You'll see, for example, in Blogger that one of the page elements you can embed is a feed from another blog. So when you do find someone else saying something useful, just link to them and you have their content available through your page. It's often just a case of typing their blog's address into the dialog box when setting up the page element. You might also want to let the blog owner know that you're linking to them. There's always the chance they will reciprocate, but don't be upset if they don't.

Perhaps the most important add-ons to your blog are those that allow people reading your blog to bookmark your posts and to pass them on or recommend them to others.

There's a bewildering array of these – often with their own peculiar process of registering. A quick way of covering most, if not all, the bases is to use a widget like Addthis (www.addthis.com) which simply gives you a button to insert in the template for your blog. You must register, but in return you can set up buttons for websites and blogs, even for e-newsletters (see Chapter 7). Addthis will also track usage statistics for your button so you can see how your posts, blog or Web pages are being followed.

Figure 12 *A simple button like this is invaluable*

You should also make your blog, indeed anything you regularly update, available to others as widely as possible. Feedburner (www.feedburner.com) and others are central storage points for content that people can subscribe to. Though you may not know how well targeted or publicised your feed is through these, it makes sense to be there as it's free (at least for the basic version) and, if your blog really takes off, people will look here for it.

What else can you add to your blog?

There are countless other ways of linking your content that may prove useful, such as Digg and StumbleUpon, but most of these are options on the Addthis button, so committed users can pick the link of their choice. We'll say more about some of these in Chapter 7.

In Chapter 12, we revisit some of the other online services that might make running your business a little easier – including phone services that can be linked to your Web pages. For example, Grand Central (www.grandcentral.com), recently acquired by Google, promises to be able to direct all calls to a single number and to enable call-screening and recording. At the moment it is in 'beta testing', which means that you can only reserve a number at present, and not yet in the UK or Europe, but the features look impressive. When it does become available, it could be useful in encouraging customer enquiries from blogs, websites and other online locations – another response mechanism. For alternatives, look at Chapter 12.

Talk to your customers

If you think your customers or contacts would benefit from hearing your voice – or your music or drama or . . . well, any noise – then you might want to think about a podcast.

At its simplest, you make a recording and make it available for people to listen to and/or download. It's called podcasting because of Apple's iPod (and similar devices) on to which such sound files can be loaded. Lately the notion of podcasting has been rather overtaken by the rise of the 'vodcast' or video blogging, mainly due to the increased availability of broadband access and the tools to deal with video (see Chapter 10).

It sounds as if it's a pretty simple matter to make a sound file available online, and in a sense it is. The files can be uploaded like any other files, but the trick is in making a podcast that is worth listening to.

The Web is awash with detailed technical advice about the many, many ways in which you can do this, and much of it points out the problems of making an audio file listenable. There are several stages to producing your own podcast, and this isn't the place to repeat the abundant advice that is available online. So here are the extremely basic rules.

The better your original recording, the better your end result can be. It's possible to record directly on to a PC, but a high-quality microphone helps, as does some dedicated software to record with. Many PCs have a noisy fan which, in normal use, you don't notice. However, you can't miss it on a recording, so a dedicated digital recorder is often better, along with a way of editing the sound file such as Audacity (http://audacity.sourceforge.net), which is free.

The 'studio', which may be your office or even your bedroom, needs to be as acoustically 'dead' as you can make it. Lots of curtains and soft surfaces help to prevent echoes. It goes without saying that extraneous noises like passing trains need to be listened for and cut out as far as possible.

One product that does seem to make recording a podcast simpler than most is Pod Producer (www.podproducer.net), which is free and has a user-friendly interface. It allows you to emulate many of the effects of a professional radio show such as mixing sources.

If you want to include music you can, but you need to be careful about performing rights. There's more information about licensing music at www.mcps-prs-alliance.co.uk and about music you may not have to pay for at www.podsafeaudio.com (see also http://tinyurl.com/5dazuc).

Making your podcast available to those who want to download it to an MP3 player or to their computer is a matter of 'burning' it using the services of Feedburner (see above) and/or the Apple iTunes platform at http://apple.com/podcasting, which includes some guidance on creating audio and video podcasts.

What to write or say!

Well, clearly I can't tell you what to write. For most people, however, writing a blog (or a podcast) starts off as a confession – usually about your own ignorance as to what you should be writing. Don't try and write everything in one hit. A brief introduction to yourself is fine at first. Your second post then might be something about your aims for the blog and the business you're running. Remember to think about who you think your audience might be – or who you intend them to be – and write for them. Above all don't write essays – just link your readers up with things they need to or would like to know.

The GooseLoose people would write about the sports they and their customers have taken part in. They would be constantly on the look-out for other sources of information, announcements of new products, offers and ideas that their customers might be interested in. The main aim is to get visitors coming back time after time. You won't sell anything without an audience so keep providing the information your customers need – sources of bargains, unique products, trade secrets and more – and they will keep coming back to you.

CHAPTER 4

THE SIMPLEST WAY TO A WEBSITE

If a blog (and some of the other ideas linked to your blog in the last chapter and later on) doesn't seem to meet all your needs, then you may just have to bite the bullet and think about getting your own website.

There is no shortage of free website builders and hosts offering a free deal or a free trial. By and large, the free trials are difficult to evaluate since they often require you to sign up for a service and spend time setting up your account and your pages before you can really judge whether it does what you need.

Some services offer very little customisation, and make their money by selling advertising in *your* site! Whilst this might seem a good deal at first, I guarantee that as you get more proficient at managing your website, you will want to use some of the valuable (and limited) space on your pages for yourself. When you have little control over your pages, you may find that getting even the most basic data (about who is visiting and why) difficult to obtain. You'll also miss out on any advertising revenue you create, and you may not be able to maximise traffic to your site. The final disadvantage of these kinds of sites is that visitors may be confronted with a page dominated by advertising that just isn't relevant.

In the end, there is no way to evaluate the competing offers other than to have a look and read the terms carefully. It's also a good idea to look hard at the service's own website. If a site seems to be offering a good deal but leaves out much of the detail, doesn't tell you much about itself or doesn't give you links to existing customers' websites, then it's probably not a great prospect. If it doesn't look good itself, then the chances of your site looking good are slim. One of the many, but which does actually look reasonable, is Freewebs (http://members.freewebs.com/index.jsp). Alternatives are suggested throughout this chapter.

You also need to think carefully about the functionality you need. Do you want to be able to quickly and easily list products for sale? Would you like the e-commerce (a 'shopping basket' and secure payments) to be handled for you? The answer to the latter question is probably yes if you're selling direct, but if you just want a brochure then these add-ons may not be necessary. Fortunately, it's getting easier to buy modular services that enable you to trade – one of the most important is PayPal (see Chapter 6) – but increasingly, free and off-the-shelf Web services are accessible to all.

Of course, you can construct your own pages using HTML which we mentioned briefly in the last chapter and, if you download the Mozilla browser including the Composer application (free of course), you can do this relatively easily – see www.mozilla.org or http://tinyurl.com/d65s8. However, just building pages doesn't make a website – they need to be updated and connections *between* pages need to be set up and maintained (known as 'content management'), and you'll need a host computer (from a Web hosting service) that will be available 24 hours a day and can handle the numbers of visitors you hope for.

Another big issue with free or cheap websites is security. In the early days of the Web everyone was a pioneer, and there was always the risk that a great service provider could break down, either technically or financially. Consider that if a free Web provider goes bust, there's not a lot you can do to retrieve all the 'assets' – the pages, pictures and even details of customers and their orders from your site – and that could be fatal to your business.

Fortunately, now all these complexities can be forgotten because the 'big three' providers of online products, places, services (and much more) Google, Microsoft and Yahoo take ease of use and continuity of service very seriously.

Of course, it's perfectly possible that, by the time you read this, there will be just a 'big two' – if Yahoo has been sold – or *more* than two –

if completely new competition has sprung up from some of the sites mentioned in later chapters. It's also possible that someone will disagree with my choice of major players, but I've chosen these as offering fairly stable and free (or virtually free), useful and usable business tools. And don't forget that much of what you will do with a simple website can often be achieved with a blogging platform such as Wordpress as we mentioned in Chapter 3, and some of the alternatives at the end of this chapter.

Whilst the big three are in competition with each other, they also come at the Web in very different ways. Microsoft has been predominantly a software company, and so has an interest in keeping within the model of usability of its seemingly ubiquitous Office suite. Google, by contrast, has been online all its life, starting with revolutionising the search business, and has clearly grasped the value of collaborating with users and of gobbling up smaller companies with good ideas. The result has been a culture of continuous improvement. Yahoo, although sometimes overshadowed by the other two in terms of development, is still very popular, claiming to be the most visited home page in the US and partnering with Kelkoo, possibly the leading shopping search engine in Europe.

We'll deal with some of the other services of the big three in the next chapter, but for now we'll concentrate mainly on how you get access to their free website and Web-hosting offers, and a few of the extras they make available.

But first, some planning . . .

When you read the simple instructions that follow, I hope you'll be encouraged to get online and have a go. That's great, but you'll also need to think back over the kinds of questions we were asking in Chapter 2. You may also want to think about how relatively static Web pages fit in with your blog (if you have one), or you may be starting with a Web page that may be subsequently linked to a blog or other service.

Before you start composing Web pages, you need to have a pretty good idea of your 'story' or your brand, and of what you want your

Web presence to achieve. You'll also need to think of your customers and their point of view. These are the 'outside-in' and the 'inside-out' views we discussed. It's always useful to look at what others are doing, so look at the website for Cyndi Rhoades's Worn Again brand at www.wornagain.co.uk and its relationship with www.lowcarbontravel.com, Ed Gillespie's travel blog.

So take a large piece of paper and map out what you need the website to say immediately, such as your name, product and contact details, and prices, and then branch off to what you would like to say in the future. Then, with a blank piece of paper, look at your site from your customers' perspective; sketch out what they would need and like.

The strategic decisions you've already made shouldn't be derailed just because there's a neat trick you can do online, like making words flash or your logo spin: they should instead be reinforced time and time again. Every time you make a design decision in the rest of this chapter, ask yourself if it is supporting your strategy.

Microsoft

Microsoft has a suite of Web products for small businesses which sells partly on the reputation and popularity of their Windows and Office systems. Whatever you think of Bill Gates, Microsoft does seem to be committed to making useful software available for all.

Going to Microsoft's www.officelive.com gets you to a simple sign in/up screen where you can see two services. We'll look at the 'workspace' product later (in Chapter 12) but for the moment we'll concentrate on the 'Office Live Small Business' option.

As the panel on the right of the screen says, you can sign up free of charge. The sign-up process only takes a few minutes and, as usual, you should keep a note of what data you enter to that you can be sure to retrieve your account in the future.

If you already have a Hotmail e-mail address, you can use this as your sign-in to the Live services. Otherwise you simply have to provide an e-mail address.

Figure 1 *The two main Office Live services*

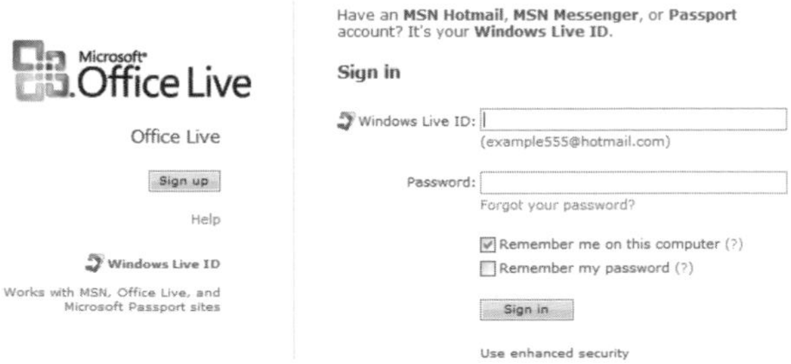

Figure 2 *Sign in with an e-mail address*

Early on in the process, you are asked to fill out some rather general information about the sector your business is in and how many employees you have, but these can be altered later and needn't be completed at all at this stage.

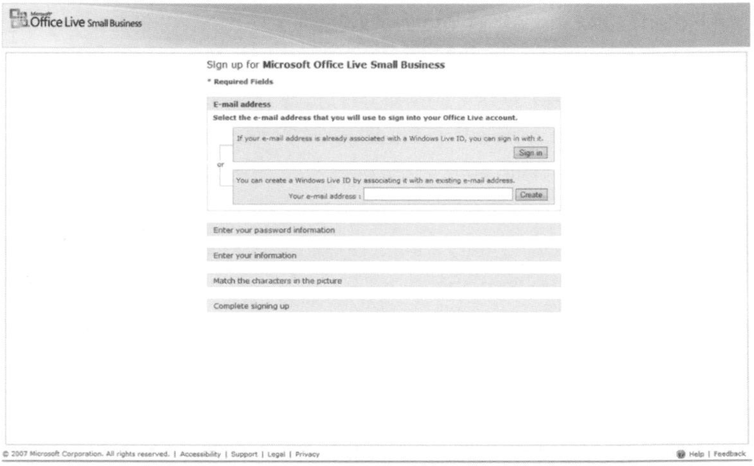

Figure 3 *Sign in with an existing Windows Live ID, or create one*

After another click or two, you hit a blue button to go to your account's home page. This is where you will be taken each time you sign in and where you can manage your site and other Live services. You can see immediately that Microsoft are generating advertising income from your account – you have, after all, told them you are in business, so mobile phone and computer companies buy ad space here[1].

Your Hotmail e-mail inbox, if you have one that you used to sign in, should show up as a small panel on this home page, along with a panel showing how many visitors your site has had – none so far. But Office Live Small Business allows businesses to manage most aspects of their business online, only some of which are absolutely free.

At the top of your page you will see a range of services available under the heading 'Get started with Microsoft Office Live Small Business' (Microsoft seems to go in for long and obvious titles). You can, if you like, get a Web address or domain name which is, typically, free for the first

---

[1] It's not great targeting though – they are mostly US-based companies even though the site was accessed from the UK.

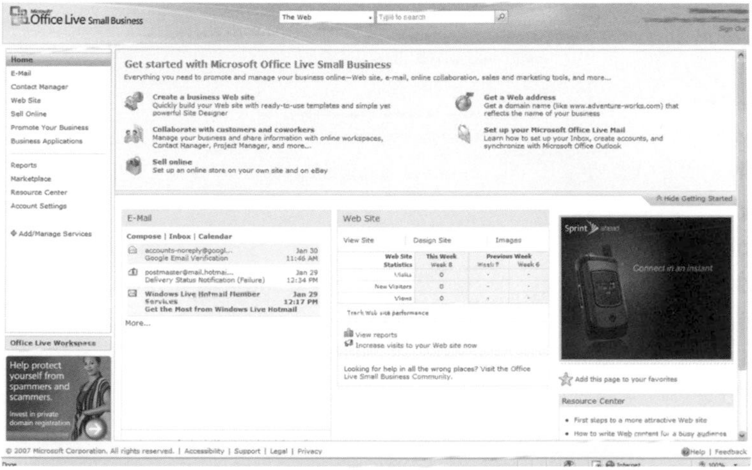

Figure 4 *Your home page on Office Live acts as your 'dashboard'*

year. Microsoft isn't the only source for such domain names, and you may want to think quite long and hard before signing up for one. Just as with your blog, the name has to be right for your business and for your customers, both existing and prospective.

However, back to Office Live: if you click on 'Create a business Web site' you'll see how rapidly you can set up some home pages. In fact, using only the information you have put in so far, Office Live has set up four basic pages for you. All you have to do is edit them.

If you now click on 'Design your Web site' towards the top of the page, you'll see roughly what your free Web pages look like.

You'll see that you have a site heading with a line that says 'Add your site slogan here'. Under that you'll have a basic menu leading to pages labelled Home, About Us, Contact Us and Site Map. To the right of this, you'll see the actual content of your home page divided into 'zones'.

It's all fairly disciplined and so looks reasonably professional. The design employs stock photography – that is to say, photography that is free to use (see Chapter 10) – so to Web cognoscenti your site will look off-the-peg rather than bespoke.

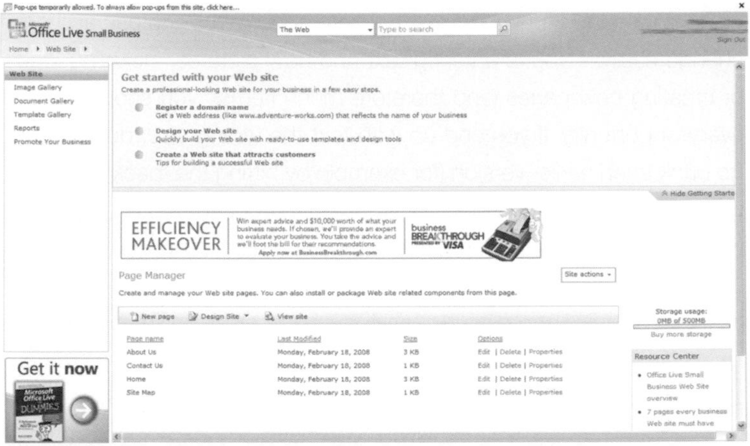

Figure 5 *Your website will have pages created automatically*

Figure 6 *One of the standard layouts*

You can easily play around with any of the settings on this new page, changing the text in the main heading or at the foot of the page, adding in a logo (if you have one), and choosing from one of the present themes or colour schemes.

Any time you navigate away from this page, you'll be asked if you want to save what you've just done. Be careful! As there isn't any kind of

Undo command you should just be clear about what you can and can't change easily. If you're entering text and new pictures, including logos, or creating new pages (and therefore menu items), you should save at every opportunity. If you end up with text the wrong size, don't try and go back to an earlier version (for example by hitting the 'back' button on your browser); it won't work. My advice is to concentrate on getting the words right first, keep saving, and then edit the size and typeface later.

If you're simply choosing options from the menu bar at the top – such as themes, styles and colours – saving isn't so crucial. Whatever pre-set style you choose can be switched later without affecting the words and pictures you've added. It's just a question of seeing what works best.

The interface is pretty intuitive if you have any experience of using computers and any kind of design tool. It can be fun just trying out different colours and layouts. A couple of words of caution: don't spend too long on the look – in the end, they're all pretty much variations on a theme and they won't add much impact to your website. Later you may want to include a logo that you use elsewhere, and then some of the design elements may become annoying. Concentrate instead on getting the description of your business right and *short*. You want it to communicate to potential customers quickly.

Incidentally, as you type in your text (often referred to as 'copy'), you might find you have trouble spacing paragraphs. One tip is to experiment with different spacings by using shift *and* enter instead of just the enter key. The former gives what is called a 'hard carriage return' or in HTML a 'line break' (symbolised by
), whilst the latter gives a 'soft carriage return' signifying a paragraph break which is adjustable according to the style parameters of that paragraph. You may have to experiment with these if you select a different paragraph style for your text.

Also, see if you can add your own photos: unfortunately, you can't do this in the main website heading and title. To add photos, click on an existing one, or under 'Site Designer' click on 'Logo'. You can also add from the 'Page Editor' tab at the top left of your screen, and then by clicking on the button marked 'Image'

You will find you have to load to your computer a small application, but this only takes a few moments – when prompted just click on 'Upload' and then the 'Run' button[2]. The application allows you to find and upload pictures on your computer, and gives you some basic editing ability before you place the picture on your Web pages.

It's pretty easy to add your own pictures if you have a digital camera, but be fussy. Don't add a blurred or badly-lit picture. If you want to demonstrate that you are a local business, consider having your photograph taken with a local landmark in the background, or even the town's name on a sign. You might also include a photo of your vehicle if, for example, you visit customers in your van. All of these things can make your business seem more accessible and reliable to potential customers. See Chapter 10 for more on putting images online.

As you edit elements and add in text, it's always worth using the right mouse button to see if there are any shortcuts to make the thing easier. In the case of photos, a right click will allow you to change the way the picture 'floats' with the text (or to delete it altogether), and this can be useful if the picture doesn't look quite right where it is.

If you need to add detailed information such as multiple contact details or scales of pricing, consider using a table. Again, this is a fairly simple option via the Page Editor tab and the Table button. It's best to set up a new page to play around with this rather than overload your home page

To see what you could do, I tried setting up a website on Office Live for a fictional 'Flying Plumber' based in Greenwich, London. A home page can be put together in just a few minutes.

By and large, your home page should contain the basic information that every visitor would want to see – and in one screen. If you find your page is getting longer and a visitor would need to scroll down, then move some information to another page and put a meaningful link, like

---

[2] If you have any anti-virus software installed, you may have to click another button to allow the installation and, as always, you may not be able to install at all on a PC that isn't yours – either in an Internet café or on a network.

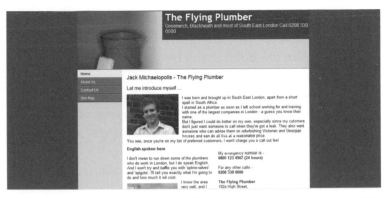

Figure 7 *If you're lucky, the standard image at the top may be nearly right for the business*

'How much I charge' or 'What my customers say' on the menu shown on the left of Figure 7.

Once you have your basic information finalised, you can think about adding other functions too, some of which we'll deal with in Chapter 5. By clicking on the 'Module' button (on the Page Editor tab) you can add a map, a weather report, a slide show or a blog, or a range of other, more complex options including HTML which, potentially, enables you to insert almost anything.

Google Page Creator

As you would expect, Google also has a simple way of establishing your online presence. We'll look at Google's directory-style listings for businesses in the next chapter. Here we'll look at an alternative to Microsoft's Office Live pages.

If you visit Google at all, you'll be familiar with the look and feel. It seems far cleaner and more open than some of the Microsoft space. At Google's home page, you can click on to the 'more' link towards the top left of the screen, and find their 'pages' product ('Page Creator') tucked away under the heading of 'Labs', where you can see some of the products Google invites you to test. Even quicker: point your browser to http://pages.google.com.

If you have a Google account and you're using your own computer, then you may well be recognised. You can see in Figure 9 that there is a blue login box towards the top right. If you haven't already done so, create a Google account (it will come in handy time and again) and then navigate back to the 'Pages' link above.

Once you're logged in, you'll be greeted by an illustration of a page and the terms and conditions of the service which you must read and

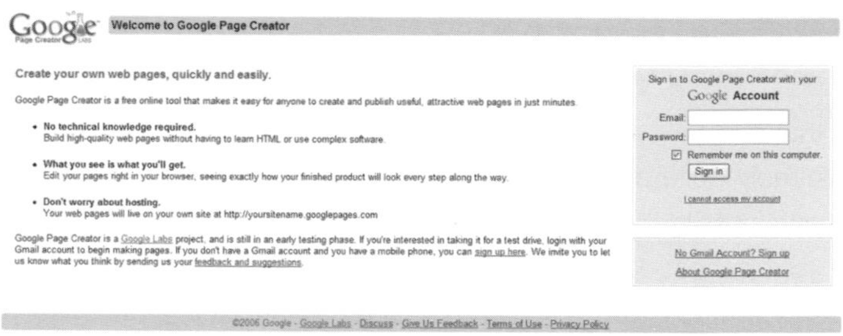

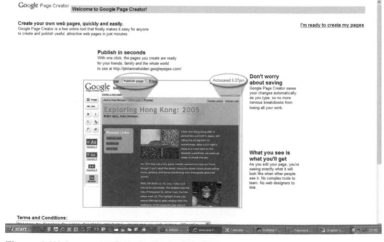

Figure 8 *At the moment, Google Page Creator is experimental – hence the 'Labs' logo*

Figure 9 *Welcome to Google Page Creator*

agree to. It's worth pointing out that you and you alone are responsible for your pages, but that Google is well within its rights to remove your pages and notify the relevant authorities if they deem anything you publish to be illegal – or even just suspect.

You can't immediately click on the very obvious link at the top right-hand corner of the screen – instead you'll need to agree to the terms and conditions, and click on the white button below them. Then you'll be taken to a generalised home page, which is rather less 'designed' than the Open Office equivalent. This will become your home page, but don't worry – you can redesign it.

Look towards the bottom left of the screen and you'll see a blue bar that tells you what the Web address (or URL) will be of your page – probably quite a mouthful. Don't worry too much about this as it's perfectly possible, as it is with the Open Office version above, for you to buy your perfect domain name and have it automatically redirect to the pages you've created. You can also have links to these pages to your blog, if you have one: the visitor won't see the long address.

You can start to enter words into this home page immediately. Again, like Open Office, if you try to navigate away from this page you will see it automatically saved. As before, the most important thing is to get the information and words right at this point. Looking at your 'outside-in' view of the business (back to your sketched maps), what is it that customers need to know as soon as they get to you? What will they be looking for? What is your best 'offer' to grab their attention and make them stay or click or communicate or even order? Can you offer them any reassurance about dealing with you online?

At any time you can click on the options at the top right of the screen to change the layout or the look. There are over 40 (generally pastel) colour schemes which don't include any stock graphic like Open Office, and just four alternative layouts. You can, though, put your own pictures into the heading, so you would be able to put your logo there.

As you can see, having more options doesn't automatically lead to a better design . . .

Figure 10 *Adding text is as easy as typing on to the screen*

Figure 11 *Heading and page design changed*

. . . but at least we can include the van with the logo.

As we've already said, dealing with photos is tricky. In HTML pages, it's difficult to get photos and logos (collectively called graphics files) to sit exactly where you'd like. Notice that the main heading is sitting at the bottom of the box whilst the photo is standing up above the text.

In Google Pages, you can at least drag photos around the page a little to see if they end up where you'd like. You can also edit them – cutting them down, changing the contrast and so on – without downloading additional software. However, the preview you get isn't a guarantee that everything will look OK on someone else's computer screen.

As we touched on in Chapter 3, some HTML is very useful, but the templates in Google and the others are controlled so that you can't really edit the look of pages in much detail.

Incidentally, the solution to the heading and logo problem for the Flying Plumber could be to produce a graphic just for the heading that incorporates the website title and the picture and can be placed in the topmost box. Some experimentation is needed to get the size and shape right. The image used below was around 600 × 160 pixels.

Figure 12 *Replacing the standard heading with a 'banner'*

Apart from putting in text and images, you can also add links, which could be potentially useful if you have other pages, a blog and so on. Google prompts you to link to other pages which you can create as you go along.

However, the other links are relatively limited. You can link to external Web pages (such as your eBay store or blog) and you can include e-mail addresses. If you choose the latter, the prompt helpfully reminds you that any e-mail addresses on Web pages are easy for spammers to pick up and use.

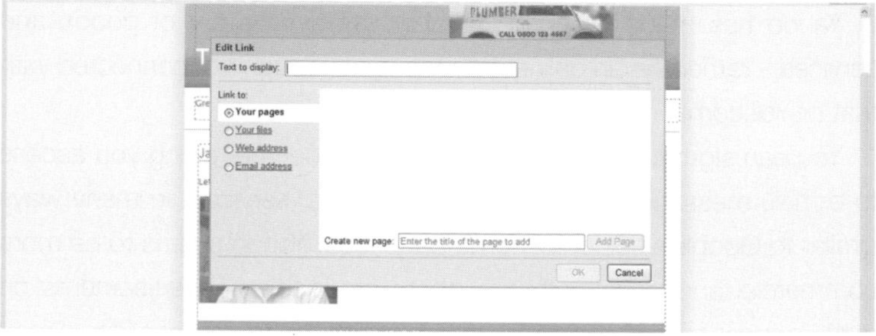

Figure 13 *You can add pages and links here*

Unlike Blogger and the other blog providers we looked at in Chapter 3, the Web page providers don't seem to be into connectivity. It's not so easy to include photo albums, feed or links to other, more social, sites and services except as text – so, unfortunately, no easily recognisable logos or buttons. However, it would be fairly straight forward to include a link to a forum or a collaborative working area (such as those described in Chapter 12), perhaps for certain clients or co-workers. A plain text link would then lead on to a login screen and be reasonably secure.

Now go to top left and see 'Back to Site Manager'.

Yahoo

The third giant provider of Web services (at the time of writing, at least: there has been much speculation about its future) is Yahoo.

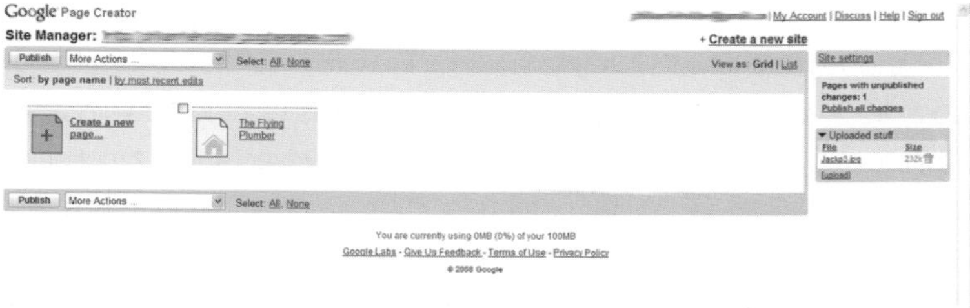

Figure 14 *The Site Manager area shows you what pages you have created*

Yahoo has made its name primarily as a directory of goods and services – rather like an online yellow pages (though not connected with that or Yell.com).

You can sign up for your local Yahoo service free, giving you access to e-mail, messaging, groups and many other services. In many ways similar to Google's 'iGoogle' home page idea, Yahoo seems to be more commercial and visual – that is, there are display advertisements on many pages, and you have to search a little bit to find services aimed at you as a business owner. You could say that Google is a bit more 'geeky', aiming for a simplistic interface; Microsoft is 'corporate', fitting in with its software, and Yahoo has more of a commercial-TV feel about it.

Yahoo's small business services are based on their US site – yahoo. com – and so are naturally biased towards business there. It's unlikely that companies based in the UK or the rest of Europe would want to use Yahoo for recruitment, for example, but you could investigate the merchant services or the promotional tools. You can check it out at http://smallbusiness.yahoo.com and click on the 'Web Hosting' heading shown in Figure 15.

Yahoo's Web hosting offer is, however, strictly a paid-for service – on offer at about $9 per month at the time of writing. It works in pretty much the same way as Microsoft's and Google's offerings, giving you templates to fill in with your own information and pictures. As a paid service, Yahoo offers you unlimited storage space, which may be valuable if you are likely to upload a large number of images or videos, for example. It's also much more amenable to customisation – if you know what you're doing with HTML and other authoring tools – and supports Flash animations.

Yahoo currently offers a number of incentives in its basic charge, such as some free advertising and credit towards Google Adwords (see Chapter 7), and there is a 30-day free trial. However, a fully functioning e-commerce site costs from around £20 a month, and offers you extensive support for selling online, including order handling and many other features. To its credit, Yahoo gives you links to example sites for you to explore, so it's fairly easy to see if you can achieve what you want.

Figure 15 *Yahoo's small business offering*

My recommendation is to try setting up what you absolutely need using one of the free providers and see how it looks. You can use Yahoo's own directory to find alternative free hosting services at http://tinyurl.com/6mfdwx. As you develop more expertise, you may want more control over the look and feel of your site, but you may find (especially when you've read Chapter 6) that you can generate all the sales you need without a complex e-commerce site.

Alternative listings and Web space

BT Tradespace (www.bttradespace.com) is an alternative way of giving you a Web presence. In its basic form, it's free and lets you select a number of categories in which your business can be listed. Unfortunately, the free version only allows you to list up to five products for sale, on which BT charge you 5 per cent of each transaction – so it's not ideal for e-commerce. There is the opportunity to blog and upload a limited number of pictures and videos, but also to develop an online community, which might be a good place to interact with customers. The full version, in which your product listings are unlimited, costs up to £134 (+VAT) a year, and BT reduce their charge to 3 per cent on transactions. Your Web address for this service would be http://youraccountname. bttradespace.com – probably not the most user-friendly, but as with other such services you can often add on your own domain name and redirect it to your BT page.

To investigate further, see http://about.bttradespace.com, but don't expect to find much in the way of visitor figures to convince you to sign up. The traffic across the whole site seems low, and the newly-introduced communities seem inactive. Still, it's early days, and BT may get behind it more and build its popularity.

Of course, there's no reason why you couldn't be listed on BT Tradespace as well as others, including Google, MSN and Yahoo. The more often your business is mentioned online, the more chances you have of being found. However, you'll need to judge this against the extra time taken to update multiple sites; it's not clear that you can automate much of this with the BT site. For example, your blog in BT Tradespace would be entirely separate from any other blog, and both would have to be updated.

Going further

Once you have an online presence, you might find you want to take the next step and design your site, having it hosted independently.

A good halfway house is offered by Squarespace.com (www. squarespace.com), which offers a very well-designed website and sophisticated add-ons such as blogging, photo hosting, podcasting and more. It's easy to sign up and free to try (and from $7 a month thereafter), and seems to offer easy-to-use tools for managing your site. You can compare it with Ning in Chapter 9, which has a similar approach but is based on a social network model.

Of course, once you get to a certain level of traffic, or you want more sophisticated tools such as the ability to manage subscriptions, you will have to pay more, but it may be worthwhile for a very manageable website with most of the bells and whistles you could want.

Many off-the-peg website-building services don't offer sophisticated e-commerce functions. There are, however, many providers such as Bluepark (www.bluepark.co.uk) which offer a full service, including website building and hosting, that could be worth exploring. Virtually free options such as CubeCart (www.cubecart.com) offer integration with Google's Checkout product and PayPal (see Chapters 5 and 6), but require a compatible hosting service where your website will be located.

Joomla (www.joomla.org) and Xoops (www.xoops.org) are free 'content management' and Web-building platforms that you can download and use on your own server space. They are commonly used by professional Web designers, are constantly being improved upon and have a high level of community support for novice users.

You should also look at OSWD (Open Source Web Design at www.oswd.org) which has some well-designed templates to download free. In fact, just search for 'open source Web design' and you'll find a mountain of free page layouts and some considerable help out there – also see Chapter 11.

It's still a good idea to understand many of the opportunities the big players offer. The next chapter covers some more of the services of Google, Microsoft and Yahoo, where Web users are already searching for products and suppliers.

If you still want to sell direct to customers online but find the prospect of your own e-commerce site daunting, then Chapter 6 offers a couple of easy ways to start selling that will grow with your business and don't incur the heavy start-up costs of establishing your own website. And eBay and Amazon also have millions of customers already online and searching, ready to buy.

Generally speaking, the more you move away from the free or virtually free options provided by Google, Microsoft, eBay and Amazon, the more you are likely to need experienced help to set up and run your site. Again, see Chapter 11 for some ideas and contacts.

A well-designed site like Mr Humbug (www.mrhumbug.com) has successfully carried through its fun and tasteful approach to its business from the (real-world) candy and sweet store to the site. The challenge then is to attract customers to the site, and that's what we'll deal with in Chapter 7.

Figure 16 *Mr Humbug is a good example of a bespoke e-commerce site*

I'd recommend using the guidance in Chapters 5 and 6 to get some experience of online trading first. At least having sold *some* product using virtually free tools, you will have some experience upon which to base the design of a more tailored website. You will also then have solved the problems of accepting, processing and fulfilling orders.

And, crucially, you will have developed your system of keeping track of and in touch with your established customers, and will be developing a sense of what you can provide . . . that they really want to buy.

CHAPTER 5

THE BIG THREE . . . AGAIN (AND WHAT THEY CAN DO FOR YOU)

As I suggested in the last chapter, the big three are Google, Microsoft and Yahoo. Keeping in touch with what these can offer your business (while still checking out some of the smaller, and sometimes more innovative, alternatives) is vital. Google itself is pretty creative and productive and they, along with the other big two, offer a sizeable market opportunity for the small business.

Apart from anything else, all three have a community of committed users – biased towards the US, it must be said, but increasingly well represented in Europe and elsewhere.

Start with Google

For many people, Google *is* the Web; it's the first page they see when they switch on their computer. Increasingly, it seems that Google has a product for everyone, and there are certainly many free Google services you can use, if you invest a little time.

Perhaps the best starting place is to use the site to search for people and companies who seem to offer the same products and services as you. You may even find yourself listed because of other directory-type sites. This kind of basic market research is extremely valuable and, of course, virtually free.

The kind of keywords you might use will vary (as we saw when we were looking for blogs), and it's a good idea to keep track of which search terms get results. Fortunately it's quite easy to keep notes of your searches. In the latest versions of many browsers (including Microsoft Explorer and Firefox), you can save searches and tabs to come back to. The keywords you use may help you later on when you are designing your own pages or advertising (see Chapter 7).

To use the full range of services Google has to offer, you'll need to sign up for a free account. Apart from being able to search Google, you can also use maps, get products listed, set up a website, set up an online store, run an ad campaign, and generate income from others' advertising. You can even place Google maps and other elements in your own Web pages, and you can embed a search toolbar in your browser.

To get the free account up and running, click on the 'Sign in' link at the top right of your screen and simply provide your current e-mail address and a suitable password. You'll get an e-mail fairly quickly with a link you need to click to verify your account.

You can elect to have iGoogle as your default page when you start your browser, and once you've typed in the security characters further down, you're ready to go. You'll be given another chance to change your home page with a few options as to the content and graphics, but nothing particularly sophisticated at this stage. If you are keeping track of several important pages (such as news) or blogs, you might find the iGoogle page useful – even more so if you download the Google toolbar. Built in is a newsfeed reader so you can set up your home page to display certain feeds as soon as you log in. Very useful for checking on what's being discussed and what you may need to respond to.

Local business for local people?

Remembering what we said about knowing where your customers are in Chapter 2? Now's the time to use this information. If you rely predominantly on customers in your town or district, Google's local business maps are a useful place to start. For many such businesses, simply being on the high street and being noticed is a good start, but what happens if you sell things that are less frequently purchased?

Or if your premises are off the beaten track, but your customers are still local? Or suppose you need customers to visit you from far afield – maps, directions, opening hours and of course phone numbers and e-mail addresses are all useful things to have out there, readily accessible.

Google maps and their local business centre are easily found. When you sign in or you go to Google's home page, you'll usually find a link that says something like 'Business Solutions': in fact it appears at the foot of almost every Google page. Wherever you are in Google, you'll also probably see a list at the top left that says:

Web   Images   Maps   News   Shopping   Mail   more   ▼

You can always click on 'more' (and then sometimes 'even more') to get to other Google services. Eventually, for services you use frequently, you may want to personalise your iGoogle home page so that they are easier to find.

The first section to look at is headed 'Business information'. You have to sign in again (!), but then you can start to fill in the details of your business with contact details and a short description. As you do so, a preview of your listing appears on the right of your screen. In this case, as I've gone back to grab the screen shots, you can see all the other information filled in, such as payment types and opening hours.

You then get to add in up to five categories under which your business may be listed. As a plumber you might want to be listed under 'Services', which has a sub-category of 'Plumbing', but in order to add another sub-category such as 'Heating, ventilation and air-conditioning', you'll have to click on 'Add another category', select 'Services' again and so on.

It's worth looking through the categories and sub-categories in some detail to determine which are most appropriate. Our plumber might, for example, want to be included in the category 'Real Estate' and sub-category 'Property Management'. These can always be edited and revised at any time in the future. My example isn't a great one, since

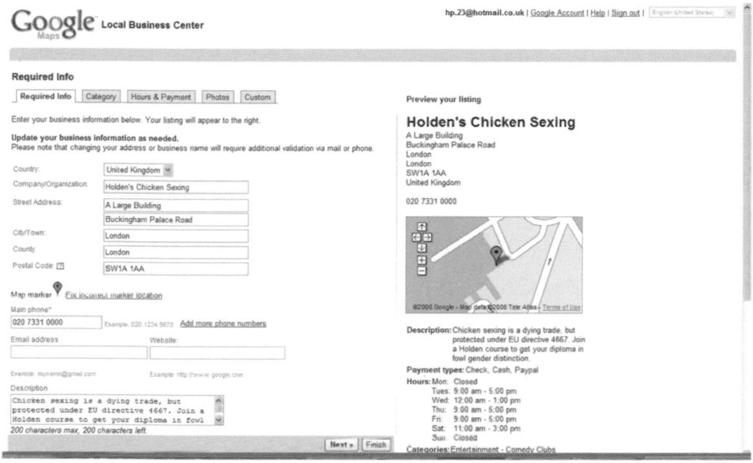

Figure 1 *Starting to fill in your business details – here the details are plotted on a Google map*

apparently I can't decide whether chicken-sexing is for fun or profit . . . but you get the idea.

You're next asked about your opening hours and the methods of payment you accept. For all businesses, these are pretty important facts to get right, so don't forget to update your Google listing when these change or you'll end up with disgruntled (non-)customers.

Next, you can add up to ten photos that may give some indication of your business. For small businesses it's not a bad idea to have a picture of you, the principal, up there . . . assuming you look trustworthy. Don't upload a photo unless it's a good one and it's yours to use. Of course, product shots and photos of your gleaming premises or van are also reassuring in some cases.

You can also link to videos such as those from YouTube. Again, you can come back and add pictures at a later date, and we'll look at some photographic and video tools in Chapter 10.

The next section is more complex, as you have the opportunity to say much more about your business, how you charge and attributes that you may want to add. You can even add in e-mail and Web addresses

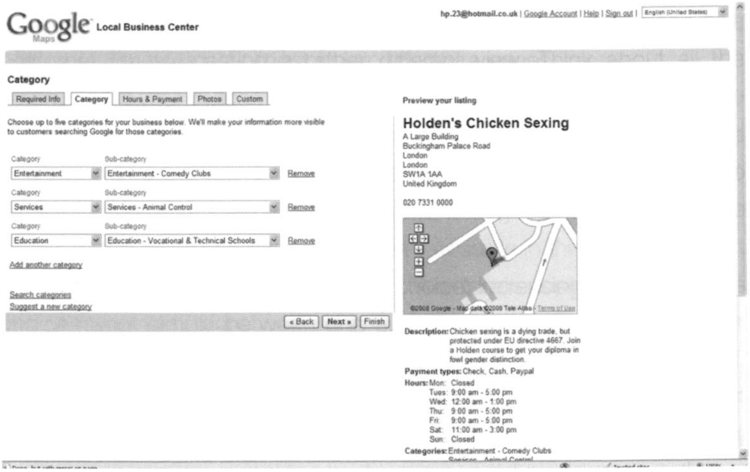

Figure 2 *Choosing the categories under which your business will be found*

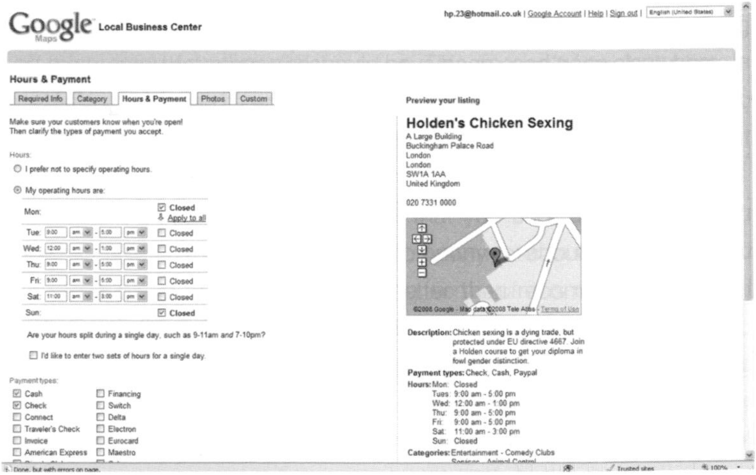

Figure 3 *Enter your opening hours and acceptable payment methods*

here: practically any simple fact you think enquirers might want to know. This is a perfect opportunity to link together your other pages, blogs or online stores; in fact, anything that could be of value to your customers.

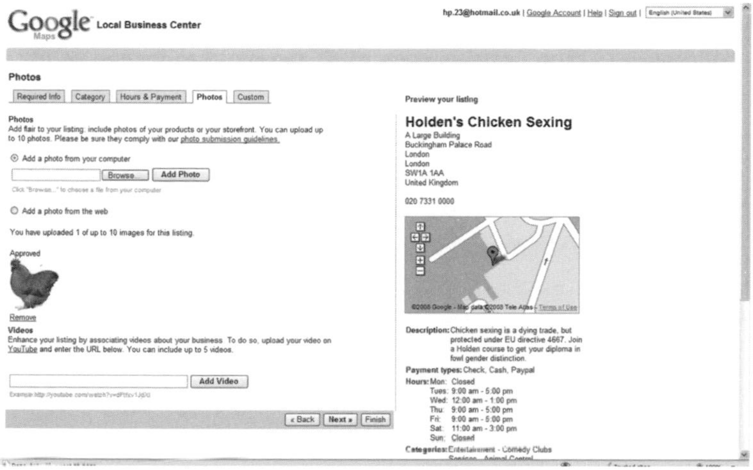

Figure 4 *Photos and videos are easily uploaded*

Again, you get a preview of your listing so you can review it to make sure it says what you want.

Having done all this, you validate the listing immediately by photo or text message, or you can, rather quaintly, request a postcard. Hit the Finish button and follow the instructions, then you're all set. Incidentally, when you do activate your listing, you'll probably start receiving offers about using Google for advertising, and we'll look at this again in Chapter 7.

If, at this stage, anything about your listing seems to be amiss, there is a useful help centre at http://maps.google.co.uk/support, and there is also a self-help group at http://groups.google.com which covers thousands of issues that other users have experienced. Any problem is worth researching here and, if you still haven't got an answer, posting in the same place for other, more experienced, users to offer solutions. The help groups are amongst the most useful for every aspect of Google's service.

If you've activated your listing immediately, then you can try searching for your service in your area and see how prominently your entry appears.

However, bear in mind that Google reckons on updating these listings only every four weeks, so it's hardly rapid. You can, of course, go back and edit details.

By the way, don't contact me if you do have any chickens.

Start promoting straight away

One of the instant things you can do within Google's Local Business Center is issue discount vouchers. This is obviously attractive for a local bar or café (less so for chicken-sexing classes). So, if you are still logged in to your Google account, you can navigate your way to the Business Center where you'll see a blue tab at the top entitled 'Coupons'.

Again, there is a fairly straightforward form to fill out, along with a preview of how your coupon will look. Bear in mind that you are completely responsible for the content of the coupon – Google includes what you specify in its directory – so make sure the terms of the offer are very clear. If you run a restaurant, say, do you only want to offer 25 per cent off one meal, do you mean a single dish, one item from the menu, excluding drinks? The simpler and bigger the offer, the more powerful

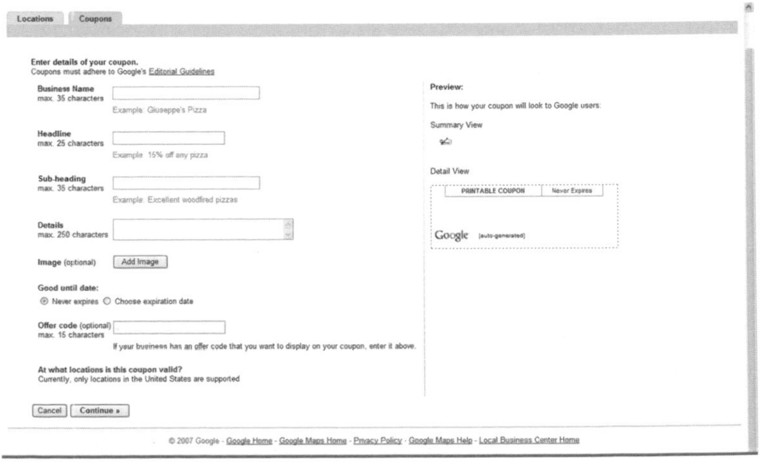

Figure 5 *How you specify a coupon*

it will be. It also helps to make it time-limited: having a £10 voucher expiring in your wallet is like money going out of fashion.

If you're in a business where customers search for alternatives (the nearest Italian restaurant, the nearest live theatre) and make decisions in a relatively short space of time, coupons can help them make the decision in your favour. Don't forget to read Google's own editorial guidelines before you decide on your coupon offer and (in the UK) check your obligations under the various codes of conduct and regulations by looking the Advertising Standards Authority website at www.asa. org.uk.

Selling things?

Perhaps the next thing to look at is Google Base, where you can list products. You can find it at http://base.google.com.

In a way, Google Base is just another kind of listings site like Yellow Pages. You fill in a fairly simple form allocating your product or service or event to a category, and it ends up being searchable on Google.

To look at the service you can click on some of the 'popular item types'. This will take you straight to a list of items posted by others. In most cases you will also see a form at the top which enables you to sort all the entries in that category. For example, you might be looking for a certain kind of recipe, or a job in a particular industry with a salary over a certain amount. It's worth looking at the most appropriate category for your product or service to see how your competitors show up, noting any strengths and weaknesses of their listings.

Don't worry if you can't find exactly the right category. When you come to generate your own listing you can suggest a category and, as with the Local Business Center, choose several.

To start building your own listing, you'll have to sign up and agree to the terms and conditions of Google's service; these are in addition to any you've signed up to so far.

Of course, simply listing a product isn't enough; you'd like to sell it too, and you'll notice that some listings have a Checkout button next to

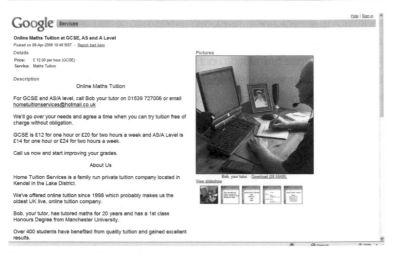

Figure 6 *You can list services as well as products*

them. Google Checkout (www.checkout.google.co.uk) is an easy-to-set-up selling system which is virtually free. It costs nothing to set up or to transfer funds, and Google handles credit card transactions on your behalf. Instead there's a straightforward charge of 1.5% plus 15p for every transaction. If you spend money on Google's Adwords search advertising (see Chapter 7), you get credit towards these fees each month, so that buying £50 of advertising would allow you £500 of sales in the following month without charge.

Your customers must also sign up to Google Checkout in order to buy (they have to give credit card details and so on), but can then buy simply by signing in. Google claim that the Checkout button increases the rate at which listings are clicked on by 10 per cent.

Once you're signed up to Google Checkout, you can integrate it with your own Web pages simply by inserting the code for a 'Buy it now' button next to items you're selling. Therefore you don't need any e-commerce functions on your own site.

When orders are made, you can access all the details you need to fulfil the order online via the 'Merchant Center' in your Google Checkout

Figure 7 *Google Checkout gives you an easy e-commerce function*

account. Every time you log in, you'll be notified of new orders and can process them, saving any details you need to fulfil the order and sending a confirmation e-mail, via Google, to your customer.

You can see examples of Checkout in action via Google's website. For example, Bedworld (www.bedworld.net), which has a fully-functioning e-commerce site but has a Google Checkout button as an alternative.

There's no doubt that Google is a reassuring name for many Web users, and small businesses can benefit from this. Checkout lowers some of the barriers of online selling at very little cost, but you'll want to consider other sites, especially eBay and Amazon in Chapter 6.

Should you consider MSN?

Well, the short answer is yes. But MSN is not as accessible to the small business as Google, and some of the functions centred on its 'Windows Live Spaces' product are better executed by others.

MSN itself has a huge audience and a considerable emphasis on e-commerce. However, there are few opportunities for free marketing. Maybe it's me, but the Microsoft offering seems to be stuck in the past, trying to be a portal for everyone.

If you want to advertise, there is a conventional media sales outfit that will sell advertising across much of the Microsoft empire – some of it on a pay-per-click basis – but see Chapter 7 for more accessible alternatives.

A large section of MSN is concerned with shopping, and as such utilises a network of other sites such as Autotrader. It is possible to promote your brand within the various product sectors, in specialised 'gift guides' and alongside search results, but you have to go through their ad sales department, and it's certainly not free. Go to http://advertising.microsoft.com for more information.

You can also set up personal pages ('Spaces') in Windows Live Spaces (in the UK http://msn-uk.spaces.live.com[1]) which seem to have some social networking features, although when I visited it didn't seem to be working so well with broken links, spelling mistakes and quite a few 'coming soon' messages. Even the 'Help' link didn't work.

'Spaces' can include linking up with other people with shared interests, maintaining friends' lists, uploading photos, and blogging. There is a suggestion that blogs do improve your search performance in MSN, so you might want to consider this – if you identify MSN as a source of customers. However, it's not clear if you can automatically feed posts from another blog into a Live Spaces blog, so you'd have to manually update this.

Promoting yourself on Yahoo

Yahoo has a listings facility for merchants through Kelkoo (www.kelkoo.co.uk), which includes the websites of GMTV (www.gm.tv) and Loot (www.loot.com). The listings are free, but you must pay for clicks through to your page or website. To find the details of costs and audiences you need to contact the Kelkoo sales people.

If you have a high-traffic website, you might make some money by becoming a Kelcoo affiliate (http://tinyurl.com/5ldztu), carrying ads on your pages. If you know what category of product your site's visitors are interested in, then you can specify the kinds of ads that appear.

---

[1] http://msn-uk.spaces.live.com was a truly hideous page when I visited; I daren't even show it on this page. Just to confuse matters, you could also find http://specials.uk.msn.com/spaces or try the US site at http://home.services.spaces.live.com both of which are bland but at least readable.

Advertising on Yahoo is often shared with MSN, and covers other search sites such as AltaVista. It's a straightforward 'pay-per-click' offer, and you can manage everything online. As we'll see in Chapter 7, any pay-per-click advertising has to be evaluated on its merits: if it leads to sales at the right price, then why not use it?

Search engine submission

Of course Google and Yahoo listings are all about getting found, but just because you have a website or a blog, or you've listed your products elsewhere, doesn't mean you will be found. Having information pages in industry directories can help – certainly Google indexes its own pages very well – but you can do more to help the process.

One way of improving your visibility is to ensure that MSN and Yahoo can find your blog (or website), and to do this you'll need to go ahead

Figure 8 *You can sign up online for Yahoo's search-based advertising*

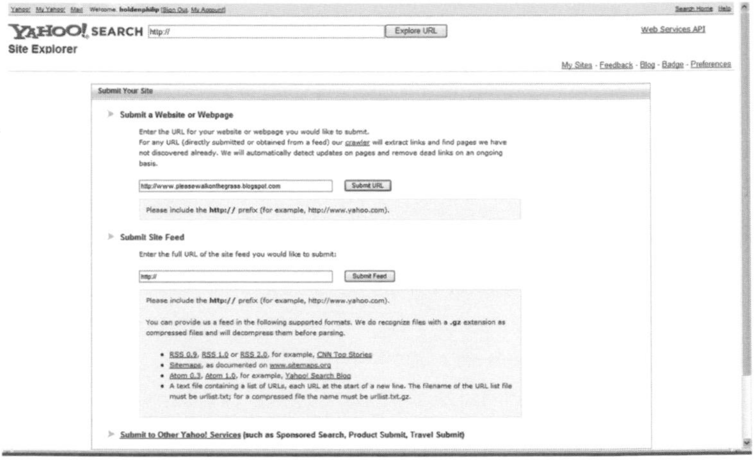

Figure 9 *Submitting your site to Yahoo*

and sign up for both sites (even if you hardly use them afterwards). If you've set up your blog, you need to find your site feed URL (in Blogger that's under 'Settings' – see Chapter 3) which may look like http://pleasewalkonthegrass.blogspot.com/feeds/posts/default.

Now, sign into your account at Yahoo or MSN and go to your home page. On Yahoo you'll have to click on 'My Yahoo' on the left and then go right to the bottom on the next page to find a link that says 'Publish on Yahoo'. Alternatively, sign in and simply go to http://publisher.yahoo.com/rssguide, and it's a simple matter then of pasting the feed link into a box.

A further alternative is to visit http://search.yahoo.com/info/submit. html where you can submit both a feed and a website URL. This also includes submission to AltaVista.

On your Yahoo home page you can also personalise the page (a tab towards the top, shown in Figure 11) and have your blog postings appear automatically there too. Likewise in MSN, you can add content to your home page by clicking on the 'Add content' link to the top left (see Figure 10). A small window will open into which you can enter your feed URL or search for any other content you want to add. Then click the green arrow.

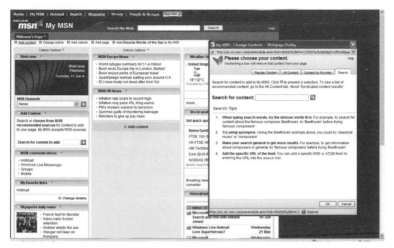

Figure 10 *Ensuring your blog is known by MSN*

Figure 11 **Submitting your page to the MSN search engine**

Both Yahoo and MSN may take a couple of days to update their databases, but you'll soon be able to find your blog in their search – as well as seeing it on your home page.

If, as is sometimes the case, MSN can't find the feed you are directing it to, try searching for the full address of your blog or Web page. If it still can't find it, there is a form for submitting pages (that you know exist) at http://tinyurl.com/5nbwbq.

As well as MSN and Yahoo, don't forget you can also add sites to Google at www.google.com/addurl, but once you've done that you shouldn't need to notify any others. Sites like AltaVista, AOL and AllTheWeb use search provided by the big three[2]. You should also visit DMOZ, the open directory project (www.dmoz.org/add.html), which is an authoritative list but can take up to six months to update. The only other search engine that might find you is Ask (or Ask Jeeves) at www.ask.com or www.ask.co.uk, which doesn't accept website submissions.

Search engine optimisation

Once a search engine knows of your existence, you might think it's easy for customers to find you. Search engine optimisation, or SEO, is the art of improving your chances. In itself this doesn't sound much of a problem, but the few searches we've carried out in earlier chapters suggest otherwise. The problems are many.

First of all, there's the sheer size of the Net, a problem that Google was probably the first to address in a committed way. The founders, Larry Page and Sergey Brin, knew that in order to offer meaningful search results quickly, they had to have dedicated servers with sufficient capacity working very hard – recent estimates are that they have nearly half a million servers around the world[3]. Even then the issue of the relevancy of results wasn't solved instantly.

In order to produce results that were likely to be useful, the Google search algorithm had to take into account how Web pages were constructed: not just the words they contained but also the links into and out of them. Essentially, Google's servers regularly analysed and kept a copy of the World Wide Web so that when a query was entered into their search field, it was compared with that analysis to find the best responses.

---

[2] Consequently, the many websites offering to submit your website to 'all' the search engines are, in my view, pointless.

[3] According to David Carr in *Baseline* Magazine, July 2006 http://tinyurl.com/2djop4

The second issue is that there is intense competition. In any search for a product or service, there are thousands of companies that would like to capture all prospects, and so a market has grown up in promoting businesses, products and websites in search engines.

Search engine optimisation itself has a reputation as something of a black art, and there are hundreds of firms out there who offer SEO services. A few are very good (but none has the magic formula and can absolutely guarantee that you will be at the top of a results page), while many charge for their time rather than by results. Yahoo also offers search-based marketing services and a useful simple guide at http://sem.smallbusiness.yahoo.com/searchenginemarketing.

For our purposes here, we want to look at techniques that can be virtually free, and that means putting some time into understanding how your online presence is discovered and tracked, and what you can do.

There are, more or less, two aspects to search engines. The first is simply the subject matter of your site, represented by the words you use on your pages. A little knowledge of HTML is useful here, since some search engines look at words that are hidden as well as those clearly visible to browsers. Hidden text, usually at the top of a page and called 'meta tags', can describe the content of the page or site and attract the right kind of attention. In the early days of the Web this feature was quickly abused by website owners trying to attract casual surfers, especially to pornography or scam sites.

Some would argue that this isn't SEO so much as being search-friendly, and I would argue it's good manners to make sure your Web pages are not misleading. It's good practice to have important words for your industry somewhere on the page but, if they can't be clearly shown in text, then meta tags and similar devices can be useful. If your business is about garden design, then it's permissible to say so in the tags even if the specific page is, say, about the types of pots you have for sale.

To get an idea of how your Web pages might be viewed by various search engines, go to www.submitexpress.com/analyzer. At the same website you can use the various free tools to assess the meta tags in your pages or to estimate the popularity of various keywords.

Some key words are obvious. For example, you should include the common descriptions of what you do: – if you sell fresh flowers then you'd want to include several phrases such as 'fresh flowers' and 'florist' and maybe also 'delivery'. There would be a whole list of other words that might be used to search for your service. A tool like Wordtracker (http://freekeywords.wordtracker.com) or the one provided by Google itself (http://tinyurl.com/qkfuh) will give you an indication of the most popular searches.

Wordtracker's free search shows that out of over 120,000 searches including the word 'flowers', some 6,166 are for 'wedding flowers' and 1,355 for 'send flowers' so these could be useful phrases for your site (and for advertising). Google, on the other hand, suggests a range of phrases and words related to your initial phrase and also gives an indication of their popularity, and the phrase 'flower delivery' might also be worth considering.

Over and above the use of keywords in advertising (which we deal with in Chapter 7), we can use them to increase the relevance of our Web content. If you have been writing your own company pages (as suggested in Chapter 4 or 5), or even wondering what you can write about in your blog, these keywords are, well, key. It also follows that this aspect of optimisation is ongoing – every time you check on keywords and searches you will find something new to emphasise on your pages.

It's often taken as a rule of thumb that about 200 to 400 words of good quality content, well seeded with your chosen keywords, will help your page be found. All the keywords should be noted and included in the relevant meta tag. Likewise, the keyword should be deleted from the meta tag field if it is omitted from the page. The trick is to do all this naturally without your copy reading like a list – "wedding flowers delivered; send flowers, flowers, cheap flowers" . . . and so on.

Given that 5 per cent of all searches for flowers relate to wedding flowers, if you were a florist (or a wedding organiser) you'd probably want to make sure you wrote frequent articles about wedding flowers. It's really as simple as that. You should also make sure that, as far as possible, titles of pages are relevant to the content. This is one of the disadvantages of some off-the-shelf websites – you don't have this much control. But it's fairly obvious that no search engine is going to put you at the top of a list just because your page is called 'home' or 'index' (along with billions of others).

This kind of internal SEO, where you manage the content, appeals to Yahoo and MSN but is less important for the Google search engine which, as we've said, is also concerned with links into and out of a site. External SEO is about getting other people to have links to your website. You can do this by blogging and commenting, providing articles for other websites, and ensuring that you always have a link back. By and large, the more current and controversial the subject on which you comment, the more likely it is to be searched for and linked to by others – it's called 'link baiting'. Just be interesting and committed; a single comment on a site or blog about an issue won't have much effect, but a dialogue over weeks or month could. Likewise, don't be satisfied with one or two links to other useful sites: try and be comprehensive.

There's a lot of useful stuff about online marketing, keywords and search engine optimisation at www.sphinn.com and at the Marketmou blog – www.blog.marketmou.com – and a useful source with an emphasis on small businesses, Hobo (www.hobo-Web.co.uk) and Search Engine Watch (http://searchenginewatch.com). We'll say more about driving traffic to and through your site in Chapter 7.

Online advertising

For the really small company, advertising seems like an extravagance, and doing it online can seem dauntingly complicated. It's true that it's difficult to make online advertising campaigns really effective but, conversely, all such activity should be measurable. Advertising is generally sold on the basis of paying for how many people see the advertising or how many people click – pay-per-view or pay-per-click.

We'll look at Google's advertising product in Chapter 7, running advertising in Facebook in Chapter 8 and some other options in Chapter 9 – and explain why this can be so well targeted. However, before you go promoting what you have to sell, it's as well to make it available for people to buy. Rather than set up complex stores you can, of course, use channels that are already there, and we'll look at two of the most famous (and a couple of others) in the next chapter.

—

CHAPTER 6

SELLING THROUGH eBAY AND AMAZON

It's no surprise that Amazon and eBay represent a huge chunk of online buying and selling. Despite the apparent dominance of Google, Yahoo and MSN, these two sites represent the great successes of the dotcom boom.

Specialists in various industries will tell you these are not *the* most important sites. For example, those selling motor cars will find an account with Autotrader.co.uk essential, whilst estate agents will look to Prime Location. Many small ads – especially looking for flat shares but selling all kinds of items – go through sites like Craigslist in the US (www.craigslist.org) or Gumtree in the UK (www.gumtree.com). But for an introduction to online selling, eBay and Amazon are perfect. For literally thousands of sellers in thousands of categories, from artworks to zoology textbooks, Amazon and eBay *are* the marketplace. And, yes, cars and houses are sold on eBay too.

Perhaps the most important thing to note is that, by and large, eBay is concerned with auctions and Amazon is not. In actual fact, an increasing part of eBay's business is from non-auction transactions and, though you'll struggle to find them, Amazon runs auctions. But, for most purposes, the two sites have different strengths, and it's as well to play to them in the way you market your business. You can, of course, sell products in both.

In this chapter we're going to look primarily at selling, although it's quite likely that you'll want to use these sites to buy your business supplies or even stock to then resell. Most eBay users find that they can't help but use their knowledge to grab a bargain as they're browsing – see the example of Paul Harrison later in this chapter. In any case, in order to sell you have to know how each of these sites works, and the best way to do that is to be a buyer.

Amazon, of course, has a well-established reputation for books, CDs, DVDs and computer games, but increasingly also for electronics and other products. The popular perception of eBay is that it offers bargains, or at least the chance for a competitive deal, in all kinds of products. It's hardly a scientific analysis, but the categories with the most items for sale on eBay are consistently 'Collectables' and 'Clothes, shoes and accessories' but these categories (as we'll see below) mask an enormous range of products available both new and used from all over the world.[1]

While Amazon seems to stick closely to its origins as a bookshop, eBay caters for some fairly wacky tastes. Both sites are mainly for physical products, though that's not to say services aren't sold this way. There's also no end of eBay sellers offering get-rich-quick schemes, to unlock mobile phones or transfer video to DVD, and some very strange things have been offered for sale over the years including fighter jets, a meal out with Rupert Murdoch, and New Zealand (the latter as an act of protest).

Amazon also has its share of 'How to earn $5,000 in a week' and these are often just a download of a pretty useless e-book. The notion of an eBay auction for a service is pretty strange – unless it's exceptionally rare, and perhaps for a charitable cause – and so the vast majority of items on eBay are just that: items. The site also has a category for 'Speciality services' such as the personalisation of products, art, computer help and, interestingly, services to help you sell on eBay.

Given our approach to marketing for small businesses, we're going to focus on what these sites are best for: attracting a lot of customers who are either looking for something pretty specific or are browsing. Either way these sites offer you an online presence with pretty good traffic

---

[1] You can get some interesting insights into eBay categories from www.auctionsoftwarereview. com and both eBay and Amazon themselves track the most popular items and categories. Amazon at www.amazon.com/gp/bestsellers and eBay at http://pulse.ebay.com/

(the equivalent of 'footfall' through a shopping centre) and ready-built e-commerce functions. Crucially, they are low-cost, and you can test your marketing as you go along with fairly minimal outgoings.

eBay – a market for everything

To start with, we'll look at how eBay works for consumers: a bit of research. Go to www.ebay.co.uk (or your local version[2]) and you'll see the 'entrance' to the marketplace. If you're already a user the site might even welcome you by name.

Spend a little time familiarising yourself with the site. You should certainly look around for the kind of products and services you may be offering online. Take on the role of a shopper and find out the different

Figure 1 _The first thing you, and your customers, see of eBay_

[2] There are at least 26 versions to my knowledge, from Australia to Singapore as well as of course, the biggest in the US and the potentially huge eBay China.

ways you could come across the right product.[3] Remember the 'outside-in' view of your company? You will be judged, initially, by your listing of a product – only later may a prospective buyer investigate you further.

So, let's suppose you're looking for a particular brand – FatFace, for example, which is a high street brand of casual clothing that also sells online (www.fatface.com). Not only does FatFace have a particular design look, but it also has clear associations with surfing. In addition, FatFace is associated particularly with certain items such as sweatshirts.

Potential customers will probably search in many different ways. For our purposes we'll divide them into the 'hunters' and 'grazers'.

Customers as hunters

The hunters already have a clear idea of what they are looking for so they may go straight to the long search box at the top of the eBay page and key in a precise description of what they want. Let's say 'women's blue FatFace sweatshirt' and hit the search key. The next page to load rapidly gives the hunter the results – in this case none at all!

What happens next is interesting, because although there were no perfect hits, eBay immediately gives hunters choices. They could try refining their search by using the advanced search link, or they could go back to the search term they entered (it's still there in the long white search box) and try a different term.

Hunters are very likely to take these options if they know precisely what they are looking for and are familiar with the product, even down to its pattern name. So they might go back and enter 'Calista' (one of the FatFace product names) to see if that brings up anything relevant.

It's a universal truth of searching that the more precise a search term is, the fewer hits it will generate. So, instead, hunters may broaden their search terms by excluding, in this case for example, the colour – the product might be described by some as grey. Except that eBay

---

[3] Bear in mind that if you follow me step by step you won't get the same results, because eBay has around 250 million registered users and millions of products are put up for sale every day.

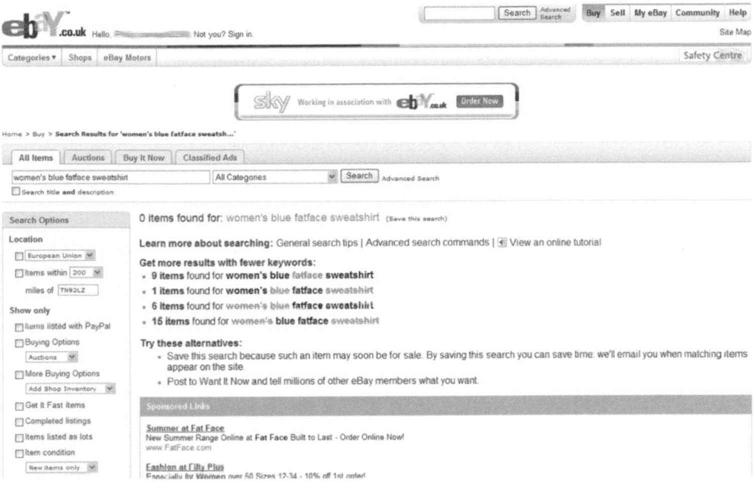

Figure 2 *eBay prompts searchers to look at near matches*

does that for you. The links you can see in Figure 2 cleverly repeat the search terms used but with some words crossed out. In other words eBay has done five searches whilst you only asked it for one (with four words).

That makes it easy for the hunter to turn into a grazer and start seeing what's out there that's nearly what he or she was looking for.

Since FatFace is the key term we'll check out the second item (however ungrammatical it is):

1 items found for **women's ~~blue~~ fatface ~~sweatshirt~~**

Clicking through brings us straight to a listing of all the products for sale, in this case one. But if we click on

6 items found for **~~women's blue~~ fatface sweatshirt**

then we'll end up with a list of other FatFace sweatshirts, any of which could be what we want.

You'll probably notice that there are, indeed, some relevant items here. You'll also notice that they seem to use the term 'ladies' instead

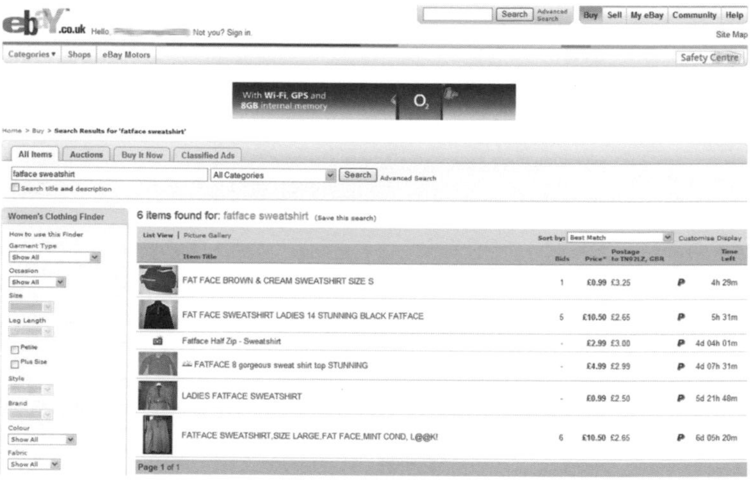

Figure 3 *A list of items resulting from a search*

of 'women's', which would be useful to know if you want to be found alongside all the other similar products, or if you want to stand out. We'll discuss preparing your listing later on.

Before we go on, if you scroll down from this initial list you'll see another product in a different kind of list – shown in Figure 4.

The lower half of this screen then shows one product that is for sale through an 'eBay shop', which you'll notice isn't an auction. We'll come on to these later in this chapter. For the moment, however, notice that this result was not on the first search results screen we came to (Figure 2), nor was it on the first screenful when clicked through on the alternative search terms (Figure 3): we had to scroll down to find it, significant if you want your product to be found easily. A large proportion of visitors – some argue as much as 80 per cent – never scroll down to the lower half of the screen.

The items at the top of the screen, to which eBay generally gives preference, are all items for sale through an auction. So these have links to pages describing the item more fully and columns to the right showing how many bids have been made, what the current price is, postage rates (to my home postcode, because I've signed in and it recognises

Figure 4 *Scrolling down the screen shown in Figure 3*

me!), a letter **P** (for PayPal which we'll come to later) and the time left before the auction ends.

The default order of the items listed puts those auctions about to end soonest at the top. As with an auction in the real world, this is where the action is – just before the hammer is about to drop.

At this point we could just go ahead and have a look at items and decide to buy them, or at least bid. Notice how you're immediately drawn to the products with photos. In Figure 3 you'll see that the third item doesn't have one so it's almost invisible. Determined bargain hunters may look at it, but if there is no picture at all would be unlikely to bid the £2.99 opening price. Maybe later I'll report back to tell you if the item sold.

If I choose to look at the fifth item (it's blue and it's only 99p!), I'd click through to it and find that it's my wife's size and looks OK. It's not exactly what I was looking for but it's the price that seems attractive – £3.49 including postage. I could bid for it or I could just click on the link towards the upper right that says 'Watch this item'. Clicking on this immediately puts a summary and link to this item in 'My eBay' – my account page if I'm a registered buyer.

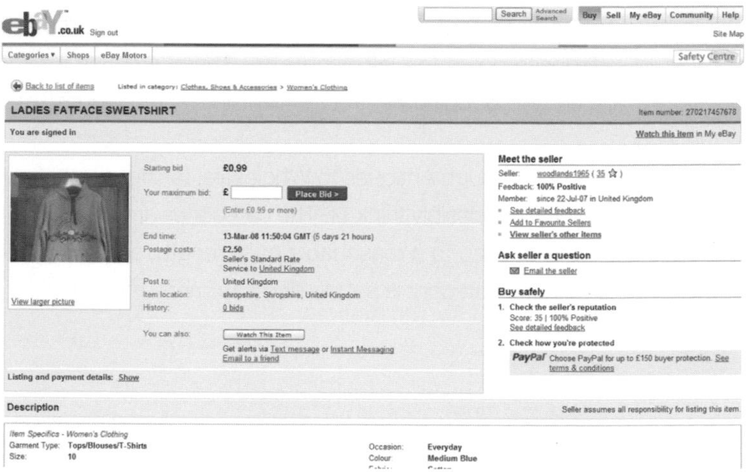

Figure 5 *A single item for sale on eBay has its own page like this*

This really shows the most basic of product pages. A simple photo and prominent easy-to-use buttons to place a bid. Actually if you scroll down again, you might find more extensive details, more photos and more 'design' (the inverted commas are necessary as the page designs are rarely tastefully restrained on eBay).

More importantly for us as sellers (and as cautious buyers), to the right of the screen there is information under the heading 'Meet the seller'. This is a key part of eBay. This seller has sold before (35 items – next to the yellow star), has been registered since July 2007 and has 100% positive feedback from other eBay buyers and sellers. All of these can be clicked on to be examined more closely and, for expensive items, buyers often do.

A buyer can also ask questions of the seller and find out what else is also being sold by them.

Not buying, just grazing?

Of course grazers – who comprise roughly 25 per cent of buyers – do things differently.

Go back to the front page of eBay (as in Figure 1) and you'll see a number of categories down the left-hand side. These are just like the directories you find in shopping centres, except this is the biggest mall in the world.

The categories go through Antiques to Wholesale, taking in just about everything else you can possibly think of. The categories are constrained mainly by the need to keep to a reasonable page length, as you'll see if you click on one: each category is subdivided into many more. Let's try 'Musical Instruments'.

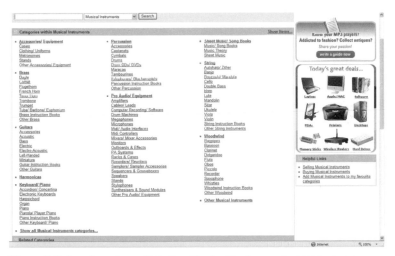

Figure 6 *Sub-categories within the Musical Instruments category on eBay.co.uk*

This leads us to over 100 further categories, including the catch-all 'Other Musical Instruments'. Click on any of these and you come to a listing of products for sale. So, if our grazer was interested in looking at, let's say, a set of bagpipes, they would come to a list of perhaps 90 categories and may not scroll down very far to find that bagpipes are indeed listed (under 'Woodwind'). Clicking through then brings us to a listing of over 200 items. Bear in mind, however, that these items are not all actually sets of bagpipes: some are parts, some may be music, items of jewellery that look like bagpipes or even completely unrelated items that appear to have been put in the wrong category.

Again, as a seller, you should note that below the main category listings, you could scroll down to another screenful of related categories, eBay shops and products for sale. If your product or store is listed down there, it's highly unlikely to be seen.

Of course true grazers may just click on one of the pictures on the first page of eBay, or be following an interesting link from a search engine site such as Google. Someone interested in bagpipes may have been searching for information on care or repairs, looking for local concerts, or they may have simply entered a search term such as 'bagpipes for sale'. We've already seen that this kind of search brings up more than enough information to keep the casual (potential) customer busy for hours.

How to sell

So what have we learned by being a customer?

It's clear that eBay is huge and that it's quite precisely segmented. People who are looking for something specific can find it fairly easily by refining an initial search until they see what's available. Conversely, some grazers will just mooch about the site looking for something interesting.

Actually there are many more kinds of customers. Some go 'sniping' for bargains and buy (almost) anything that is for sale by auction and close to (sometimes within seconds of) its end time – with one proviso: it looks undervalued, maybe even with no bids. There are programs available to help you to do this such as Bidnapper or Hammersnipe (www.bidnapper.com or www.hammertap.com; the basic version of Hammersnipe is free).

Some sites and programs even help these snipers pick up on incorrectly spelled or described items that the hunters wouldn't normally find: for example, Searchgnome is free from www.searchgnome.com. If you described the item you had for sale as 'Fattface' without noticing that you'd hit the 't' key twice, you may not appear is a search for 'FatFace'. Even 'Fat Face' is a different search term to 'FatFace'!

The seasoned snipers may then go on to resell the same items believing that they can get a higher price. So for some buyers, eBay is also just a form of entertainment; the fun of the auction and the potential to get a bargain. For others it's almost a way of life and certainly offers the potential for a great home-based business.

The other immediately obvious thing we've seen looking at customers is that if we have an item for sale, it may simply not be seen by them. They may search for the wrong thing or look in the wrong category – or, strictly, we may list our item in the wrong place using the wrong words to describe it, and so remain hidden.

We also saw that, in auctions, the action happens at the top of the screen, and in other kinds of selling (stores and fixed-price sales) further down. So the first conclusion we have to draw is that we should try conventional auctions before we stray into the more remote areas of the eBay empire and, as always, we must be thinking about what customers are looking for to meet their needs – not just what we have to sell. We're choosing to be on the main street rather than the slightly posher shopping street just off the main drag.

Another issue is that of pricing. In many categories (try looking for small electronic goods like iPods and similar) you'll notice that some sellers have several identical items for sale – they tend to be auctions finishing at different times. They also show different prices – starting prices, reserve prices and, inevitably, closing prices. Sometimes as you look around, you'll notice that some identical items sell for a high price one week and fail to sell at all another week.

What even experienced eBay sellers can't tell, in advance, is what price an item will sell for. So there is a sound argument for testing various price points. If you frequently sell the same or similar items, you can test auctioning the item (with or without a starting price or a reserve price) or a fixed-price sale. All of these can vary and may influence the success of your sale.

Setting up an eBay account

There are two essential things you'll need to set up shop on eBay. You'll need an eBay account (obviously) and you'll need a PayPal account (perhaps not so obvious).

To start with the obvious: your eBay account gives you the ability to track everything you're interested in within the site, and it keeps your basic records of transactions – no small advantage of trading online. eBay uses your account details (and those of its millions of customers) to ensure, as far as possible, that people trade honestly. We saw that with the feedback scores both buyers and sellers get.

To set up a simple account is easy. The key link was at the top left of the very first page we looked at.

As we said before, you might be greeted by name, and if someone else who is already a registered user of eBay has been on this machine you might see their name at the top of the screen. Whatever else you do, don't try and use someone else's account – it's illegal. If you're not registered or you are not greeted by name, you click to sign in or register and will be taken through a series of fairly simple forms.

You have to expressly agree to eBay's privacy terms, and it's worth reading them thoroughly looking at them. Selling online is all about confidence, and eBay makes sure it can act quickly if anyone is caught cheating – buying or selling illegally. Every bit of information you input can be used to track you down – but then your customers are in the same position, so it should be reassuring.

Having an e-mail address is, of course essential. You will be asked to confirm this, and eBay requires more from those with Web-based e-mail addresses such as Hotmail or Yahoo.

Given that you are planning to use eBay to sell, you should be quite happy to submit your personal information to eBay. You will have to make a few decisions (such as your user ID) which have some bearing on the way you appear in the marketplace. Nonsensical IDs such as 'fthf73737' are sometimes seen as coming from someone listing a single item with no intention of continuing in business – off-putting. Better still to use a short but potentially meaningful name. If you're planning to sell collectible model cars you could call yourself 'dinkyman' . . . but there is already a *dinkyman*, and a *dinkyfan* and a *dinky-mad* so it may take a while to find a suitable name. You can add numbers as many other users do. The key point about this name is that it stays with you as long as you are registered and appears alongside everything you sell.

When people look at your trading history in a few months or years, because you keep the same name, they'll be able to see exactly what you have sold (and bought) and will quickly get an impression of how specialised you are. A mixed bag of purchases and sale depicts you as a dabbler (maybe a grazer?), but a long list of similar sales, along with very good feedback, marks you out as a specialist.

You have to choose a password, and eBay usefully tells you how secure your chosen word is, as well as asking for security questions in case you forget some of your account details. Once you've finished and confirmed that you agree to eBay's terms you just have to check your e-mail to confirm your e-mail address. After following the instructions in the e-mail you receive, you'll be ready to start buying, but not selling . . . yet.

To be able to sell, you have to click on the 'Sell' link at the top right or log in to your account. Before you get too far, you'll be expected to give more information including a credit card **with the same billing address** as you gave as a seller. You'll also give them your bank account information and decide how you want to pay the eBay fees. Once it has your authorisation, eBay will take its payments every month.

To encourage first-time sellers, clicking on the 'Sell' link at the top right of the screen from almost anywhere within eBay will take you to a quick way of listing your item for sale (as in Figure 7). You'll have to sign in eventually to finalise your item.

There's quite a lot of useful information linked from this page, and you can drill down to a 'university' of advice, literally: go to http://pages.ebay. co.uk/university to view or download a series of tutorials, from the basics up to 'turbolisting' and 'powerselling' for the serious business.

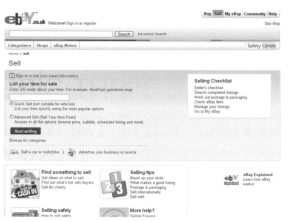

Figure 7 *The page first-time sellers see on eBay.*

How to list an item

Finding an item to buy is, as we've seen, a question of searching with the right keywords or browsing in the right categories. So, logically, when you come to selling you should think hard about how you describe an item and to which categories you assign it.

As you go through the rest of the form to sell an item, you'll be asked to make a number of decisions about the promotion of the product. Remember in Chapter 2 we discussed how you might regard your marketing strategy, broken down into four areas – ways of looking at your customer's needs – each of which might be adapted for a different target group of customers. It may sound laborious, but certainly until it becomes instinctive, try asking yourself what customers are really expecting from the product, the delivery and the price and then how you should talk to them in your listing.

Presenting your product

First and foremost you'll need to write a title that will help buyers find your item. Don't try to be clever with typography – too many sellers still think writing 'L@@K!!!' induces buyers to click through. It doesn't, and I can guarantee that word and spelling are never searched for.

You're not allowed to use misleading titles such as 'not a Cartier watch', or to use offensive words or to suggest that the item is illegal. Any of these can get you reported and banned. Again, honesty is the best policy.

In some categories you have the opportunity to enter item specifics, for example colours, sizes, condition (new or worn) and genres, especially for music CDs. These help buyers find a close match to their needs but, as we've seen in the search example above, don't mean you're ruling yourself out of consideration for those who just search the item titles.

It's almost always worth including a photograph. We say more about photos in Chapter 10, but suffice to say here that the quality of the photo makes a difference. A dimly-lit product on a cluttered background, with flare from the flash or, as frequently happens, an unwanted reflection of the photographer in the frame makes you look like an amateur. If you don't care about how your product looks, you might not care much about its condition or about packing and dispatch; buyers will avoid you.

For many categories, two or three photos allow the customers to examine your product from various angles. At 12p for an additional photo, you might test this. Just 15p for a photo alongside your listing is almost always worth it, as we saw in our FatFace search above.

Incidentally, don't copy other sellers' photographs or lift pictures from commercial sites without permission. It's illegal and can get you banned from eBay.

Think about convenience for customers

You will also have to decide what kind of a sale this is. An auction can last from one day to 10 days. If it is a concert ticket for the weekend ahead then you may have to be quick, but the rarer or more in demand the item, the longer you should list in order to get the highest price. A 'Buy it now' price may induce someone to pre-empt the auction, but this largely depends on the item: something that is fairly mundane but reasonably urgent, like a small car part, is likely to sell this way.

Fine adjustments are also possible with the start time (and therefore the end time) of your auction. For example, it will cost 6p to make sure your auction ends at the weekend or, if your main customers are in another time-zone, when people are likely to be looking. It seems obvious, but most home-based buyers buy at the weekend and evenings, and most bidding action happens then.

You should always state the location of the item. Some buyers see this as a proxy for reliability or cost and speed of delivery. Still there are many Hong Kong-based electronics suppliers who claim to be in London; smart buyers can see through this. Again, be honest.

In a highly competitive category, you might find you have to pay extra to upgrade to bold type or to otherwise highlight your listing. The great thing about eBay is that you can test these variables. After some experience you will get to know when it's necessary and if it tends to lead to a higher sale price – but you need to keep good records.

Assuming your heading and choice of categories are correct and your photo works, your description of the item to be sold is the next most important part. Your description should be detailed enough for the customer to make an informed choice – be honest about faults, but don't undermine the reason for buying the product. You could point out the scratch on the mobile phone you are selling but not the fact that you find it difficult to use; that's irrelevant. Take a moment to think through why people might be buying – a gift, a cheap alternative, a rare example – and make notes before you write your description.

Always specify payment options (see below) and postage information – the latter demands some investigation[4] – so that you don't have to deal with too many queries. Complete information also shows that you are well organised and therefore likely to be reliable in any subsequent sale.

---

[4] You can find this information easily for the UK at the Royal Mail website (www.royalmail.com and see http://tinyurl.com/gwqqy) where you can also create an account and print your own postage – great for the home eBayer.

A returns policy sounds dangerous, especially if you are new to eBay, but again you need to place yourself in the buyer's position. A frequent barrier to making a purchase decision (especially online) is 'What if it's not quite right?' or 'What if it doesn't fit?' In appropriate circumstances, you should endeavour to offer a return and refund. Generally customers don't return products, but if they have to and you are helpful you will get good feedback – and that is valuable in itself. Look at the hassle involved as a marketing investment.

Pricing

Do plenty of research before setting prices. You can look around eBay (and Amazon) to get a feel for the competition and what people are looking for and, usefully, you can opt to look for 'completed' items so you know which sold and at what price. This may also give you a clue as to the layout used in a successful listing. The various help applications below can be of use here too.

One potentially valuable tool, even though it's aimed at US buyers first and foremost, is mpire.com (www.mpire.com), which can give you a slightly different perspective on the market price. In Figure 10, for example, you can see the results of a search for an iPod nano. Interestingly, it shows the US trend in pricing as well as giving links to current products for sale in online stores, eBay and other sites including Amazon.

Finally always, always, always review your listing. Clicking on the review link you will see a preview of your listing page. Check it for looks but also for spelling. The way you write and describe your item says a lot about you and can turn people away. If you see something that needs to be changed, click the Edit link next to the part you want to change.

If you're happy, you can click the 'List your item' link to go, but I would recommend taking a moment to make sure you have a record of what you're offering and when. Even when you've listed the item, it's worth checking again and noting end dates so that you can be ready to dispatch as soon as you have a buyer. It's crucial to keep up to date with your record-keeping; eBay only keeps track of your sold items for

Figure 8 *Mpire usefully tracks the prices of items over time*

60 days. You will need to monitor the cost-effectiveness of the various listing options above to maximise the profitability of each sale.

What does eBay cost?

Remember, setting up your eBay account costs nothing. You only pay once you start selling. You can see a summary of the fees online at http://pages.ebay.co.uk/help/sell/fees.html (or http://tinyurl.com/dtce3). These are pretty complicated and vary with categories and the type of sale. You will pay a listing fee and for any additional features on your listing such as photographs, and you'll also pay a fee based on the final sale price of your item, assuming it sells.

To help you calculate the fees, you just need to go into qicture.com's site (www.qicture.com/calculator.html) where they have a useful free fees calculator (and a useful eBay service for your mobile phone, *not* free), or there's a downloadable application called, imaginatively, eBay Fees Calculator 1.3 which you can download free from http://tinyurl.com/yskolp.

You can also visit Ecal at (http://tinyurl.com/yo5v5l or www.ebaycalculator. co.uk) for alternatives. The latter also allows you to calculate profit (or loss) by including the cost of goods and the real postage and packing costs you have incurred. This kind of calculation is essential if you are going to make serious money from your eBay account – exactly the same as any other marketing activity.

A question of looks

One area I haven't mentioned much is that of design, by which I mean the adding of the borders and colours to your listing, which you will have seen from other sellers. eBay offers some standard ones which are adequate but hardly compelling, and you pay to use them. Alternatively, there are free templates such as those from www.auctioninsights.com, or you can download software that allows you to prepare your listing, including its design, offline before you put it on to eBay. Some of these are listed below.

As to whether it's worth doing this, only you can tell as you test your eBay market. However, if you start to build up a business there is value in using the template to increase recognition of your brand. With your own distinctive template, you can ensure that buyers know just how good your feedback is and how satisfied other customers are. You can direct them to your blog or website and even to your eBay store.

Setting up shop

Many eBay businesses get by just fine without ever opening a store but once you get to a certain level of sales, a shop can give a boost to sales and make managing them easier. You can also sell products at a fixed price from your 'Shop Inventory' list, for which eBay charges on a different scale.

To open a shop you just need to have a feedback rating of 10 and to set up automatic payment of your fees by direct debit. If you have a PayPal account you can use this and need only have a feedback rating of 5.

The main advantage of your own store is that you can cross-refer between items for sale, meaning that customers interested in your category might be drawn to look at your other products – which could be at a higher prices than those at auction. Some store owners use auctions to clear damaged stock but have full-price items in their store.

Your store can be personalised to your business – in fact, it must be, since you decide what appears in the heading of each page. Again eBay offers templates for shop pages, all of which have fairly strong eBay branding, but you can add your own logo and adjust colours and typefaces. There are some easy interfaces to help you tailor your pages and to upload graphics and logos (see http://tinyurl.com/6j7unf for extensive help and http://tinyurl.com/6pxgs9 for the FAQ – frequently asked questions).

Store wars?

To set up your store go to http://tinyurl.com/26rgaw and simply follow the instructions. You need to be registered as a seller and then you need to meet the minimum requirements above.

A basic shop will cost £6 a month and is the logical place to start. This level of subscription includes five pages of information plus 1Mb of storage for photos and up to 1000 e-mails a month – useful for newsletters and notifications to proven customers.

Selling Manager Pro is available for an extra £5 a month. It is a program for automating many of the tasks associated with selling on eBay, and is useful once you get to listing many items per week. In particular it automates e-mail communication with your customers, so making sure you reassure them once they've decided to buy. But note that there are other programs, some free, that can do much of this too. See 'Virtually free help' below.

All store owners regardless of level of subscription get sales statistics from eBay. For regular sellers this is available at £3 a month and gives you a breakdown of sales by item and category as well as by format of sale (e.g. auction, 'Buy it now' and so on), and reports on the fees you've paid, making possible a useful analysis of the cost of sales.

You can upgrade your basic shop at any time, and a 'featured' store costs £30 a month including the Selling Manager tool. A featured store benefits from more pages and reduced-price additional picture storage. You can send up to 2,500 e-mails and you also get useful additional information about the traffic through your store, including pages visited and some visitor profiles.

Incidentally, if you want to concentrate your attention on eBay for selling you might also want to consider it for hosting your blog (http://blogs.ebay.co.uk). As long as you have a selling account you can use this to communicate with buyers, and it seems eBay blogs get a lot of attention, especially from search engines.

How eBay changed my life

Paul Harrison explained to me how eBay transformed his small business. He runs Elstree Props (www.elstreeprops.com) specialising in sourcing and supplying movie props as collectables. Paul's father had worked on the *Star Wars* films in the 1970s, but Paul himself ended up running an IT company until he decided to downshift.

Figure 9 *Paul Harrison's eBay store*

Paul started by selling a few things online for a bit of extra cash and buying online as a way of saving money. Paul realised that there was some potential in his link with Elstree Studios, where his father had been involved in making some of the props of some very famous movies. He began to make display cases for the props – especially from *Star Wars* – including lighting and effects, along with certificates of authenticity, that made the props look every bit as good as they did in the movies.

After being ripped off by a dealer, Paul found out on eBay what the props he had were *really* worth – it was whatever serious collectors were willing to pay. Paul calls it 'proper fair trade!' where the buyers decide the price – and it was invariably more than Paul had anticipated.

Paul's best month saw a turnover of £30,000, but even when the takings are lower he doesn't resent the charges eBay and PayPal make. As Paul says, 'Show me any other business model where you get paid up front with assurances (always use PayPal!) and deliver afterwards! If I make something and put it in a shop, I would only ever get the price or less.'

Over five years on, Paul and his wife are buying and selling all kinds of things on eBay – he reckons much of his home is furnished from online purchases. He visits his small workshop in Elstree once or twice a week, leaving him free for the school runs, time with his children, the odd lie-in or game of golf when many other people are stuck in the office. The Harrisons haven't suddenly become rich, but they have a worklife balance that many would envy.

Virtually free help

If you're interested in emulating the people who make their living on eBay, you can find numerous free online tools to help you. Selling Manager is one of a range of tools eBay offers to help you – just click on the Help link at the top right of every page, or see http://tinyurl.com/dm4no.

For buying, sniping tools like Hammersnipe (www.hammertap.com) are free, and for selling Auctionpixie (www.auctionpixie.co.uk) is a free and simple range of tools that helps automate listing and has a number of other useful functions. Similarly, Adcreator (www.auctionlotwatch. co.uk) helps you professionalise the presentation of your sale items and Auctiva (www.auctiva.com – also free) is a popular provider of photo hosting and templates for selling on eBay. Also look at www.ebaitor.com and www.freeauctionhelp.com.

Auctionsplash (www.auctionsplash.com) is useful for managing a number of auctions from your desktop without having to go online, and it's free. For just a few pounds – up to around £30 – you can buy some incredibly useful management tools (some of which allow free trials) from developers such as Raje Software (www.rajeware.com), whilst more advanced services such as Auction Hawk (www.auctionhawk.com) offer a monthly subscription rate starting around £7. This is a pretty good option to consider when you get established as an eBay seller, since many eBay-related services charge a percentage based on your selling price.

One very promising tool is that developed by Kulveet and Harjeet Taggar and friends at http://auctomatic.com. Their site enables you to manage auctions, your inventory and your photographs easily. At the time of writing, it's free to register and start using the tools, and indeed to use their 'quicklister' service you don't even have to sign up! If the whole service is as good as it promises, then you won't mind paying a little in the future.

PayPal

Remember the **P** we noticed on an eBay listing early on in this chapter? It simply denotes that the seller of the item accepts PayPal as a payment method – around 90 per cent of eBay purchases go through PayPal for the simple reason that it's quick and secure. As PayPal themselves reasonably point out, when you pay by cheque, you hand over all your bank details and a sample of your signature! No wonder PayPal now claims over 150 million account holders – and eBay bought the company in 2002. From 2007 onwards, sellers have had to accept either PayPal or credit card payments (or both) in addition to any other methods.

To get your PayPal account, you will need to go to www.paypal.co.uk and follow the 'Sign up now' instructions. As with eBay, you will need to give name and address details as well as bank and credit card details. You'll set up a user name and password which, for obvious security reasons, should differ from your eBay details.

One important decision you have to make is about the type of account you will have. It's best to start off with a personal account and then, if necessary, you can upgrade to one of the other accounts available – premier or business. The essential difference is that whilst all accounts enable you make payments out of your account without charge, personal accounts can only process **two** credit or debit card payments in a year. This may seem a severe limitation, but remember that the vast majority of payments are made from PayPal accounts to other PayPal accounts and these are still free for personal account holders.

In fact, PayPal seems to be one of the best business payment service providers; they can process credit card payments and handle shopping carts and integrate payment forms with your website should you wish. The fees are broadly comparable with others such as WorldPay and Nochex[5], but PayPal also tends to accept sellers without extensive form-filling. They also offer seller protection, for example in the event of non-delivery of your item, of up to £3,250. The details of the service are worth checking (http://tinyurl.com/ldwek) as you are contractually obliged to conduct your business responsibly in order to gain this protection, which is only available to premier and business account sellers.

Of course the PayPal service is an extra cost – per item you sell or payment you receive – but as marginal/variable costs these are predictable and, I think, reasonable. If you get to the point where you're processing hundreds of thousands of pounds through a PayPal account, then you may want to look more closely at alternatives which may offer

---

[5] www.worldpay.com and www.nochex.com

savings. However, there is much to be said for the reassurance and simplicity of PayPal for your customers and you.

As far as signing up to the standard PayPal account is concerned, you'll need to read and agree to the PayPal terms, and again you'll receive an authorisation e-mail to activate your account. Should you want to increase the ceiling on amounts you can transfer, you may also be asked to carry out a small test transaction – just a few pence – to confirm that your bank account is active.

Amazon isn't just for books

As much as eBay dominates online auctions, Amazon is the site most people would think of for buying books online. As we've noted, they also sell CDs, electronics and many other products and, like eBay, they offer small (and quite large) sellers the chance to get in front of millions of buyers worldwide.

Setting up an account on Amazon is pretty straightforward. As on many other sites, you'll need to give credit card details and confirm your account via e-mail, but the process is relatively easy. Beyond that, however, there is a bewildering range of selling programmes: Amazon Advantage, Amazon Marketplace, Amazon zShops, Amazon Auctions, Amazon aStore, and some 'pro' versions of these!

Be careful about the options you choose, as some demand monthly subscriptions which can swallow your profit from a few items, and some involve you providing stock to Amazon for them to sell. It can be confusing, so here we'll look at the simplest options.

To start selling you'll need to see if the item is already listed in Amazon's 'Marketplace' – if it isn't there you can't sell it (unless you have a zShop; see below). For most books and CDs, this isn't a problem, you simply click the 'Start selling' link, search for the exact item (with books be careful about distinguishing between hardback and paperback versions) and then click on 'Sell yours here'.

You have to specify whether the item is new or used and what condition it is in. You can also add a fairly short comment or description.

Figure 10 *This box, to the bottom left of each page, links to the services for sellers*

It's important that you are seen to be honest here. Point out any defects or any features – an interesting description can just tip the balance in your favour.

With Amazon, the price is a very important aspect of the presentation of your product. Put simply, yours will be desplayed alongside other identical products and (usually) they will be arranged in order of price. If yours is the cheapest, it will be at the top.

Amazon provides the picture of the product in its standard layout, and yours becomes just a listing amongst many. So all you have to do to proceed is specify how many products you have and where in the world you are prepared to send them. Then submit your listing.

How much does it cost?

Unlike many other sites, Amazon tells you what to charge for postage and packing. It's usually enough to cover postage and, in fact, can be the source of most of the profit on many a small item that is competitively priced. Always include this and your costs of packing and despatch in working out your profit.

The details of Amazon's charges are at http://tinyurl.com/26oa22. They don't charge you for listing an item but do charge on completion, so all the costs are deducted before you see anything. By way of example, every item is subject to a completion fee of 85p and a further 17.25% is deducted for most items. The charge goes down to 11.5% for electronics or photographic equipment, but it's still a chunk out of your revenue. You can then add back around £2.75 postage allowance for a book – and you'd add this for every book, even if you'd sold multiple copies to the same buyer!

Items remain listed for 60 days and can be re-listed as many times as you like so, with multiple items, it's often worth experimenting with different prices on multiple listings and selling in smaller batches – if you can get a higher price, so much the better.

How to set up a store

By all accounts Amazon's zShops are difficult for smaller businesses and don't seem to get much traffic, whilst an aStore is a more accessible option to start with. While a zShop attracts reduced selling fees, you also pay a £25 monthly fee to be able to set up and maintain your shop. There are some tools to help manage your listings (like eBay above), but you have to be able to sell more than 30 items a month – and cover that £25. You also have to sort out the delivery of your products yourself, although you have the advantage of Amazon handling payments for you.

In practice, however, if you have a website and you want to sell books or other items already on the Amazon inventory, you should become an Amazon Associate and set up an aStore – you're actually just getting commission for linking buyers to Amazon. You don't have to carry any stock whatsoever!

The opportunity here is that if you have a customer base to which you could sell books or CDs (or indeed anything that is already on Amazon), you could have a book (or other) shop up and running within hours. Selling more to existing customers is, as I pointed out in Chapter 2, a valid marketing objective.

Without going into great detail here, signing up as an associate is free and relatively easy: see http://tinyurl.com/y6rczo. You can set up your aStore with a name that reflects your own brand, so Goose Loose could end up with a URL that is simply http://astore.amazon.co.uk/

gooseloose (with a number following to indicate the region such as 21 for the UK). But this address need not appear anywhere, as Amazon provides numerous ways of linking their content into your site through 'widgets'.

Building this kind of online store is as simple as following the step-by-step instructions which include searching and selecting products from the Amazon listings. Each one comes with a picture, title and price, but you can add your own text to describe the item.

As we noted, with a zShop you can to list your own products – those that don't appear elsewhere on Amazon. It's perfectly possible to have both sorts of store.

Interestingly, while the charges on zShops are lower than they are on conventional sales, through an aStore (where you don't have to hold any inventory or despatch any product) you can earn at least 5 per cent commission on sales – a greater margin than the writers of some of the books you might be selling!

You can adapt the pages of an aStore as shown in Figure 13. Step by step, you can make it fit in with the corporate image and colours of other

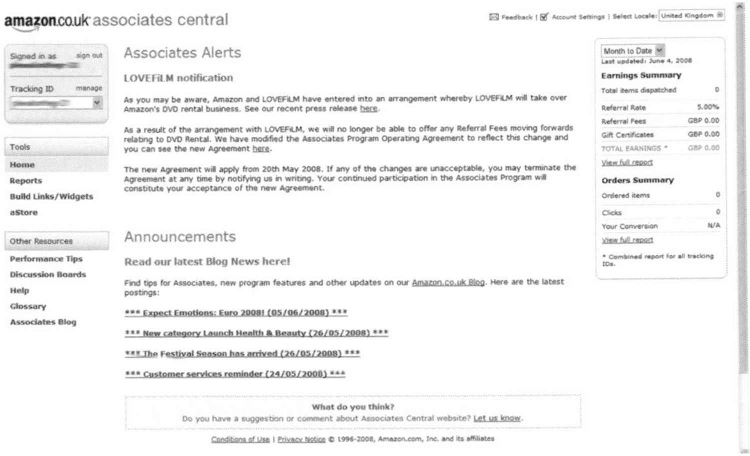

Figure 11 *What you see as an Amazon Associate*

sites you may have so that visitors follow the link without feeling that they are leaving your pages.

It's also possible to build multiple stores for different sites or different pages of your website, reflecting different customers' interests. Each of your aStores can have as many categories of product as you need. You could have a book shop and a music shop for example, or just pick adventure books or just items of a certain colour or related to travelling in hot climates or DIY plumbing – the choice is entirely up to you.

You then specify what your store is to look like, choosing colours and some design elements rather like the Web pages we looked at in Chapter 4. You also have the opportunity to have your heading linked to a graphic hosted somewhere else on the Web – you can't just upload a file, but the header could be where you keep your blog, website or other assets such as photos (see Chapter 10).

You can add to your store sidebar widgets which include other dynamic content such as wishlists or recommendations. These can be useful to make buyers aware of similar products they may be interested in, or to remind them of items they had searched for before. You hope, of course, they'll buy though your store.

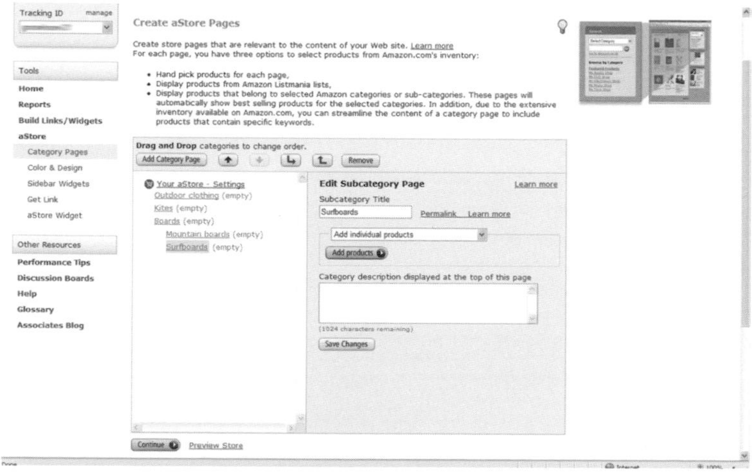

Figure 12 *How you start to build your store*

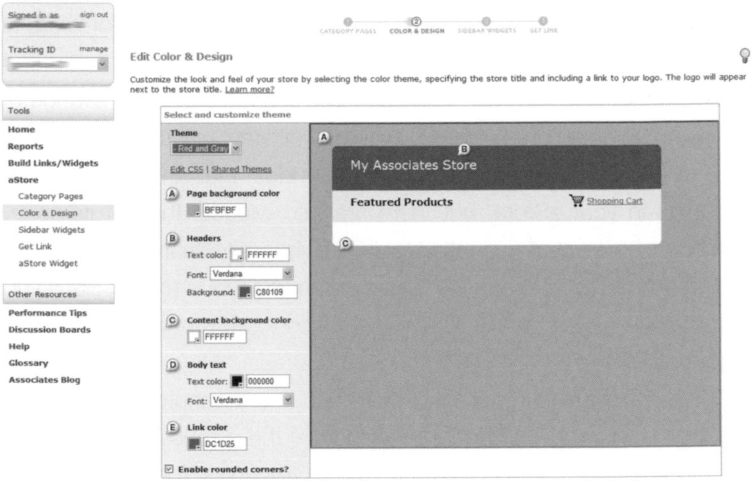

Figure 13 *Selecting colours for your store*

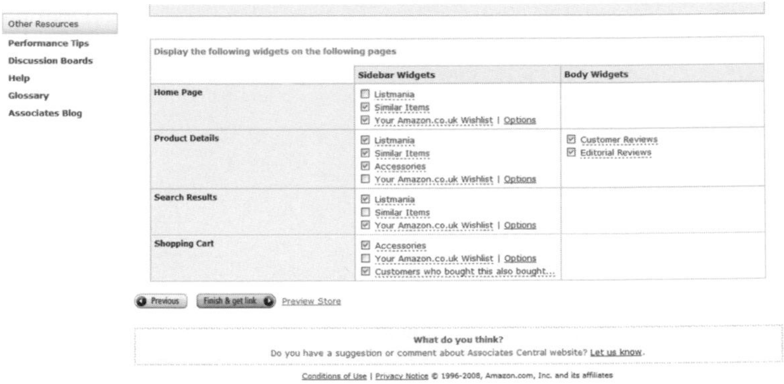

Figure 14 *Some of the standard widget options for your store*

Having selected products for your store and chosen the layout, your store can then go live but, at this point, no one will know it exists. To be able to show products in other pages, such as on your blog, just click on 'Build Links/Widgets'. These are like mini adverts that you can embed in your own pages to link potential buyers to your store.

It's often necessary to play about with the various options for widgets so that they fit where you want them. The good news is that you can make as many as you want and each one can have a different range of products, and can present them in slightly different ways. At the bottom of Figure 16, for example, you can see a widget that simply links to the products in your aStore, but there are also widgets that list items by subject or show photos or allow your site visitors to search.

Many of these widgets are, in fact, open to anyone to use. But if you want to earn your commission you will need to register as an associate first.

There is also plenty of help under the 'Other Resources' heading to guide you through the range of widgets – the discussion boards are useful. Alternate widgets, layouts and sizes work for different sites (including blogs and some of those dealt with in Chapters 8 and 9), and someone will have tried them all before you.

You may recall that when you set up your Blogger blog[6] in Chapter 3, there was the opportunity to include 'page elements' which included

Figure 15 *Some of the widgets you can use to promote your aStore*

---

[6] What do you mean, you haven't done it yet?!

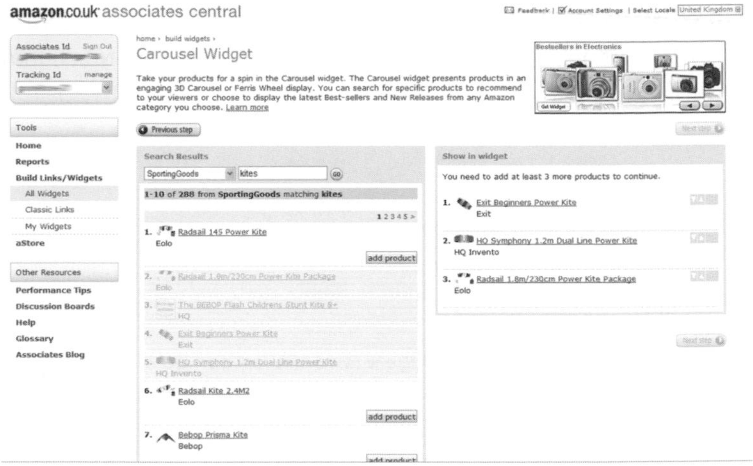

Figure 16 *Adding products to a widget – in this case at least six*

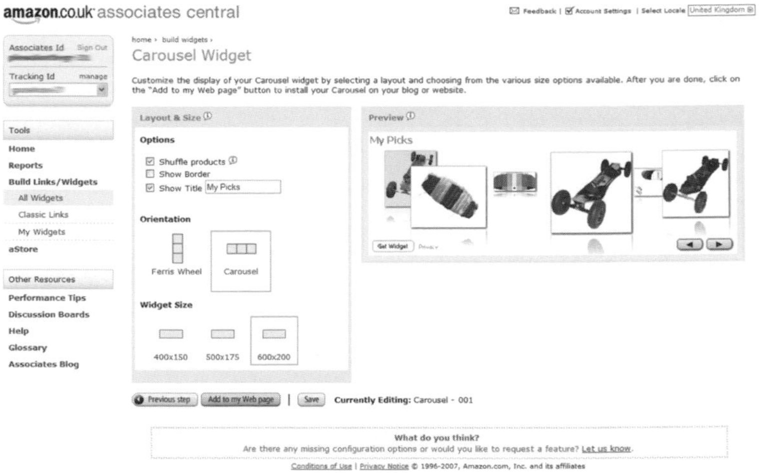

Figure 17 *A preview shows your widget and some options*

HTML or JavaScript from other sites. An Amazon widget is one such element, so you can have your Amazon selections – favourites, wishlist, aStore and so on – appearing there too.

How am I doing?

Once your widgets have been embedded you can keep an eye on their effectiveness just by signing into your associate account. The data is

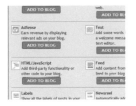

Figure 18 *Links from Amazon widgets (and similar) can go into your blog layout*

fairly clear and will help you keep your accounts in order as well as monitoring the effectiveness of your links.

Figure 19 *Amazon gives you reports on your earnings from all sources*

To further confuse you, Amazon also offer further options such as being a 'Pro Merchant' (again for selling more than 30 items a month) and a fully customisable e-commerce platform called Webstore (http://webstore.amazon.com) which can be trialled free for 30 days but which costs from around £40 a month plus 7% commission. Probably not the place to start.

A few final points about online selling

There is no doubt that Amazon and eBay are making it easier for people buy and sell. It's interesting, though, to look at what business they are really in.

The two websites, ignoring all the bells and whistles they can add for you as a seller, are marketplaces. To be slightly more accurate, they are 'marketspaces'. Amazon and eBay 'own' these customers but they are more than happy for you to sell to them.

Each one has created a destination for potential customers to go searching for what they want. In fact, so successful are they that many people who would often normally visit the high street or out-of-town retail park also go online to check out products and prices. In this way these marketspaces are, for many people, always on the shortlist. If you have a real-world store, you are already in competition with them.

Where would you go to buy a CD or an iPod? Where would you look for that particular book? Increasingly, the same kinds of decisions are being made about clothing, toys, cars and even original artwork. The marketspaces that are already there with customers visiting in their millions cannot be ignored. Amazon and eBay can offer reasonably cheap ways of handling sales for you, too.

As we've seen in both eBay's auctions and Amazon's Marketplace (respectively the most popular parts of their sites) the emphasis is on price. In other marketspaces such as Primelocation and Autotrader (and quite a few others), you know that customers are comparing alternatives all the time. As the credit crunch squeezes, these markets will grow.

The challenge for you, if you enter these spaces, is to be competitive on price but to stand out on every other aspect of the exchange – reliability, quality of information, service, friendliness, however you express them – in order to make customers eager to come back to you and maybe even pay a little more to deal with you. Remember these sites are fairly level playing fields – you just want to tip them in your favour, and that means taking advantage of all the selling support these sites offer and some of those free programs mentioned above.

CHAPTER 7

PROMOTION ONLINE . . . AND OFF

Okay, so you've got a blog. You've got a website. You've got a listing on a directory somewhere, and you've started to sell online. So what?

Well, unfortunately, so nothing. One of the first, and most disappointing, things you notice about being online is that few people notice. In fact nothing that you can do online guarantees the kind of coverage the dot-com heroes enjoy or the success many of them have had in subsequently selling their businesses for millions of dollars.

You may have a great idea but, as a small company, your short- to medium-term aims (which you considered in Chapter 2) are clear. You want to build up your business by keeping your existing customers and/or getting more like them.

You also have your 'inside-out' view – your core brand values – and your 'outside-in' view which is how customers see you (your brand image) and the product or service you're offering. These would normally be written down as an important part of your strategy – a working document that you can keep looking at to remind yourself where you're going and to make sure you're still on course.

This summary of your business and marketing plan is also a good point of reference when it comes to promoting your business. Let me just say at this point that the kind of promotion I'm talking about here is not broadcast 'shouting' about your business in the hope that someone influential will hear your. No need then to bemoan the fact that you can't afford to advertise on television or in the *Financial Times*.

If you have developed a strategy for your marketing, you'll have a number of target groups of customers you would like to communicate with, and you need to concentrate on these first and foremost. Logically, the work you are doing to position your blog and website online, and the way you use any of the sites looked at so far may already be bringing you to the notice of your target customers. By definition, remember, eBay listings, and particularly an online store with them or Amazon, positions you as providing what certain customers are actively looking to buy. After that, customers will make their own judgements about value.

So if you are writing regularly about, say, flower arranging and selling florist supplies online, perhaps through eBay or Amazon, then you will be coming to the attention of some customers. Maybe even enough customers to keep you busy and meet your initial targets.

Go carefully

If you are already meeting your objectives, then you might be tempted to expand and simply try and sell more. Okay, but be cautious.

Firstly, you may not be sure that your current business is sustainable. You need to have very good relationships with your first customers to ensure you know why they are buying and if they are totally satisfied. Again, this is an area we cover in *Marketing & PR*. You need to have a realistic view of the size of the market. One old client of mine built industrial-size cement-mixing machinery – they knew everyone in the UK market by name. In fact, they would probably have fitted in their boardroom.

The closer you are to the market, the clearer vision you have of who they are and where they are, the easier it will be for you to predict when (and if) they will come back to you for their next order.

The second reason for caution is a more tricky issue – slightly outside of the scope of this book. Nevertheless I'll try and give you a couple of pointers.

Not all sales are the same. You can take on new customers relatively easily by selling products at very low prices. As we've seen on Amazon, for example, it's possible to undercut the competition simply by checking their prices online and deducting whatever you choose, thus placing yourself at the top of the listing. Job done.

You might then, for example, be tempted to put in a big order of those _____ (fill in the blank with your cheapest product) and joyously create your multiple listings waiting for the orders to roll in. You may even create the listings *before* you stock up – think of the positive cash flow!

Well, it's not difficult to see how such a plan can come unstuck. Orders come in but stock is suddenly unavailable, or delayed or more expensive. Or maybe you just can't keep up with the packing and despatch. Or postage costs go up.

There's no guaranteed way of avoiding all such setbacks, but you need to plan for some of these – and make sure that in scaling up your business you are not putting too much strain on the market (the few customers who wanted that product), yourself or your working capital – the money you need to be able buy stock, before you get paid back by customers[1].

What kind of promotion?

So the purpose of this chapter (and of your promotional activity) is twofold:

1. getting your customers to come back to you time and time again

2. getting more customers

– probably in that order.

'Virtually free' publicity is the kind of networking and involvement that I've been urging up to now and to which we'll return in the next few chapters when we start looking at social networking sites.

This kind of promotion is an essential element of your day-to-day activities which should include, as we said in the first few chapters, researching your business, customers and competitors. Simply getting your name known and always giving people the link to your e-mail

---

[1] For a good guide to managing sales growth without falling into these traps, see Bob Gorton's book *Boosting Sales* published by A & C Black in 2007.

and website addresses should be routine, and you should make time for this.

If you've set up your Google alerts and subscribed to the feeds from your best sources of information, you should also be reasonably well connected. If you are blogging regularly and commenting on other blogs and sites (in your own pages and on theirs) then you will find yourself slowly getting some kind of traffic.

You won't be the most famous person in plumbing or flower arranging or adventure holidays, but you should know and connect to those who are, and that's the key: to be amongst the main players.

Your watchwords should be 'consistency' and 'integration' . . .

Consistency

Consistency is one of the keystones of branding. Since you *are* the brand in most cases, you need to be aware of this. I've said before that everything you do that impacts on the customer is marketing. Likewise, everything you do that a customer might see needs to give an impression that is supportive of your aims and your company/brand position and values. If this sounds like marketing jargon, that's because it is. It simply means however that you have to look at everything you do (and say) *from the point of view of the customer* and ask the questions "Does this give the right impression?" and "Does it give the same message?"

It's here that it is difficult to stick to the 'virtually free' ideal. Of course it is possible for almost anyone to draw a logo and to design a letterheading (as we'll see below), but it won't necessarily be a good one. Having said that, if your business is at all creative you might be tempted to have a go, but you could also seek some help as suggested in Chapter 11.

If you're carrying out a lot of your business through eBay, you can take advantage of their advice on promoting yourself (http://tinyurl. com/5ccwh6) and their free templates for offline promotional material too (http://tinyurl.com/5ccwh6).

Whoever produces the visual part of your brand identity – always, always, always get a second or third opinion from someone unconnected with the business. And make sure it's an honest opinion by pushing them to explain what they think of your logo or advertising and why. If you have an online group of customers (regulars on your blog, eBay store or on Facebook, see Chapter 8) then you could simply ask them.

Figure 1 *The Goose Loose logo*

The logo for Goose Loose in Figure 1 was created in an hour or so using a free version of Serif's Drawplus program (see www.serif.com and Chapter 10). The branding is clear and their 'offer' is too. 'Everything outdoors' sums up what they do and are interested in, but the words printed above also suggest the range of activities they are involved in.

Once created, the logo can be used over and over again. Drawplus, like many similar programs, enables a single graphic to exported at almost any size and file format, making it a simple matter to apply the logo to printed material and online.

When you have come to a decision about the look and 'feel' of the public face of your company, then you have to police it jealously. Remember, your image and what people think and believe about your company are important assets, and any damage to them can result in damage to your income and profitability.

If you are concerned that your brand appears amateurish or gives the wrong impression, then change it. Change it now and be prepared to put some work into improving it. And be prepare to change it again if circumstances demand – but make sure that once it's changed it is applied everywhere, every time.

Integration

By 'integration', I simply mean that everything should be linked. There is no excuse for issuing any kind of message, from a simple flyer to an invoice, without also including all the possible ways in which your customer might contact you. Your business card, if you use one, should be packed with contact names and numbers, websites and URLs.

If this is true of printed (real-world) material, then it's even truer for anything online. Your blog should refer to your website, your eBay store, your various pages and groups on Facebook (see Chapter 8). Every product description on eBay should include your e-mail address, your Skype number (see Chapter 12), your Web address, your Facebook links (Chapter 8) and, for example, the fact that you take credit cards through PayPal (see Chapter 6). You get the picture . . . everything should link to everything.

Looking back at Dave McClure's 'platform wars' map in Chapter 2, each of these can describe a marketspace in exactly the way we suggested eBay and Amazon do in the last chapter. So whichever way a customer first comes into contact with you, he or she should be able to see quite clearly where else you are.

Quite simply, you can't afford to have a customer who currently uses one or more of these think that it's too difficult to contact you. You certainly can't afford to have a *potential* customer unsure about how to enquire after your services or place an order. So you give them every opportunity you can; it's like having a shop in every virtual high street or shopping centre.

In time, all these technologies will change, of course: Amazon may not be the best place for you tomorrow, but you will change with the technologies and you will add new sites and widgets as you go along.

If you have something really good to offer then you should want everyone to know about it. And if everyone you can think of amounts to

50 people, that's fine. If those 50 people also think it's a really good offer, they can then go on to tell 10 others each. Suddenly 551 people know (including yourself of course). If the 500 tell 10 others, you have 5,051. It's how very popular sites and blogs grow: virally.

The only way to be very famous is to start off famous. But you don't want or need to be famous just yet; you just want to be known by enough people to meet your objectives. These will be people who want to, and are in a position to, buy what you have to offer.

The power of linking

As we noted in Chapter 5, Google and other search sites are increasingly sophisticated in the way they rank pages and blogs, and although keywords are still important, they are not the only important factor. Remember search engines also look for links – into and out of the site – and for currency – how recently the pages were updated.

So the best way to make your site popular, then, is to keep working on establishing links with others and to update it regularly. It should be a part of your weekly routine. A blog is an ideal way of doing this, doubly so if you have readers who comment; and, of course, readers may include people you work with – business partners and customers.

You can work on exchanging links with fellow bloggers and with related websites. Never be afraid to contact these – even if they seem to be in competition. For example www.canefurniturewarehouse.co.uk based in Essex invites link swaps with related companies and has an extensive list of websites categorised for its visitors. As the site itself specialises in conservatory furniture, it's only logical it should invite links with companies like Planet Conservatories (www.planetpvc.co.uk).

Both companies could, however, do a great deal more to make the links more prominent – when they are hidden (on both sites) some way down a list of 'useful links' they just don't get used. Far better to make a feature of suppliers you have investigated and that you trust on a panel on a front page, then customers can see the range of information and services *you* are offering. You can even test out their customer service and review their products in your blog and invite comment – all give visitors a reason to stay with you and return.

Enlightened businesses often recognise the importance of linking and want to avoid their site being a dead end. If your customers can't find what they want on your site, it's a good thing to be able to point them in the right direction. The corollary to that is if you *do* have what they want, put it on the very first page they see to avoid them going elsewhere!

As I said when we were looking at setting up basic first Web pages, you should always be checking that customers can get what they want the moment they visit. As an example, imagine you are about to build a timber deck in your garden and want to look at suppliers to check out designs and prices. Then have a look at the website of the building supplies company Jewson (www.jewson.co.uk). Despite the obvious quality of the design, I don't think it will take you long to find the fault(s) with this website.

Leaving aside the issues of designing your pages and your essential information, links are your pages' lifeblood. One idea is to join an existing link-exchange scheme. These kind of intermediary schemes are, like SEO services, common and of variable quality[2]. Some want to charge a fee and some offer a level of free service.

Some link exchanges are relatively low-tech and industry-specific, such as www.accountancymarketing.co.uk/linkexchange.html and www.a1transport.co.uk/a1transport/links.aspx which relate to accountancy and transport services respectively. Both manage to get themselves reasonably high in search engine results.

Of course there may already be such programs in existence for your industry, and a good place to start looking would be your own industry-specific websites and journals. Don't worry if there aren't, though. You

---

[2] They include www.freerelevantlinks.co.uk and www.britinfo.net which is a listing site but also has a link exchange programme.

should be able to build up a resource of your own that is useful to your customers, and you should invite them to contact you with any useful links they find or if they need help locating other suppliers.

The richness of links will help your page ranking anyway – especially if the links are in 'cognate' areas – that is, that they deal with similar or related subjects. Again, even linking to your competitors could have the effect of rating your site higher than theirs. In the end, what really counts for search engines such as Google is the content of your site or pages. It must be interesting and relevant enough for customers to bookmark and share and to link to if they can – a point we touched on in Chapter 4 and reinforced in Chapter 5.

Getting social

As we discussed earlier, just looking around and contributing to other discussions is good in itself. As you get more proficient and you have more to talk about, you will be able to cross-refer to your own Web pages – on your blog, on eBay and others – and you should never miss an opportunity to do so. Remember to observe the netiquette we mentioned in Chapter 3.

If you are concentrating on one market or one category – like Goose Loose on outdoor pursuits and adventure sports – then you can start to build up collections of links in different places. There are again marketspaces where like-minded people gather to seek or swap information. Del.icio.us (http://del.icio.us), Digg (http://digg.com) and Stumble Upon (www.stumbleupon.com) are sites designed for sharing links and content with others. This 'social bookmarking' can be a way of making lists of useful websites or interesting stories, pictures and videos available with a single link, but it also acts to build up popular sites and links by a kind of voting system – the more people search for and use your links, the more highly they are ranked.

You may have noticed that many of these sites are options on the AddThis tool I recommended in Chapter 3. Different visitors to your site will use different sites for keeping track of their bookmarks and links, so a flexible tool like this enables them to note your site and, by extension, inform other people with similar interests.

With Del.icio.us, for example, lists of all your links can be embedded in e-mails, Web pages and blog posts just by including a link such as 'http://del.icio.us/gooseloose', where the end of the link is your user name. To include links relating only to a single subject you could use a link such as 'http://del.icio.us/gooseloose/surfing', where the last word is the tag you've given that subject.

Del.icio.us also allows you to automatically share links on your website or blog, or to automate the posting of links to your blog. This can take some of the work out of updating your own pages and so keep your content current.

Digg is a similar story, but intriguing in that it is built to promote that which is popular and 'bury' that which is found by its users to be less useful. The aim, of course, is to get to a critical mass of users who like your content. You start by submitting content links and so on – but submitting your own content or blog postings is frowned upon so, instead, you should encourage your existing visitors to 'digg' your content (providing them with an easy button, of course). Within any category, the most popular digs are featured on the front page, giving them further exposure.

StumbleUpon works in a similar way but aims to reduce information overload by directing exploration on the Web using popular recommendations. Put simply, other people with similar patterns of interests to yours rate pages they have 'stumbled upon': their recommendations affect the pages StumbleUpon offers to you, and your recommendations affect which pages are offered to others. You can see a demo of how you leap from one site to another (dependent on your interests, rather than scrolling through search findings) at www.stumbleupon.com/demo.

Encouraging 'word of mouse'

You can probably see how 'seeding' a few keen buyers to recommend your site might pay dividends in the online equivalent of word-of-mouth recommendations. It's important to understand that this kind of promotion can be slow to take off (it depends upon your content being discovered and liked), but when it does is fairly effective.

Whilst De.licio.us is fairly anti-commercial, Digg allows a kind of display advertising on its pages (handled, incidentally, by Microsoft). StumbleUpon goes further with an advertising product (www.stumbleupon.com/ads) that allows targeting of particular users and offering up complete Web pages rather than adverts (which may or may not be clicked on). Stumblers are then likely to give your page a 'thumbs up' or a 'thumbs down', which they can do simply by clicking on their toolbar – useful feedback about your campaign and your website.

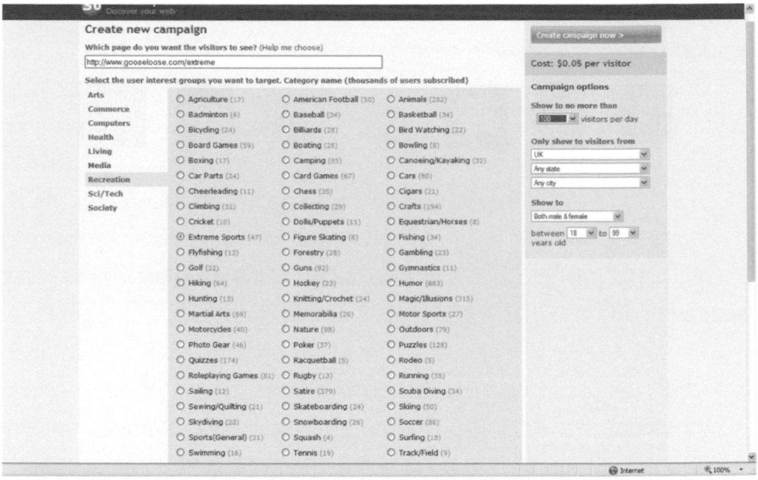

Figure 2 *Targeting StumbleUpon's advertising*

Given that StumbleUpon users have actively stated their interest in a subject, it's likely that your page will be examined rather more closely and critically than other advertising – indeed, it may not even be seen as advertising.

To set up your campaign, all you need is an account, a Web page or a blog that you want your potential customers to see, and a PayPal account. You can find out more at http://tinyurl.com/69tu9y.

Other social sites worth looking at for different subject areas include – Slashdot (http://slashdot.org), Fark (www.fark.com), Reddit (www.reddit.com) and Truemor (http://truemors.com).

Flaunting your expertise

Squidoo (www.squidoo.com), the brainchild of marketing guru, and author Seth Godin, is actually just another way of making link-worthy content and being available to those who are looking for your expertise.

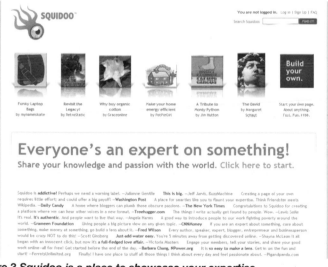

Figure 3 *Squidoo is a place to showcase your expertise*

Squidoo 'lenses' – pages covering a particular subject – show up quite well in searches and are pretty easy to set up and re-edit. Graeme Hatt, for example, has a blog (http://graemehatt.com) which he uses to promote his book *Gardening Secrets*. His lenses include tips on building a patio, terracing and growing tomatoes (www.squidoo.com/lensmasters/graemehatt). It's a good example of the integration mentioned earlier.

Graeme also makes extracts of his book available for download and has a regular newsletter at his website www.gardeningsecrets.org.

Figure 4 *Graeme Hatt's 'lens'*

Graeme's lenses include his photographs and blog postings. Other people who visit can rate a lens, bookmark it in all the usual ways, print and e-mail it.

Linking offline

Of course, not everything you do to build your business happens online. Anything you do to get people to search for or visit your site can affect your ranking on search sites. This kind of promotional activity we've already referred to as "external SEO", and it is probably most important in getting your site known.

If you write an article for a trade magazine or a local newspaper, or if you can get an interview on local radio, then it's acceptable for you to ask that they include a URL. Whether they will or won't, you can always refer to your site in order to direct readers or listeners to more information or a way of contacting you. These links will very often also appear in the online version of the magazine or on the station's website, and your credibility can rise as a result.

If your online content involves giving instructions, as Graeme Hatt's website does, you can also think about podcasting, making a video (see Chapter 11) or making a PowerPoint presentation and putting it on SlideShare (www.slideshare.net). See also the entertaining slide presentation by Andy Sernovitz (author of *Word of Mouth Marketing*) on just this subject at http://tinyurl.com/5s7d2t.

E-mail, newsletters and press releases

Never underestimate the interest people may have in what you do. A single e-mail to a blogger, a magazine, an online journal or to your customers can generate a lot of response. Of course such response could be negative, but if it gets people engaged in discussion then that in turn can generate attention. The point, of course, is that what people receive has to be of interest – it's a question of giving some thought to what is of use to those customers or journalists or blog writers.

You can do this by reading the blogs and sites concerned and, of course, engaging in a dialogue with customers, but your content should always be tailored, and you can always negotiate with the newspaper or radio station to offer some kind of promotional giveaway or prize (see below). Don't forget conventional journalists use the Web for their research. You can e-mail them too if you're sure you have a valuable story and you know the reporters cover this subject or area. To make it easy for them, write a press release which includes a usable photograph, background information and your contact details.

It's worthwhile having a page of press releases on your website anyway, as these can also get picked up by search engines.

Sales promotion

This kind of sales promotion is just about giving customers a reason to buy now instead of later. If that's your aim, then any kind of incentive should be time-limited to make customers think about when they can realise its value. Such promotions needn't be money-off offers. Single prizes, free consultations, samples – all work to get attention, and can get you free coverage through commercial radio stations and newspapers.

Promotional vouchers can work online too. We've seen that these can be set up within Google (in Chapter 4), but there are also sites which specialise in collating Web offers for their visitors. AgentB or RetailMeNot are two (based in the US) used and recommended by Nataliya Yakushev (http://webmill.blogspot.com) to promote her client's line of children's clothes. AgentB (www.agentb.com) categorises offers by segments and by type of offer, while RetailMeNot (www.retailmenot.com) offers widgets to add on to browser toolbars which customers can use to call up context-specific promotional codes.

There is a host of sites in the UK which offer similar services, including www.myvouchercodes.co.uk, www.vouchercodes.com, www.latestdiscountvouchers.co.uk, www.freeinuk.co.uk and www.discount-voucher.co.uk to name just a few. These are generally less developed than in the US. Most of them require you to search for the retailer by name and to sign up to get the voucher. It means that

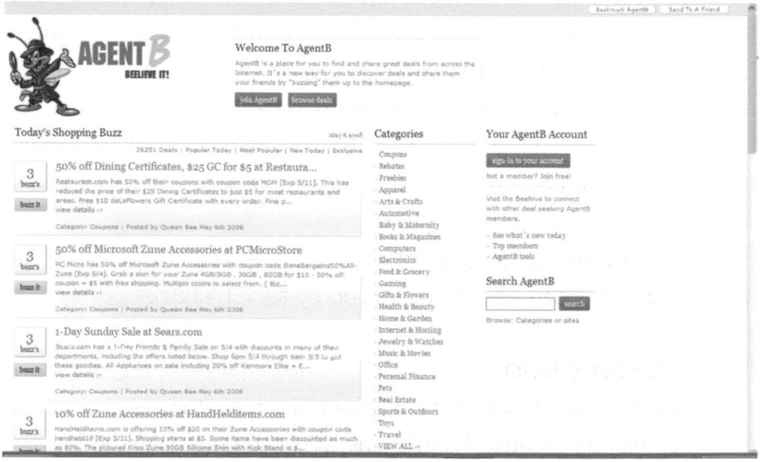

Figure 5 *Agent B is a site for sharing special offers*

Figure 6 *Coupons are also made available through sites like RetailMeNot*

customers are more likely to look for money-off vouchers on brands they have already heard of.

Trophy Pet Foods (www.trophypetfoods.co.uk) uses the freeinuk site to distribute a free sample offer which is then fielded out to one of its franchisees for its home delivery service.

No doubt these kinds of sites will develop in the UK and, when they do, could be attractive for even small online retailers and service providers. In the meantime they can be an inexpensive way of prospecting for customers since vouchers are, by definition, only redeemed by those buying.

Self-liquidating promotions

Nothing to do with suicidal intentions of marketers, 'self-liquidating' refers to the fact that the promotion is paid for by the customer.

Items can be as simple as T-shirts or caps printed with your logo, but there is an almost endless range of products that can be personalised with many suppliers online. Both CafePress (www.cafepress.com) and Spreadshirt (www.spreadshirt.net) stores are free at the basic level and offer various ways of integrating your online store with your website, and we return to these and others in Chapter 11.

Goose Loose could certainly set up a range of products relating to certain sports without incurring any set-up or ongoing costs, and if people like your brand, why not give them a way of showing it?

If you need to think of an incentive, think of the most valuable and desired product or add-on service your clients could want and start with that. To an office cleaning company, for example, free cleaning for a year may seem a costly offer. However, if this is a prize in a free-to-enter draw, then it may persuade many companies to give you information about their office cleaning needs. How many contracts would you have to gain to pay for one client for a year?

Clearly, if you can't afford it work backwards to what you can, but always start with the most powerful benefit or promise which will generally have the most powerful effect on your prospective customers.

Sometimes it's acceptable to offer something that is not directly related to your business. 'Fifty iPods to be won' is a fairly attractive offer (and you might be able to source them quite cheaply on eBay!) but be careful that it doesn't detract from your company/brand offer. In the above example, you want to attract people who have a need for office cleaning, not those who simply want a free iPod.

You should also be careful that any such promotion is legal. For example, it's not legal to give a *gift* only to those who become customers, but you can offer a prize based on a game of skill. To check the rules, (in the UK) go to www.isp.org.uk (http://tinyurl.com/5n7sxy) or to the Advertising Standards Authority www.asa.org.uk (http://tinyurl.com/5595go).

Not-so-free promotion

Sooner rather than later you should experiment with paid-for advertising. Since there are many options out there, the key to making a choice is to be clear about the value of advertising at the outset.

Again, without going into great detail, advertising is just a way of getting someone nearer to your business and nearer to the point of making a purchase decision. Your advertising hasn't contributed anything material until it results in a sale. It's the way of most advertising that while thousands of people may see it, only a few respond and fewer still buy. So those who do buy must pay for advertising to all those who do not.

For example, an ad that costs £100 and attracts 1000 enquiries, of which 10 actually buy anything, has cost you £10 per customer. Furthermore, that advertising only works if your profit from those customers turns out to average more than £10 each.

Fortunately, online advertising works in a very measurable way, and Google AdWords is fairly simple to set up and monitor.

Google AdWords

Google adverts appear on the pages alongside search results. You will have seen it in your own searches. When you look for 'kiteboarding equipment' (as in Figure 6), you get results at the top and to the right (sponsored results) that are there because the companies concerned have paid for one or more of the keywords you have used. The other results are there because the Google algorithm determines they are most relevant.

Most conventional advertising is still priced according to the potential audience: traditionally, media rates show a price per thousand (abbreviated to CPT or CPM) but they mean a thousand people who have the opportunity to see your ad. One of the attractions of online advertising with Google AdWords is that you can decide on your own budget, paying only for clicks on your ad rather than for 'views'.

You can decide how much you want to spend for your whole campaign and adjust how much you are prepared to pay for each clickthrough. It follows that you need to monitor your advertising closely, and Google provides you with useful metrics as part of its service.

As an example, here I've put together a test campaign for Goose Loose to promote its online store for extreme sports equipment. The starting point is to determine what search terms we'd like our ad to appear close to.

It's possible to get Google to scan a website in order to pick up relevant keywords for advertising. If you've already optimised keyword tags in your site (as in Chapter 5), you can use these words in your list. In any case, you can choose the words by entering terms into the central box, and you can choose to omit certain words – then click to get keyword ideas.

To get your own ads showing up, you will need to use your Google account and register for an AdWords account. You can choose either the Starter or Standard edition. By all means try the Starter to become familiar with online advertising, but you will soon want to upgrade. As you can see in Figure 7, your own website is a requirement for the Standard option.

There's a sign-up fee of £5 (or £10 if you intend to pre-pay for your advertising), but beyond that pricing is flexible – you bid for keywords against other advertisers. You don't pay anything until you have specified what your campaign will look like.

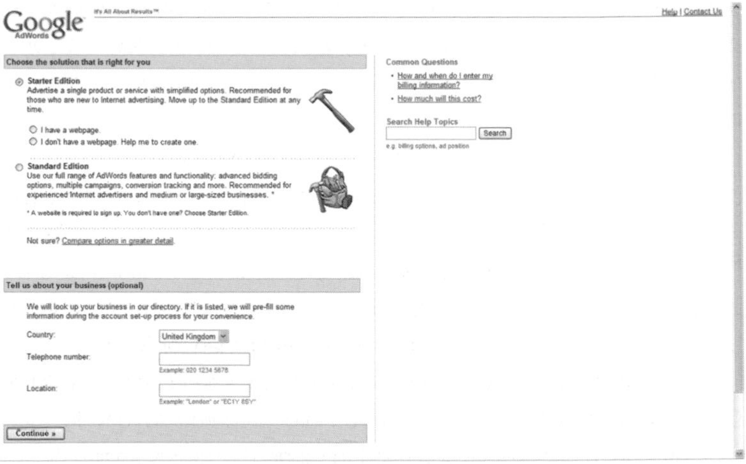

Figure 7 *Choose between Starter or Standard editions*

Google also helps you by giving a free page (in the Starter version) as the 'landing page' for any enquiries (useful if your website is not easily edited), helping to tailor your response page to the exact details of your campaign offer and the needs of your target audience.

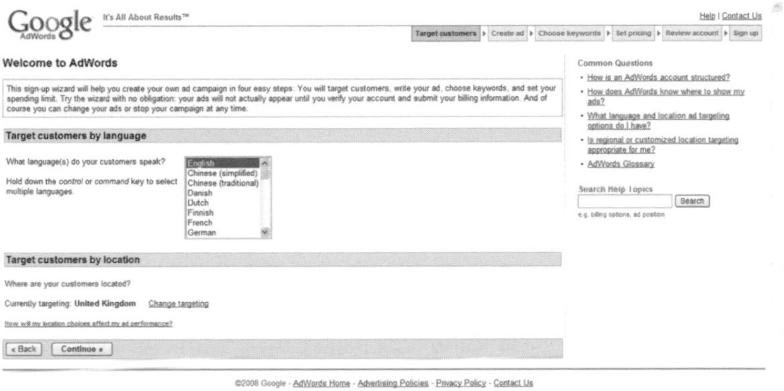

Figure 8 *Starting to target your advertising*

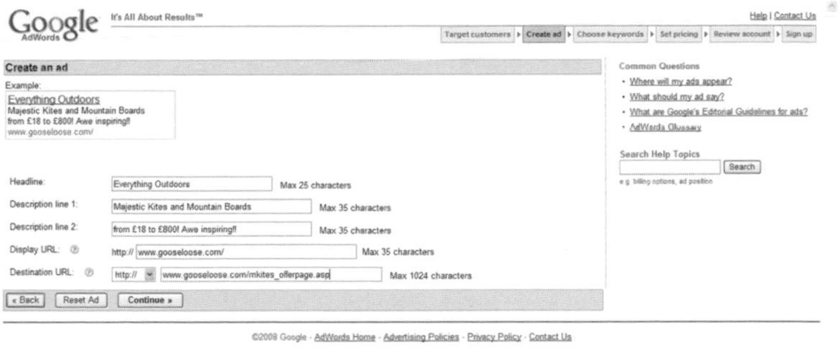

Figure 9 *Wording your ad*

As you design your campaign, you can specify who is chosen by Google to see your advertising – by language and location. There are guidance notes every step of the way.

When you write the content of your ad – less than 100 characters – you see it illustrated in the top right-hand corner. You'll need to experiment to get it looking attractive, and Google is quite particular about the content of ads – the exclamation marks in the Goose Loose ad in Figure 9 would result in rejection. It's possible to re-edit and re-submit and even apply for an exemption from some of the rules if, for example, an exclamation mark was a necessary part of a brand name you wanted to use.

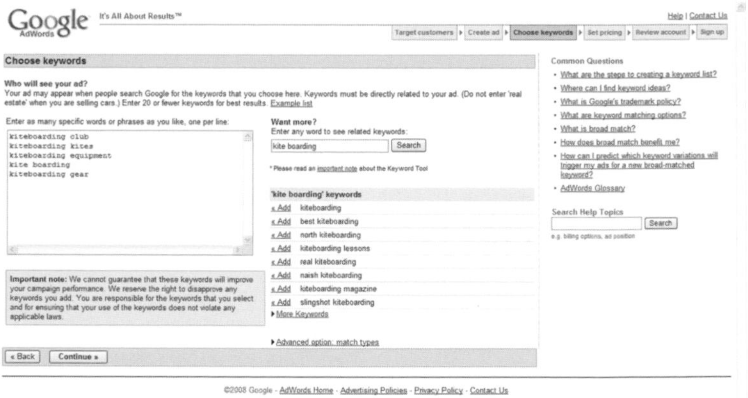

Figure 10 *Your keywords specify which searches trigger your ad to appear*

How much does a click cost?

How your ad is ranked depends mostly on how much you bid per click and your total budget. Another advertiser may bid more for the same or similar keywords and so appear above you in the list. This may not be a significant problem: in fact, the exact position of your ad is not as important as the rate at which people click through (and then go on to buy – the cost of advertising *per click, per sale* or *per customer*). The higher-bidding advertiser may, of course, hit his or her monthly budget before you, and so your ad could continue to be shown, perhaps now in the higher position.

The starter edition of AdWords automatically tries to optimise the number of clicks you get within your budget. You can accept these settings or adjust them to bid higher for clicks. How much you pay each day is a function of the number of clicks and the prices you have chosen. At 10p per click, 25 potential customers clicking through your ad to the page you'd set up would cost you £2.50. If you'd set a monthly budget of £50, your advertising would be scaled down to spread the budget through the month, so you'd spend about £1.66 per day getting 16 or 17 clicks.

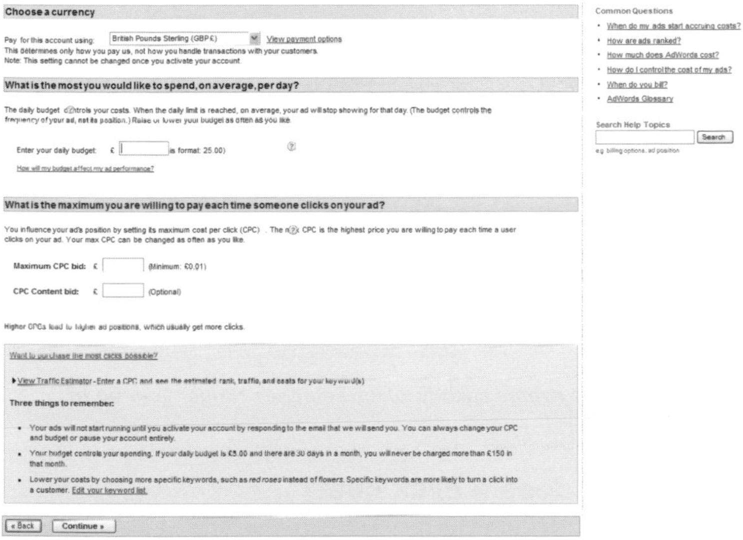

Figure 11 *Deciding how much you want to spend*

You can find much about the way ads are priced in the Google AdWords help pages (https://adwords.google.com/support) and see http://tinyurl.com/5nmtj2 for the explanation of positioning – you'll need to be signed in first.

You can see in Figure 12 that you are given some detail on targeting your ad and the likely costs. You can adjust keywords and costs until you get an acceptable balance between your budget and the anticipated response. In the end, however, there is no substitute for live testing of your advertising.

It's also worth noting that the more specific your keywords, the more effective they are likely to be – for those specific searches. For example, Goose Loose could include brand names such as *Flexifoil* in their keywords to capture searches from more knowledgeable buyers, along with keywords 'kite' and 'holidays'; it would appear higher up in the list of ads.

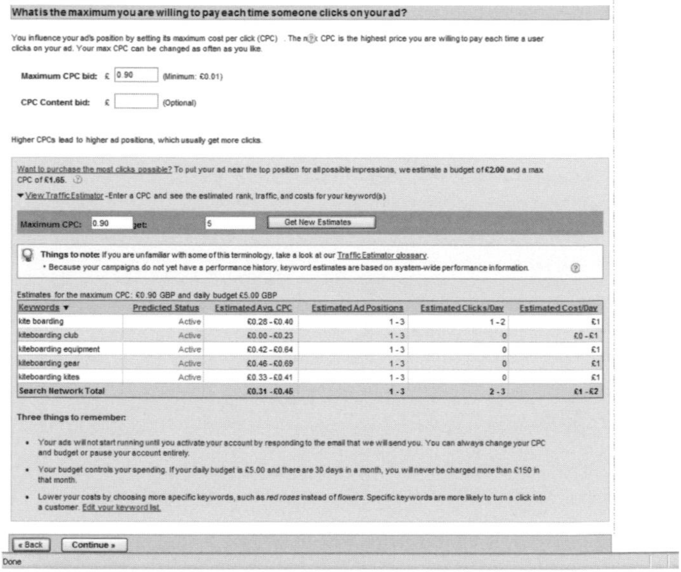

What is the maximum you are willing to pay each time someone clicks on your ad?

You influence your ad's position by setting its maximum cost per click (CPC) . The max CPC is the highest price you are willing to pay each time a user clicks on your ad. Your max CPC can be changed as often as you like.

Maximum CPC bid: £ 0.90 (Minimum: £0.01)

CPC Content bid: £ (Optional)

Higher CPCs lead to higher ad positions, which usually get more clicks.

Want to purchase the most clicks possible? To put your ad near the top position for all possible impressions, we estimate a budget of **£2.00** and a max CPC of **£1.65**.

View Traffic Estimator -Enter a CPC and see the estimated rank, traffic, and costs for your keyword(s)

Maximum CPC: 0.90 **get:** 5 Get New Estimates

Things to note: If you are unfamiliar with some of this terminology, take a look at our Traffic Estimator glossary.
- Because your campaigns do not yet have a performance history, keyword estimates are based on system-wide performance information.

Estimates for the maximum CPC: £0.90 GBP and daily budget £5.00 GBP

Keywords ▼	Predicted Status	Estimated Avg. CPC	Estimated Ad Positions	Estimated Clicks/Day	Estimated Cost/Day
kite boarding	Active	£0.28 - £0.40	1 - 3	1 - 2	£1
kiteboarding club	Active	£0.00 - £0.23	1 - 3	0	£0 - £1
kiteboarding equipment	Active	£0.42 - £0.64	1 - 3	0	£1
kiteboarding gear	Active	£0.46 - £0.69	1 - 3	0	£1
kiteboarding kites	Active	£0.33 - £0.41	1 - 3	0	£1
Search Network Total		**£0.31 - £0.45**	**1 - 3**	**2 - 3**	**£1 - £2**

Three things to remember:

- Your ads will not start running until you activate your account by responding to the email that we will send you. You can always change your CPC and budget or pause your account entirely.
- Your budget controls your spending. If your daily budget is £5.00 and there are 30 days in a month, you will never be charged more than £150 in that month.
- Lower your costs by choosing more specific keywords, such as *red roses* instead of *flowers*. Specific keywords are more likely to turn a click into a customer. Edit your keyword list.

« Back Continue »

Done

Figure 12 ***You can fine-tune your budget***

The ad itself might be for instructional holidays – "Take your Flexifoil on holiday and we'll supply the expert tutor" might attract clickthrough more rapidly than "Kiteboarding holidays . . .".

As you're in competition with other advertisers, it follows that you may not always get your ad shown, but in any case, you can limit your monthly budget (daily in the Standard edition) and specify how much you are prepared to pay per click. If you get no response you can always adjust these figures at any time, or pause or stop your campaign.

Again, Google offers some useful advice and tools on its help pages, such as the Traffic Estimator (http://tinyurl.com/5l52qp).

As far as possible you should track advertising right through to sales and profitability of customers (again there's more about this in *Marketing & PR*). You might be surprised how one particular source produces many more profitable customers than another.

The important thing to remember is that all these variables can, and should, be tested within the budget you set yourself. It can be quite a task to keep track of various ads and their success rate, but this attention to detail can be the difference between adequate advertising and great advertising.

Press and radio advertising

For a local business, local radio is a relatively cost-effective way of building up awareness of your name. Having a memorable website address that is easy to hear and understand is important. You might want to think about this if you have so far been using blogs or webpages hosted by one of the companies already discussed in Chapter 4 such as MSN or Google.

Such long addresses are difficult to find sometimes, but it's perfectly possible for you to buy a domain name specifically for a campaign which is easy for a potential customer to remember. If your name is unique, you could simply invite prospects to 'google' you. Of course, you'd have to test it first and monitor it regularly to make sure your name came up first. By way of example, a domain name like 'freepetfood. co.uk' could be bought for as little as £6 from a domain registrar such as www.123-reg.co.uk and could form the basis of a strong campaign to pet owners.

It's relatively simple to get a domain name URL to forward traffic automatically to a specific page. Depending on the registrar or host company, you may have to pay. Some host companies will set this up for you or give you access to a control panel to input the setting yourself, which is more daunting. Check on 'domain forwarding' before you buy and, if you do use this service, make sure it's set up well in advance: it can take weeks before it is functioning properly and you will want to test it.

Newsletters and e-newsletters

For people who are less connected, you might still want to have a fairly conventional e-mail newsletter. This could be simply an aggregation of your various blog posts or a synopsis of other content.

You also need to allow for those who can't, or simply don't want to, receive e-mails or subscribe to newsfeeds. In this case, a hard-copy newsletter is useful, and needn't be complex or expensive. The stories within the newsletter need only be the kind of information you are already using online. Indeed, you could reproduce all or some of them in date order as diary entries.

The door-to-door organic food supplier Abel & Cole (www. abelandcole.co.uk) do this with their weekly newsletter which is delivered with each box. The simple A4 sheet chats about what is happening in the company and especially with suppliers of that season's produce. It's also reproduced on their website – although it's not a blog and it's not very prominent. However, inserting the printed newsletter into every delivery ensures that all customers receive it, and there's no postage cost. Doing something similar with, say, every product you've sold via eBay or Amazon would be a great way of cross-selling.

Remember also that the printed newsletter must include all the other contact details customers might need: – the address, phone number, e-mail of course, but also the fact that you have your own Facebook group (see Chapter 8) or website of whatever kind. It should welcome participation. In fact it should offer a real incentive for a response and for passing the newsletter on to friends or colleagues who might be interested. Your existing customers are your best channel for finding more like them.

Some sources of help

Newsletter Manager Pro (http://tinyurl.com/5hpa6y) is a downloadable, Web-based program costing around £50 with no ongoing licence fee, unless you want to receive program updates after a year[3]. You can download and read the user guide before you buy and you can see a demo set up at http://tinyurl.com/6me3ro. It shows clearly how you go about managing multiple lists and newsletters. For a one-person company with a fairly limited requirement – say, a weekly or monthly e-mail to everyone – Newsletter Manager Pro may be over the top. For a company with various product sectors or customer interests, perhaps with different kinds of customers or prospects, or for someone running several companies, it may prove valuable.

Newsletter Manager Pro resides on your Web server, so there is usually no additional ongoing cost for Web hosting if you already have a provider. In the end, it's worth asking yourself whether you need to mass produce different kinds of mailing or whether it isn't easier, and perhaps more honest, to produce a single diary-style letter and dealing with other customers, as far as possible, on a one-to-one basis.

To produce your hard-copy newsletter, you will need a simple template in a word-processing programme like Word. It's worth getting someone who understands design to set this up for you, including the logo and visual style you have established online. Once you have a template, however, the copy (the words) can come mainly from your online updates by cutting and pasting every time you update your blog or website.

The addresses and mailing preferences of your customers still need to be managed and kept secure – remembering your responsibilities under data protection legislation (www.ico.gov.uk), and always give your customers the ability to opt out of receiving the newsletter. Some of this can be done within Outlook or Mozilla or your own e-mail or contacts management program (and you might find some of the Skype extras mentioned in Chapter 12 useful), but as your list grows you may find yourself reluctant to personalise and print every copy, and cleaning large lists can become troublesome. If your newsletter is distributed to

---

[3] Fanblast (www.fanmass.com) does much the same things as Newsletter Manager, but for a monthly fee; but see www.download.com and search for e-mail and/or newsletter management for alternatives – some of which are free or free to try.

purchasers, then it should be part of your despatch documentation. Some of the merchant tools mentioned in Chapter 6 may help you to do this.

For a conventional postal mailing that runs into the hundreds, if not thousands, then a specialist mailing company may be the best answer. Don't forget, as we said in the last chapter, it's possible to buy postage online, but it's also possible to get discounted postage if, for example, your outbound mail is pre-sorted.

A final reminder – consistency and integration

As you will have seen, there are all kinds of ways of keeping in touch with existing customers and of trying to make contact with new ones.

The more your customers are online, the more you will use online methods, but don't ignore the more traditional routes. Even door-to-door flyers have a role. If, for example, you're landscaping a garden in one house, why not tell the neighbours? If you're attending a country fair, don't just sell your product: give customers a way of contacting you directly for ever afterwards – and an incentive to do so.

The key thing here is that techniques of getting a response are improved if those neighbours and fair-goers have multiple ways of responding, each one connected to the other and each one branded consistently. These will include phone number, postal address, e-mail and Web address of course, but also – as we'll see in the next few chapters – other market spaces and social networks, too.

CHAPTER 8

FACEBOOK – SOCIAL NETWORKING FOR BEGINNERS

Unless you've been in a cave for the last couple of years you've already heard enough about Facebook to know that it can't be ignored. Having said that, being in a cave may not have hindered you: it's a pretty safe bet that Osama Bin Laden has a profile.[1]

With over 6 million users a month, Facebook is the kind of 'thingamajig' it's hard to ignore. Surely with all those users whizzing around spending more time online than they do in front of the TV, there has to be a business opportunity?

Well there is. But it's the thingamajig that's the problem. What exactly IS Facebook or, for example, Friendster, Bebo, MySpace or Orkut, Perfspot, Hi5, Tagworld, Piczo, Faceparty and Mixi or even mychumsclub. com?[2] They are all, more or less, social networking sites. And that means that they are for finding and communicating with people with a shared interest, but also (as the founder of Facebook, Mark Zuckerberg, argues) for keeping in touch with people you already know. Unlike very specialised websites that predefine the audience, these make it easy to join (or set up) interest groups so that, for example, if you collect vinyl records you can find others who do so too, like the 'Vinyl Preservation Society' group on Facebook with over 700 members.

---

[1] I've just checked . . . and he has, genuine or not!

[2] Or, for that matter, Black Planet, Asian Avenue, MiGente, QQ or Cyworld, Ryze?,flickr, photobucket, Twitter, Pownce, ScrapBook? Some of these are social networking sites, some are social bookmarking sites, some are online communities, some we'll return to later. Some are just weird.

According to data from the research company TNS Media Intelligence, only 18 per cent of UK marketers think they should be looking at social networking as a matter of urgency, and WARC (the World Advertising Research Council[3]) suggests that there may be a degree of cynicism this side of the Atlantic, noting that, as this book was written, some of these sites were seeing a decline in membership.

The truth is, probably, that some social networking sites will grow while others wither away. Bebo sold to AOL for $850 million as that media giant tries to catch up with the new wave of websites and services based on advertising revenue rather than on what now appears rather an old-fashioned business model: subscription.

In this chapter, we're going to concentrate on Facebook (we'll come on to alternatives in Chapter 9) because Facebook seems to be the networking site that has most openly embraced marketing – and therefore the tools exist to build and maintain relationships with customers. For the most up-to-date guidance on using Facebook, the site itself has extensive help pages as well as discussion groups, but I would also direct you to Justin Smith's excellent website www.insidefacebook.com which is constantly updated with useful tips and insight.

What (marketing) use is Facebook?

Facebook has the potential for many small businesses to meet the second strategic aim we referred to in Chapter 2 – getting more customers – since it seems to have reached a mass audience. The most significant point, however, is that many potential customers already use Facebook, and so it makes sense for you to be there too, rather than trying to lure them elsewhere. Think of it as a TV station or a magazine with maybe 40 million viewers or readers, or as a marketplace where you can meet buyers. And getting access to those people is completely free.

---

[3] www.warc.com/news, 4 March 2008

Where Facebook really works is in making it easy to keep in touch in various ways with a large number of friends and groups of friends in one place. For many people, use of a social networking site has replaced conventional e-mail. Of course, your contacts have to be 'on' Facebook too. It's a fundamental issue we come across with all such sites: you can only connect with the people who are there. However, Facebook is far more representative of the population than some sites such as Bebo; that is to say, the age profile of members and the range of interests are pretty wide.

Other, narrower social networking sites (sometimes described as 'vertical') cater for a particular interest, so it's worth searching for one that may be close to the interests of your (potential) customers. And, of course, there's no reason why you can't join more than one and, indeed, create links between them.

In sum, then, Facebook in particular seems to have reached a critical mass – at least amongst a younger (under 45) audience in the US and more recently in the UK and around the world, so that unless you really want to aim your marketing at Luddites, you have a pretty good chance of finding a receptive audience on the site. It's now perfectly acceptable to include on your business cards, letterheads, website (and of course blog) a reference and link to your profile, events and messages on one or more social networking sites.

Even if, at the moment, the specific people you want to contact aren't currently on Facebook, you can invite them to join and, as it's free, there isn't a great deal of resistance to overcome. As I've said, the Luddites will resist joining on principle, but six million users (a month) can't be entirely wrong.

Facebook has a mixed reputation, however; the logic of some of the applications and how you opt in or out can be difficult to fathom: it's often trial and error. There are also scare stories about accounts being suspended when Facebook members send or post too many items, without there being any specified limit. These are problems the Facebook management need to address.

How to do it

Signing up to Facebook couldn't be simpler. Just go to the URL – www. facebook.com (it's a pretty uninspiring page) – and click on the green 'Sign Up' button.

If you prefer, you can click on the 'Site tour' link at the top right, which will give you a very brief idea of the site, but there's no substitute for signing up and having a look at what the site does in reality.

You'll also see that there is the opportunity to 'Find your friends' before you login, but this seems to be limited, so that you only see a brief listing of some people before you sign up. Once you decide to start the sign-up process, it's decisions, decisions all the way.

Figure 1 *The kind of page non-members will see when they first look at Facebook*

You can set up a Facebook 'profile' page (like a homepage) for yourself or for your business. Initially it makes sense to start with an individual page. That way you can play with the features without exposing your business or brand to ridicule. Furthermore, as an individual on Facebook you have much more access to other users' profiles, so you can look around. Business accounts are really only for managing pages and ad campaigns, and are restricted in other ways too.

So I'd recommend you don't start by setting up a business account unless you are doing so on behalf of another company. The reasons are complicated, but because of the Facebook site rules and controls, you can't have both types of account. As we'll see later, however, you can set up business 'pages' (rather than profiles or accounts) once you have a personal account.

Bear in mind that unless you plan on keeping your personal use of Facebook utterly separate from your business use (with separate logins, e-mails etc) then you will be linked to your business pages. Even if you could keep these things entirely separate, it's debateable whether you are sticking to the terms and conditions of the site.

Facebook (like most social networking) seems to be based on the idea that transparency = honesty. Again, this is a change in culture for some in business who like to keep home and work separate. For most small businesses it's not a real issue and, as we discussed in Chapter 2, if you are embracing Web 2.0 you need to loosen up!

So when you first sign up, you're expected to give a name, and here's your first decision – do you give a 'screen name' or 'handle', or do you simply want to be yourself?

Well you can go back and edit most aspects of your profile, but you're pretty much stuck with your name (unless you delete your account and start again) so I suggest you just think of a name that you'd be happy to be associated with personally and professionally. For most people, it's easiest to use their own name – and why would you want to adopt a disguise anyway? It's probably the case that, like many small businesses, you *are* the company – or a substantial part of it.

As we've already seen, you can choose to create a personal or a business profile at this stage. The business option gives limited choices, none of which might fit exactly. It should go without saying that you can't use an identity (such as a competitor's brand) that you don't own – it's illegal.

So, as you set up your account, Facebook continues to offer you plenty of options. For example, you can ask Facebook to automatically check to see which of your existing contacts are on Facebook. It's usually a pretty easy process if, for example, you already use Microsoft's Outlook to manage your names and addresses. You may want to go through this rather carefully if, for example, you want your clients to be there (but not your bank manager) or your suppliers (but not your mother-in-law). You'll also want to be clear about who should have access to your phone number, for example. At first, don't include it. Later you might need to, but then having a business number separate from a private number will probably become essential.

You'll also have to choose a network to belong to – these can be colleges, workplaces or just geographical locations. They'll show up on your profile and prioritise connections with these people, but it's not the most important choice you make. Generally, the wider the network the better (more potential contacts) so, for example, 'London' is better than 'St Thomas's School'. Networks are, usefully, more tolerant of announcements and messages that are sent to all that could be seen as spam – as a member you can post on the network home page.

Immediately you can begin to see the kind of issues you need to deal with. What is your Facebook presence actually for? Who do you want to be able to see you online? At this early stage then, it may be best to add just a few trusted friends and co-workers, and start to have a look around at what is already there.

The main point to remember about your profile page is that it will be viewed by pretty much everyone you link with, and could become pivotal to your online presence. Stick to our first recommendation: set up your account for yourself and invest some time discovering what the site can do before exposing your brand too much.

Personalising your profile

It's not necessary to go into too much detail about what you can do with your Facebook profile. It's a question of playing with the various

Figure 2 *Core features of Facebook are listed on the left, other applications on the right*

applications built into the standard Facebook account. Eventually, however, you'll begin telling people about your page and connecting to your friends. It's worth therefore thinking about what you want to say on your profile about you and your business(es) and your brands. Think of telling the story of your product or how you got into it and what you're doing to develop and promote it – and be honest. Ambition is okay, as is pride in your business or product, but overt selling is generally frowned upon. If you're successful in growing your network, then others will take up the story too.

I can almost guarantee that everyone you communicate with in Facebook will check out your profile at least once, and probably at regular intervals, so it's important to get it right and to keep updating it as necessary, but the whole 'flow' of Facebook is to keep members interacting, and that includes you, so put aside time – probably every day – to check over your pages and messages, and interact. It's a bit like being at a party and circulating . . . or standing in the corner avoiding eye contact!

Marketing on Facebook

So, in order to start getting something out of Facebook, you need to put something in: you need to be active. The quickest and easiest way of building a community around your company, product or brand is to start a group. A Facebook page is, in some ways, a more powerful alternative, but we'll explore them both.

Remember the principle of marketing with these kinds of tools – engagement. You're aiming to enable people who want to interact with your company or brand to do so, and Facebook supports this with messaging and photo- and video-sharing (but see also Chapter 10).

Any photos on Facebook can be tagged with the names of people in the photos; if they are members, they'll get a notification that they are tagged, and will be inclined to check out their picture. When they do so, they'll see other people tagged and can click on to their profiles, or hunt around for other photographs of themselves in your or other people's albums. Justin Smith of insidefacebook points out that you don't have to limit yourself to tagging people who are in the photo or video – there may be occasions when you want to alert those not in it: for example, to tell people what they've missed at an event or that there's something in the photo or video they might be interested in, like a new product being demonstrated.

Messages can be useful too. In theory you can send a message to anyone. Your own contacts will, as you'll see below, have an established link with you (through a group for example) and so you can effectively 'e-mail' them via Facebook. But you may also want to send messages to people you hardly know. If that's the case, it's best to do some research first and *not* to mass-mail people. Facebook can close you down if you're reported for spamming.

Groups

A group is just a place for your contacts to gather specifically for a shared interest. This is an easy and important way to get your brand or product known, because anyone who joins the group will have their membership of the group indicated on their home page. They can also invite other people to join the group. In this way, groups can grow rapidly – especially if people feel strongly about the subject.

Once members get on to your group, they can contribute to discussions, post photos or videos, and add links. This last feature can lead to spamming, where people join simply to insert a link to another group or a website. As administrator of the group, you can delete anything that's unwelcome and, with a large group, this could be a daily task.

The other size issue is that groups with over 1,200 members can no longer have free message sent in bulk. This is a fairly recent change (the limit used to be 1,000, then 500), and Facebook seems uncertain about how to deal with this. Various reports suggested the limit was to be lifted, but currently there is a crippling charge in place for large groups if you want to send bulk messages. You can, instead, make some or all of your members administrators, so that they can invite other friends – known as 'viral' marketing.

There is clearly the potential to link with other groups too, but the groups need to be relevant and related in some way. For example, a record store could easily link to a number of groups set up for particular types of music or specific bands (like David House does with Banquet Records – search for it), but too much posting of the same link can be seen as spamming, and Facebook itself can act to stop this. If in doubt, contact the owner of the other group with a proposal to cross-refer.

It's worth bearing in mind that you can set up as many groups as you like and that you can make groups invitation-only, so you control membership very strictly. In this way, some companies have managed to use Facebook as an internal communication system, or to communicate with only certain customers – it's particularly the case now that Facebook has an instant messaging function. The security of Facebook, however, isn't quite 100 per cent, as there have been recent cases of private photographs being publicly viewed (http://tinyurl. com/2rkxom), so you would need to exercise caution with confidential documents and information (see Chapter 12 for alternatives).

Pages

Pages have a slightly different feel to groups. Whilst groups are built out of standard basic functions to communicate and share, pages can include applications and other forms of content.

Pages are also free, but have no limit on the number of 'fans'. When people become fans, their allegiance is shown on their home page, but they can't easily invite their friends to become fans (unless they do so individually within other messages or groups).

To reiterate, then: groups allow members to recruit other members easily and so can grow quickly, but you are limited in how you communicate with the group. With pages, you can contact members

Figure 3 *This franchised coffee shop has prominent branding, photos, a link to its website – and over 500 fans*

directly over and over again, but they can't invite each other. All of which means that your group/pages need to be attractive and include information that the members will value and want to share and be happy to be reminded about from time to time. They also need to change frequently, and that means you adding content and messages frequently at first, at least until you have enough active users posting and interacting with each other.

Events

For some businesses – such as music promoters, restaurants, clubs, charities and others – being able to promote an event is useful. Put simply, an event on Facebook is just a special kind of group which enables you to invite your contacts and, if you make some or all administrators, for them to invite their friends. A restaurant or pub could promote special evenings and ensure that their best customers got the notification first or were given an earlier time for the buffet than those who responded to posters and leaflets.

Of course, an event can also be online, so this is a good way of promoting sales or special offers to members or, in fact, mass-mailing members. If people respond to the event, you can send messages to all attendees easily – to remind them or notify them of changes – and these don't get regarded as spam.

Getting people to visit

Having played around with your own pages and groups, including adding friends and uploading photos, you'll also come across 'applications'. Some of these you will have already used almost without thinking about them, such as photos, video etc.

The most significant is the 'newsfeed' function. In fact, this isn't really a tool you can manage, since all users generate content that appears in their friends' feeds. Every time someone adds an application, posts something or even changes their photograph or status (e.g. 'Phil Holden is desperately trying to finish this chapter before the deadline', which appears along with a time such as 'four hours ago'), it's reported to their friends. So any interaction a customer has with your pages can echo around all his or her contacts.

Most importantly, then, you have to give people things to interact with. New events, photos, videos and updated information keeps people interested – and therefore active. The more active they are, the more people notice your pages. And that brings us to the main purpose of applications.

Applications

Most Facebook applications are not, in fact, developed by Facebook themselves. Instead they are developed by individuals and companies who are either very keen on programming, or want to make money, or both. By and large, they are annoyingly infantile – along the lines of 'Who is the cutest guy' style quizzes – but a few are genuinely useful.

The 'apps', as they are sometimes called, aim to generate visits to pages and links between users and to 'monetize' the use of Facebook by visitors. Developers want you to stick with them and recruit your friends. Because the development of these apps is part of what keeps Facebook alive, the API (or application programming interface) is available to anyone.

If you want to create your own application, it's best to outsource this unless you have considerable coding experience. You can find developers on Facebook itself, and if you see an application that seems to do something you need, you can find out about the developer, usually by clicking on the developer's name or joining and posting an enquiry online. Actually creating your own app is beyond this book, but you might like to consider the possible benefits and how you might find the skills to accomplish this. Their great strength is the tendency of friends to interact with friends and for each to look more favourably on content that seems to be endorsed by the others – viral marketing again.

It follows, then, that if you have an app that is intrinsically useful to the audience you're aiming to attract then it will a) quickly spread amongst your fans or friends and b) may well leak outside that group to their friends. The ultimate aim is to draw more people into your orbit and closer to your brand.

In some ways the targeting is similar to social ads above and, indeed, some companies will use ads to promote apps and to generate traffic to both pages and websites. Like ads, the content of an app must be attractive and relevant. It also has to be distinctive, given the thousands of apps already available. For example, a florist could provide a virtual gift-giving application (there are several already) but add information on the meaning of flowers (lilies are supposed to represent death – so perhaps not the best Valentine's Day choice!) and the ability to order online. Goose Loose (our outdoor store) could offer an application for surfers to have real-time surf reports on their Facebook profile or page.

The real problem with apps, for our purposes, is that their management is technically challenging: it's not something you can easily pick up without having some programming skills. Fortunately there are plenty of programmers or digital agencies of various sorts for hire.

One such is Wiliam, an Australian company (www.wiliam.com.au) which built the application for Fox's *Gossip Girls* TV show. One UK comparison is Logicode (http://logicode.co.uk) who developed the app for Gumtree (www.gumtree.com) that links Facebook users straight into the functionality of this popular classified ad site. You can also find more developers at www.approvedfacebookappdevelopers.co.uk which enables you to get several quotes for the work; and, of course, a short time on Google will reveal many more – perhaps the best way.

The Facebook developers' site (http://developers.facebook.com) probably gives more information than you need to know, but could be a useful reference for when you're briefing an agency. Also check out http://wiki.developers.facebook.com.

The range of applications available on Facebook means that you should exercise caution about data security. Indeed, there has been a lot of media coverage of privacy issues with social networking sites in general and Facebook in particular. Some applications allow you to skip giving too much information, many don't, and there is some resistance in the Facebook community to the perceived invasion of privacy.

Facebook's own advertising product 'Beacon' came under fire and was eventually radically altered because it tracked users' online behaviour and made this available to the users' friends as a way of promoting commercial products and services.[4] More intelligent solutions to this have, ironically, been found by Amazon, who recently launched its own apps. One of these enabled users to publish their Amazon wishlist to their Facebook page. The other enabled your friends to be notified via your newsfeed about any books you'd reviewed, but not on what you'd bought. Crucially, all these were specific applications that users opted into, rather than the original Beacon system which offered an opt-out.

Unfortunately, while the Amazon app was welcomed by some as a more mature use of Facebook than the hundred of quizzes and competitions generally seen, it only works with Amazon.com, the US site. You'd be better advised looking for an app called Junglebook, which does much the same thing but works on other sites such as the '.co.uk' version too.

If you do develop an app, remember the responsibilities you have under the Data Protection Act. There is no way around registering – the act applies to any business of any size – and if you mismanage information, the fines can be significant. For more information, see the Information Commissioner's Office at www.ico.gov.uk.

As you can see in Figure 4, there are all kinds of features and applications to get to know, but before you get too involved in applications you should look around to see who is using what. Later you may think it's worthwhile developing your own applications – think of them as promotional gifts for your visitors.

---

[4] See how Facebook 'ruined Christmas' in the *Washington Post*, November 30 2007 http://tinyurl.com/2vnmmh

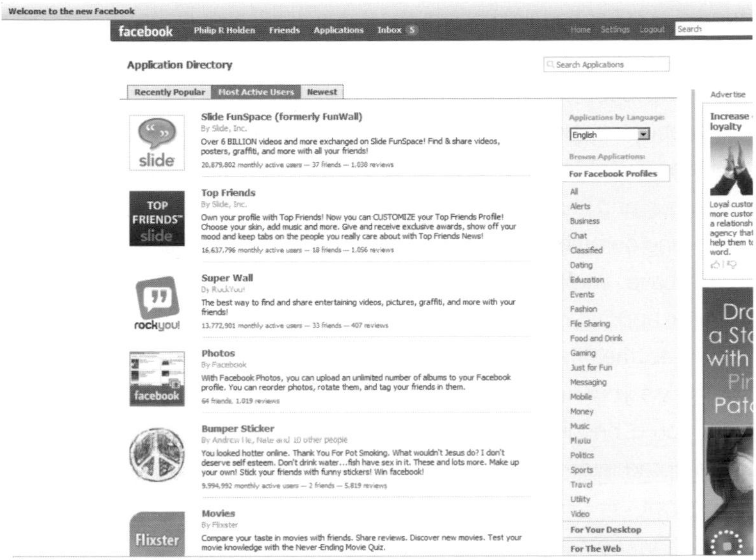

Figure 4 *There are literally thousands of applications available on Facebook*

Promoting yourself – advertising within Facebook

Creating a 'social ad' within Facebook is a simple matter of following the instructions. From any page, you need to scroll to the bottom and click on the word 'Advertisers'.

Figure 5 *Access information for advertising and business applications at the foot of each Facebook page*

Here, you'll find a simple starting page which gives you the option of creating ads or a page for your business. This is what most people expect marketing on Facebook to be about, but remember the approach we outlined in Chapter 2? Marketing is everything you do that affects customers and the following is, strictly speaking, promotion: there is a difference. But it can also be an important part of forming relationships that Facebook subsequently helps you maintain.

Before we get too involved in creating an ad, perhaps the best thing is to create a home page that describes your business and gives you a virtual base. You will have seen this as an option when you first signed up. If you signed up as an individual as suggested, you can now create a company, brand or product page.

Think of this as a kind of meeting place where fans of your brand can come and make contact or learn more about your brand. For brands such as the Red campaign for AIDS relief, there's an obvious advantage in having a presence in the site with plenty of its target audience to hand. But it's also useful both personally and for your company or brand to position yourself – showcasing your expertise.

Figure 6 *The starting page for the promotional tools on Facebook*

Advertising

The first question you need to ask is: 'Is it worth advertising at all?' The answer to this question, of course, rather depends on who you'd like to communicate with and what you'd like them to do.

Remember, on Facebook and similar social networking sites, users may be searching for you or your expertise, so it's certainly worth monitoring activity before you invest a great deal in advertising. Also bear in mind that there is not much direct selling in Facebook, although there is a thing called 'Marketplace' where you can post an ad (in one network) free. Although it's unlikely to gain you many customers, it might be worth experimenting with, as any response gives you access to the enquirer's profile – so you can find out more about them and begin to develop a relationship with them, perhaps inviting them to another page.

Figure 7 *The Red campaign has a strong presence – and it's well-targeted, attracting nearly 50,000 fans*

Having said that, all the time you spend linking and communicating on sites – especially when you cross-refer between sites and services (including your own blog and using the techniques in Chapters 5 and 7) is powerful promotion in its own right. As we've pointed out in Chapters 1 and 2, you're not announcing to the world from a distance, you're getting involved.

Advertising through social ads is a straightforward step-by-step process: just fill in the forms as you go along. You could be advertising something inside or outside Facebook, and it's easy to point to either. Incidentally, as in the last chapter, it's always a good idea to have a unique landing page for any respondents to a promotion – then you can monitor the success of your campaign. Generally speaking, ads pointing to outside Web pages are less successful than those that point to pages within Facebook, although the experience of Boso.com below was an exception.

Figure 8 *You specify what you want to promote*

The next decision is about targeting. While Facebook collates a lot of information about its users, it's not so precise as to be able to target them on the basis of their specific buying habits. You can, however, select people on the basis of the attributes they list – gender, age, education and so on. You can also choose from a long list of keywords that relate to the members' interests.

Figure 9 *You can specify who you want your social ad to reach*

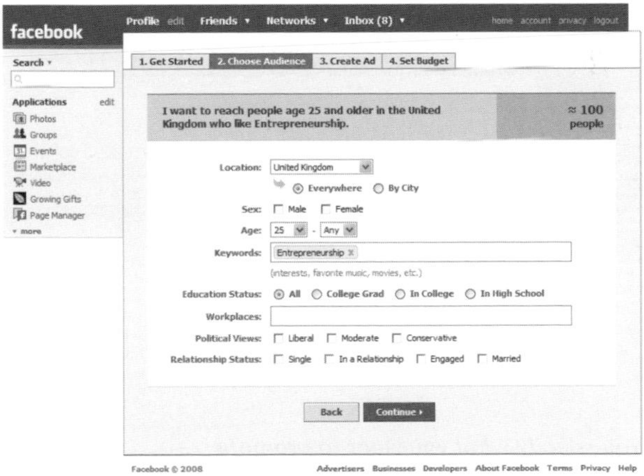

Figure 10 *Some selections will give you a very small audience*

As you make your selections, Facebook usefully tells you how many members fall into the segment you are describing, and you can adjust your targeting accordingly.

At this stage you finally get to write your ad. It's more of a classified or semi-display ad in a newspaper than an all-singing, all-dancing campaign. Nevertheless it's important to spend some time considering what it should say.

Keep in mind all the things you've decided about your brand and its values, but also add in what you believe about the audience you are targeting and the environment in which the ad will appear. Writing these kinds of small ads isn't easy, since they have to have enough impact to provoke a click and lead a user to take a detour from what they were doing. It follows that there must be a reasonable reward, and one that is relevant to the interests you are promoting.

Figure 11 *Now write the ad*

Generic appeals to greed, fear or sex appear all over the Web and are hardly ever original. Goose Loose (our 'everything outdoor' company) might decide to offer an opportunity to win a learn-to-surf holiday which might attract attention from novice surfers. A subtle change to the offer – win a surfing holiday and keep the Al Merrick surfboard you use – would attract experienced surfers who recognised one of the worlds best board shapers.

The International Fund for Animal Welfare recently ran a great ad that gave a fun and relevant incentive for people to find out more about the charity, with numerous inexpensive 'gifts' on offer.

Boso.com is an eBay rival targeting students in the UK, founded by brothers Kulveer and Harjeet Taggar. Despite Boso itself having obvious social networking attributes, the brothers quickly saw the value in using Facebook ads to draw in new users. They ran a series of ads quickly assembled while a topic dear to the heart of their target audience was still hot. After Zinedine Zidane's outburst in the 2006 World Cup finals, they ran the ad shown in Figure 13. Crucially, Facebook allows them to target particular networks with specific ads. In their case they could address students of a particular university, but it would be just as easy to target people below the age of 25 with an interest in a particular

Win a Nintendo Wii

Draw a new animal over the London Underground map to win. Also get free wallpapers, screensavers, and other cool stuff!

More Ads | Advertise

Figure 12 *IFAW social ad – fun and involving*

Oxford Flyer

Bonjour mon ami. I get angry very easily. Like the other day, some Italian guy told me that I couldn't buy or sell anything that I wanted on Boso cos i'm not a student. So i nutted him.

Figure 13 *A social ad for Boso.com – topical and humorous*

sport. According to Kulveer: 'We have a Facebook group to give us some added visibility. We try to tap in to what's hot at the moment, and consequently get loads of clickthroughs, and manage to generate a bit of buzz.'

You only have 25 characters in the ad title; you can add a photo and also decide if you want to add 'social action'. This means that responses to the ads are reported in the feeds mentioned above. Your final decision is to decide how much you'd like to spend. Like pretty much all online advertising, you can specify a budget and a cost-per-click and, since you can also time-limit your campaign, you can keep a cap on your spending. Not only can you fix the costs of your campaign on a daily basis, you can also specify how long it should run. In this way your campaign will always be within your budget, and subsequently you will be able to work out the cost per response, or even the cost per order of your promotional activity.

The two pricing models available have different strengths and weaknesses. By and large, the pay-per-click (PPC) rate is lower for any given audience than the pay-per-view (PPV) rate. Given an ad that pulls a similar level of response, the former should work out cheaper. But it's not as simple as that, since you have more control over where your PPV ad goes, and so targeting a more specific audience may lead to less wastage: that is, you don't have to pay for the views of people who are unlikely to be interested. If you can't make a targeting selection that's obviously appropriate for your ad, you may be better opting for PPC. You'll get a chance to review your ad towards the end of the process, and you can always go back and adjust things as you do so.

Perhaps the most important aspect of this advertising to acknowledge is that you will never get it right first time or every time. It's far better to think of every ad you run as a test, and to keep a record of every variable – the targeting, the ad content, the pricing and, of course, the level of response. That way you can compare responses and costs for each mini-campaign, and make better decisions in the future.

Promoting your Facebook presence outside Facebook

If this title confuses you, don't worry, it *is* confusing. So far we've been talking about promotion *within* Facebook and noted that attracting users to pages within that site is easier than dragging them out of Facebook to another site. But what about dragging them in?

At one level, it's quite easy to promote the fact that you have pages and events on Facebook: you simply tell people. Facebook provides buttons and acceptable forms of words that you can put on your blog or website, or even on printed stationery and promotional material (see http://tinyurl.com/4l4xs7) This will encourage existing Facebook users to check out your profile.

Figure 14 *The standard badge you can link to your Facebook page*

Don't forget also, as we discussed in Chapters 3 and 7, that there are tools to make cross-referring between sites and pages easy.

I mentioned Beacon briefly above and it is still around, with the modification that now users must opt into the system of tracking all their online behaviour. Unlike promotion within Facebook, Beacon is essentially code that resides on your website to pick up on your visitors' activities. If they have a Facebook account, your visitors' actions are logged, and they are given the opportunity to find out more, or to block or accept the feed being posted to Facebook. There are complications, for example, where several people use the same computer and a cookie denoting one user is used to log the actions of another – the example of a ruined Christmas mentioned earlier – so users also gets a chance to point out that they're not the person identified by the cookie.

You can read about Beacon and how it works on the Facebook help pages: just search for 'Beacon' (or click on http://tinyurl.com/598fkn).

For the moment, however, Beacon is only being made available selectively and to websites with high levels of traffic.

Making the most of Facebook

Kfir Pravda (http://pravdam.com/) a very experienced cybernaut and blogger based in Israel, recently set out his top tips and tricks for successfully using Facebook, some of which are worth repeating here.

The first is 'Be careful with whom you connect – so you can keep the network personal'. Kfir makes a point of checking every request to connect – by e-mail if possible – so that he's sure he really knows the person and his network isn't being hijacked for another's benefit. Of course, if you have a company or brand page, anyone can become a fan. It's still worth monitoring their activities, though.

Facebook groups should, says Kfir, be based around need and identified gaps. So look around to see if anyone has set up a similar group and how active it is. You may feel you can do better, or it may simply be that there is no interest. Going through the interest keywords in the social ads process – you can stop short of actually building an ad – can reveal valuable information about the size of an audience.

The general advice from Kfir, with which I agree, has already been mentioned several times. Be sociable. It's not good to hector people in groups, nor should you be constantly inviting people to sign up to apps or websites. On the other hand, you cannot be part of the community without joining in discussions and encouraging others. Often this requires no more than a posting that says 'good point' to another contributor, whether or not you agree with their views.

Kfir's final tip is, he says, the most important tip of all. As we keep repeating: join everything up. Link your blog to your Facebook pages, create events and discuss them elsewhere. Use the sharing tools in Chapter 7 to get the viral or snowball effect. Kfir reckons you should be a member of up to 30 groups. I'd say see how it goes: keep trying new groups to see if they add value and traffic, and drop the least useful.

Keep your own pages and profile active and busy – interested (in your friends and fans) and interesting for them.

Incidentally, to really study Facebook and to keep up to date with its development you should keep visiting the Facebook blog and news pages. Every so often Facebook will post on to your home page/profile a link to their own group covering updates to their service. For a more objective view and great advice, buying Justin Smith's *Facebook Marketing Bible* would be £10 well spent – see www.insidefacebook.com.

Social networking will evolve

A number of commentators rightly point out the rate at which new sites like Facebook are springing up, as well as the frequent changes and add-ons introduced. It seems clear that there will be significant developments over the next couple of years, which may include a standardised way of dealing with users' data.

Having mentioned Google previously, it is (of course) at the forefront of the development of this 'Open Social', a platform for developers of sites and applications rather like the one Facebook offers already. The idea here is that competing social networks can agree on a standard so that applications can work in different contexts. For example, an application to tag a video in Friendster could also work in Hi5 and, moreover, a user of both sites could make the same video with comments available in both.

At the moment, a number of sites including Ning, Orkut, LinkedIn, Hi5 and Friendster, and application providers such as Flixster, Rockyou and Slide, are involved in the Open Social project, and the people at Facebook recently expressed their support. According to Marc Andreeson (http://blog.pmarca.com), business users of the social Web will have to develop just four versions of their e-product – for standard Web pages, an Open Social version, one for Facebook and, possibly, a mobile version.

In the next chapter we'll look at some of the alternative social networking environments and how you could build your own.

CHAPTER 9

MYSPACE, BEBO, NING AND THE REST

Despite the title of this chapter sounding like a children's television show, there is some serious activity going on. Social networking is (are) the *mots de jour* online, and it sometimes seems that everyone is either leaping into a social networking site or announcing their imminent demise. There is even a site for pets and their owners (www.petstreet. co.uk), which may indeed be very useful for your business.

In the last chapter we looked at one of the most developed sites. Facebook is arguably the leader because it is so open to commercial use and has the volume of members to make it attractive. Here we'll look at some of the alternatives.

MySpace

MySpace, with over 200 million users at the time of writing (www. myspace.com or http://uk.myspace.com), was launched in 2003 by eUniverse employees mimicking the features of Friendster (itself still going with over 70 million users; www.friendster.com). In 2005, MySpace became part of News Corporation, prompting some concerns over its independence, and in 2006 Google struck a deal to take over the search and advertising functions.

However, MySpace certainly has a particular niche and atmosphere, as can be seen by visiting any of its user pages. Unlike some other sites, MySpace has always generated its revenue from advertising; profiles are free. According to data published by the *New York Times* (http://tinyurl. com/6hxa7c), MySpace is second only to Yahoo in the amount of data it collects on users and therefore how precisely it may position advertising.

Broadly speaking, MySpace invites profiles for musicians and ordinary users (often music fans) but also has options for comedians and film-makers. This sets the tone for much of the content as users link to friends or to those whose music, film or performances they like, and so spread the word.

Music tracks can be uploaded, and a number of high-profile bands and record labels see this as a way of promoting themselves virally at low cost. Groups can be created and membership controlled, and bulletin boards allow for announcements to be made to friends – for example to promote a gig or just plan a party. More recently, instant messaging, video (replacing the ability to embed Youtube videos, see Chapter 10) and even karaoke have been introduced. MySpace is also accessible via some mobile phones.

MySpace has been used for promoting all kinds of businesses, charities and, of course musicians, as well as for recruitment. Oxfam's first music shop, based in Edinburgh, has a profile (www.myspace.com/oxfammusic) which enables them to promote issues and fundraising events to a receptive audience.

Signing up to MySpace is easy – simply a matter of clicking on the link at the top right of most pages and filling out your details. Perhaps the most off-putting part of the process is seeing your page immediately after

Figure 1 *The main page for editing your account and pages – see the links to the top right*

you join, which is already full of advertising and content automatically input by MySpace itself.

You can instantly change the look of your page (there are standard templates available at the top of your screen) and, over time, modify every aspect of your profile. The 'stylesheet' HTML which underlies your page is editable by clicking on 'Edit profile link', which calls up a page (shown in Figure 1) from which you can amend most features of your account.

One thing you can't keep changing is your URL (the name that follows www.myspace.com/ and you can use as a link elsewhere), so choose it carefully. The easiest way to modify the look and feel of your pages is find another user whose page you like and ask how they achieved it. Most users are happy to share their expertise.

Online, you will find many people offering free layouts which can then be subsequently adapted to your needs. See www.myspacesupport. com, http://myspace.tweakyourpage.com and www.myspacelayoutspy. com amongst others.

Advertising is controlled through MySpace and you simply have to fill in a request form online and wait for them to contact you. At least one specialist advertising agency www.mysocialmarketing.com has

Figure 2 *Like Facebook, MySpace has a wide range of applications you can use or adapt*

grown up on the back of the growing desire of companies to access MySpace – and the complexity of doing so.

Darren Rowse at www.problogger.net and the Toronto-based B5media blog at www.buzzworker.com have plenty of advice on cheaper, viral methods of promoting yourself by linking MySpace into other sites, including your own blog.

Bebo

Compared to some social networking sites, Bebo (www.bebo.com) is a comparative newcomer, having been created in 2005. It has, however, grown considerably, and is of interest because it has sites and users based in several European countries as well as New Zealand and Australia. In the UK, Bebo may well have overtaken MySpace in terms of popularity with about 12 million users.

You sign up in the usual way (the link in the top right of the screen) and fill in as much of the profile details as you wish. You can add in Skype (see Chapter 11) and Instant Messenger details, which could be useful for encouraging contacts.

Figure 3 *Bebo's front page*

Bebo has several levels of privacy. If you don't join a group online, then only direct friends can see any of your information. Profiles can be made fully public if you prefer, but even then some information is only available to friends.

Since Bebo users specify which kinds of messages they want to receive and what categories of advertising they prefer, it's a fair assumption that these are well-received. The look and feel of pages is determined by a 'skin', and some companies have provided sponsored skins by which customers show their support for the brand – typically movies and computer games but also Doc Martens and Trident gum. You can make your own of course – if you have the required skills and software (see www.bebo.com/Skins.jsp).

Like MySpace, there is an emphasis in Bebo on youth culture and music, and there is an obvious commercial presence. Bebo

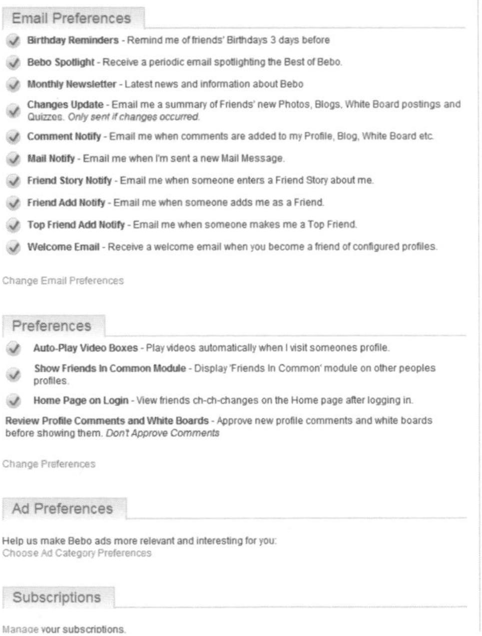

Figure 4 *You specify how Bebo keeps you informed and how the site appears*

interestingly also has a set-up for promoting your book (such as *Marketing & PR* by Philip R Holden and Nick Wilde . . . at www.bebo.com/smemarketing).

There is also a familiar range of applications developed for Bebo, some of which may help you promote your business, product or expertise both within the network or further afield.

As well as applications for listing Amazon products, others such as AdChap (www.adchap.com) allow you to create and maintain ad campaigns both here, on Facebook and in other applications such as Hi5 (http://hi5.com). With AdChap you can build multiple ads (with text and a small graphic) which are then distributed to those who have signed up to 'publish' ads from the same network. You can also publish ads, in which case you claim 75 per cent of the revenue. There's little information about targeting however, but the AdChap website gives some comparison of user profiles and, as with other advertising (in Chapter 7), you pay only per click – users have to respond before you pay.

Social music

Real Vibez Media (www.realvibezmedia.com) launched its own Web channel for Caribbean music and culture www.realvibez.com – like an MTV for reggae, dance hall, soca and calypso – in 2007.

Taking advantage of the fragmented nature of a (relatively) minority-interest music, RealVibez has secured the marketing, merchandising and distribution for musicians that otherwise would not have had access to these valuable sources of income.

According to David Mullings, the owner, when they needed to get promotion going, social networks and video-sharing sites were a natural choice, especially since some of their content was already on YouTube. They have been able to position themselves as central to their well-defined market, running advertising for companies like Def Jam, sponsoring the largest reggae festival in Jamaica, Reggae Sumfest, interviewing people like Brandy and Timbaland for their site, and touring with Sean Paul (his last album went platinum three times).

Traffic at RealVibez has gone from 0 to 35,000 unique visitors per month since the launch, mainly because of Web marketing. They have manually searched for good links and benefited from positive 'word of mouse'. Partnerships have been struck with two major social networking sites, Bebo and Imeem (www.imeem.com) another music based site.

RealVibez has begun to exploit its position by developing further links with Vuze (www.vuze.com), MTV's Flux (www.mtv.co.uk/channel/flux) and others – see Chapter 10 – where they are the only media partner focusing on Caribbean entertainment. Not bad for a company of just two people and a few freelancers – and a very small budget for self-promotion.

Specialised social networks

So-called 'vertical' social sites are springing up every week – in a sense RealVibez is one.

Cork'd (http://corkd.com), for example, is a site for wine aficionados that is free and enables users to keep track of wines they and others are drinking. As a drinks brand, it would be good to keep in touch with these people, and you could establish a personal presence online here anyway to give wine buffs a direct line to you. Several wine merchants and importers are already there with their profiles linked to websites and blogs.

Both Mothercare (www.gurgle.com) and SAGA (www2.saga.co.uk/sagazone) have launched fairly recently. It really does seem to be 'cradle to grave'! There is, inevitably, also a social network for marketers – www.marcomprofessional.com.

Kaboodle (www.kaboodle.com) allows users to build up shopping lists of fashion, gifts, homeware and a range of items from all over the Web and share them with friends, while Stylehive (www.stylehive.com) is similar but focuses more exclusively on fashion. Both represent an attempt to carve out a marketspace for a particular kind of retailing – where potential customers seek out information on labels and brands.

Nataliya Yakushev, an experienced online marketer (http://webmill.blogspot.com), promoted her client's children's clothing boutique by creating a profile on a number of different social shopping sites, including Kaboodle and Stylehive

Their sales went up almost 30 per cent the following month. Nataliya also submitted special promotional codes to sites such as AgentB or RetailMeNot (see Chapter 7) to drive traffic on to sites.

Ning

Ning (www.ning.com) is a platform for building your own social network. It's free as long as you allow Ning to sell (and therefore take the revenue from) advertising on your network. For about $20 a month, you can take control of the ads yourself. Other extras include paying to remove the 'Create your own social network' option on your pages, more storage space, or having your own Web address pointing to your Ning site. All these options are charged monthly, so it would be advisable to get your free network up and successful before upgrading.

A completely free alternative is Informe (www.informe.com) which started as a provider of forums and has developed into offering compete portals with blogs, wikis (see Chapter 12) and galleries – although arguably it's less 'social' in its approach. The interface at Informe isn't quite as slick as some, but it includes most of the features of other websites and claims to give unlimited storage and numbers of members – and your site doesn't have to be cluttered up with advertising.

Back to Ning. It is definitely positioned as a social networking platform and therefore offers you many of the functions of Facebook on your own customised and branded site. It's debateable whether customers who are familiar with Facebook, Bebo, MySpace and similar would want to sign up to yet another such site, especially in the early days with few users. Ning does potentially offer a large pool of visitors, since those joining get a ID which enables them to sign up to other Ning networks. However, your own network seems likely to work best where you already have a community, perhaps members of a club or many committed users of a more limited forum such as a Yahoo or Google group.

Crucially, Ning has already built applications that enable you to promote your content and Ning network on Facebook so you may be able to bring visitors from one to another.

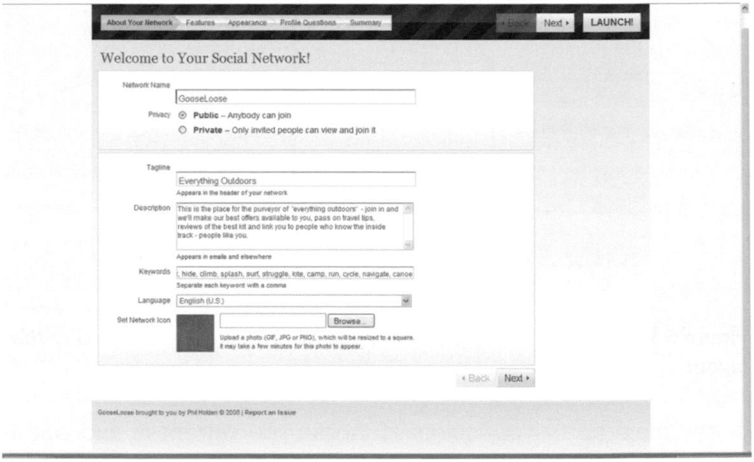

Figure 5 *Setting up your own social network is simple with Ning*

To set up your Ning site, you'll need to sign up – the usual process. Then you decide the name of your network (it can simply be your brand name) and on a description. Keywords are again important to enable your network to be found – if it's public, that is. You have the option for your network to be private and 'invitation only', so it's possible to use this platform for internal communications or for a select group of clients (see Chapter 12 for alternatives).

At this stage, you can also upload a small icon to represent your network. This gets used in listings and by messages, but it's small and tricky to get right: it has to convey your branding and be readable. You can always come back to this later, as you can with most of these decisions.

Once you have described your site, you can choose from a menu of standard features, dragging and dropping them on a layout page to the right. Text boxes usefully allow you to explain areas of your site

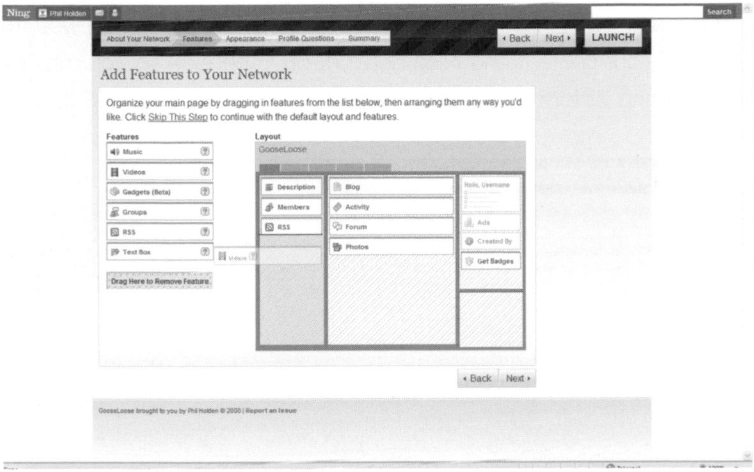

Figure 6 *You can customise your own site by dragging features on to the layout*

or say more about your company. Again, you can move and edit all these later.

Remember, just because you're online doesn't mean you can forget about data protection. It's questionable whether you a Ning

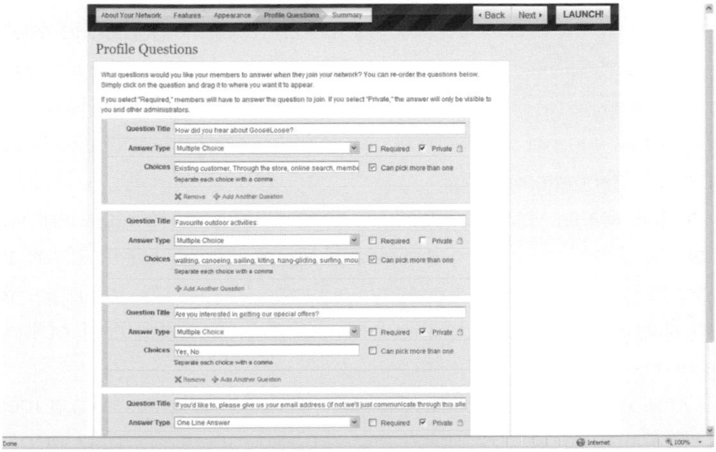

Figure 7 *It's easy to ask what members want – and to allow them to opt out*

are the data controller, but you should adopt a better-safe-than-sorry attitude.

Each question you ask should be considered carefully. You have the option to make any information provided by a member private; if in doubt, do so. Having answers to some questions permanently attached to a public profile could put some people off. Goose Loose would certainly ask a series of questions to determine the interests of members. It would be useful to know who was interested in, say, mountain boarding or kiting.

Once you've finished editing the questions, you're ready to launch your own social network.

You'll be asked to create a PIN for yourself as administrator, and will then be taken to your front page. You can, at any stage, click on the 'Manage' link at the top right of your front page and adjust the settings of almost any part of your Ning network.

Once you can see the layout of your network, you will want to start inviting people, but you would probably want to put useful information

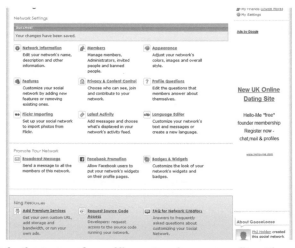

Figure 8 *As the owner of your Ning network you can edit settings at any time*

up on the site first – there should be an instant reward for people signing up and participating, which could be as simple as a 10%-off voucher. It helps if you have a number of people involved in your organisation who can 'populate' (and test) the site before it's made public.

Consider getting a few close clients to try it out and, maybe, attach some kind of reward for their help (see Chapter 7 on promotion and Chapter 12 for some sources of products you could give). It all depends on your business and your target audience. A site devoted to supporting people taking a training course, for example, might have a lot of informational content, whilst a fashion retailer's site would have more photos and perhaps links to fashion designers' pages.

You can also see (back in Figure 6) that Flickr photos can be imported and links created in Facebook. Ning allows you to create a widget just for promoting your own site on something like Facebook. This is certainly an option Goose Loose would try.

A Ning site can become the hub of all your online activity since, apart from the obvious ability to send messages and share photos and video, you can also blog within the site and promote its content to others.

Figure 9 *The finished Ning site – set up in less than 20 minutes!*

It's not entirely obvious at first, but what you have created is not simply a page but, of course, a network. Perhaps the most powerful part of the Ning platform is that all the functions you have as a member of Ning are also available to anyone else who joins. That means that people who join though your network can upload photographs and build a blog. It also means they can promote your network by, for example, giving them widgets to embed elsewhere or (if your network is public) offering feeds of blog postings.

Your customers would therefore see pretty much the same front page as you do (as in Figure 9) and interact with every part of the site. The only thing they can't do is specify those parameters you did when you set your network up (Figure 5).

Some commentators have suggested that the general-purpose social networking sites like Facebook and MySpace have a limited life and are of limited value for business. They suggest that sites such as Ning have an advantage in being able to utilise social network strengths for a precisely targeted audience.

For what it's worth, I don't think the picture is as clear as that. All these sites may be in competition (and this will drive them to change their functionality almost daily), but they will also seek ways to work together. A Ning network and a Facebook group can work together.

The main measure of strength in social network sites, however, is the size of their audience. In that sense, they are similar to other media (newspapers, magazines, TV and radio) in that they represent routes to market. However, they also represent markets in themselves, as they have active, participating members who make their interests and allegiances known when they join and as they interact.

LinkedIn

If Facebook, MySpace and others seem targeted at young people (and they aren't really) then LinkedIn (www.linkedin.com) is definitely for the grown-ups. It doesn't have, at the moment, a great visual appeal —

being mostly concerned with lists of contacts which are searchable in different ways — but there's little doubting its serious intent.

LinkedIn allows you to build your network by making contact with those from the same educational institutions or places of work in your history.

It is essential to build up your network initially by linking to people you already know or inviting them to join. These people will have their own contacts, to whom they may be prepared to introduce you.

Once you've signed in, you can begin to explore your existing contacts – you can import them from your e-mail program as with other sites. Here you don't have to be so selective as with other sites, as initially LinkedIn looks to see if your contacts are already registered. You can subsequently choose who you want to invite to link with you.

Figure 10 *The start page at LinkedIn*

The degree of connectedness with other people is shown in the listing – so you can see when others are just two steps away, i.e. they are contacts of your contacts.

Soon after joining, you may start to get contact requests from apparent strangers. Some intensive users of LinkedIn have literally thousands of contacts and seem to obsess about collecting more. Some of these can help in connecting you onwards to valuable contacts, so don't dismiss them completely.

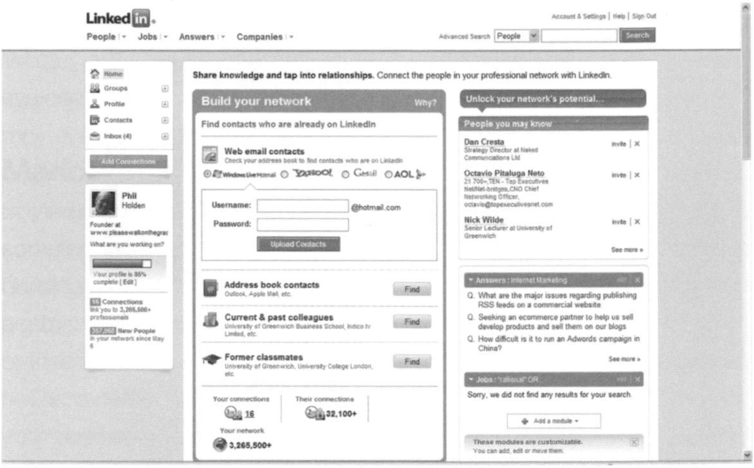

Figure 11 *LinkedIn can search your e-mail contacts for existing users*

It's certainly in business-to-business marketing that LinkedIn earns its keep. If you need to find people within a particular company (especially in the US), it's likely you'll be able to among the 23 million users. If you can't, then you can probably find someone who does.

You can search for companies as well as individuals, and for those offering particular services (see also some of the sites mentioned in Chapter 11). Usefully, you can also search for jobs, post details of a position you need filled and ask or answer a question from, or for, other members. This last facility is particularly useful since it allows you to gain knowledgeable contacts and to demonstrate your expertise to others.

Questions can range from the facile to the vital, and they are searchable by keyword and category. Most deal with professional subjects – accountancy, business planning and so on – but you will also find people testing brand names, asking for help using LinkedIn, and even asking for a recommendation on a facilities management company: that's a sales lead for someone. In any case, giving away advice which can make or save money for potential clients can turn them into real clients.

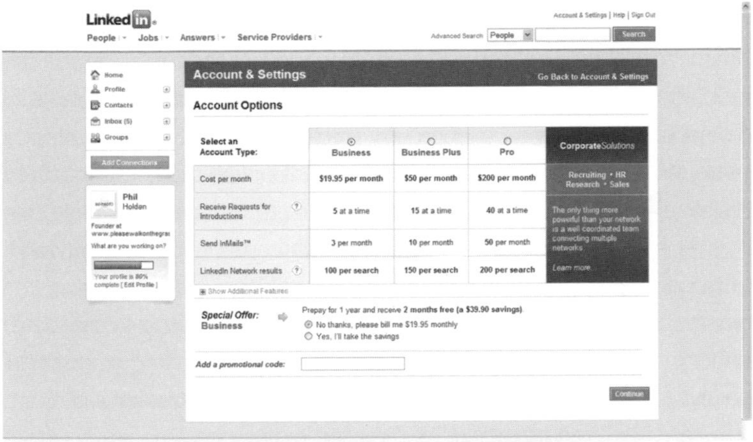

Figure 12 *Upgrading seems expensive, but there is a huge potential network*

Alternative professional networks

Numerous other sites exist which seem to offer similar networking opportunities to LinkedIn, or which might enhance your image online.

For example, Naymz (www.naymz.com) is a site which seems to offer to clarify (or even improve) information relating to you that others may find in the course of online searching. It enables you to build a 'reputation network' and collates ratings of your reputation based on at least 10 references – from people you invite – giving you a 'RepScore' out of 10.

But the rating system is complex: why, for example, should you gain points for having a nickname? And, while the free service offers to make sure your Naymz profile is found on Google (if your RepScore is nine or more), the paid service at $9 a month seems quite expensive for something with unproven benefits.

The idea is that your authorised profile from Naymz should come up in searches ahead of perhaps less-flattering information from other sites. A similar service is offered by Zoominfo (www.zoominfo.com), gathering information from the public domain and offering you the opportunity to claim your profile and correct it. It also offers itself as a research source (for potential clients, for example), although it is difficult to see what it offers over and above, say, Google or any other search engine when used intelligently. Some of the company information is brief, to say the least.

VisiblePath (www.visiblepath.com) may be a serious alternative to LinkedIn. It seems to have the most potential for a small to medium-sized company or a group of collaborators who might want to exploit their collective connections. It uses social networking theory to infer networks from interaction: that is, the more you communicate with someone, the closer they are deemed to be to you. VisiblePath allows you to search for contacts within, say, a particular company and interestingly, as its name suggests, actually shows you the 'route' to interesting people through your existing contacts. Crucially, the program keeps all intermediate contacts confidential so that, although you might request an introduction to Company A, you wouldn't actually see the details of the person connecting you unless he or she consented.

Perhaps even more interestingly, VisiblePath is available for partners to build social networks for particular markets. So, for example, if you were building a website for civil engineers, you could give your website subscribers all the functionality of a social networking site. It appears to be a more business-focused solution than Ning.

Take your pick

Your choice of social network will always involve a balance between numbers (the potential size of the market) and targeting (the efficiency with which you can communicate with the right type of customers). You can compare the popularity of sites at Compete (www.compete.com).

But this kind of comparison only takes you so far. If you can establish and build your own network with your kind of customers, or if you can find a ready-made network where your customers are concentrated, that must be worth testing before you try loosely-targeted promotion.

Your watchword for all your activities online should be 'efficiency': how many customers can you recruit for how little money? How little can it cost to keep in close touch with your existing customers?

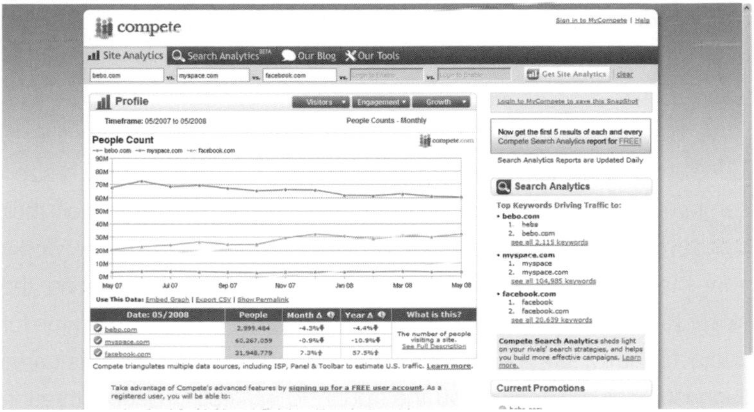

Figure 13 *Compete compares the popularity and usage of websites*

Given that you can explore many of the marketspaces described here free, the economics of social networking begin to look very attractive indeed.

CHAPTER 10

USING VIDEO, PHOTOS AND OTHER MEDIA

The use of images, photography and, increasingly, video has become standard for websites. Inevitably, if you've been setting up a blog or Web pages, or taking part in any of the social networking sites mentioned in earlier chapters, you would have been attempting to include pictures. Sometimes this is done within the application or site you're working on but, as with Blogger and Facebook, there are opportunities to have slideshows of your photographs or to embed other people's photographs within your pages.

Photographic images are pretty important online. Some research recently suggested that search results with pictures were attracting more attention and clickthrough than apparently more relevant results higher up the list.

Taking your own pictures

The first thing to note about using photography – whether of products or people – is that you can do it yourself and so, in effect, it can be free. But you'll have to work on your technique.

There are sources of photos from professionals that mean you may not have to take your own. All of the photography websites below include professionals as well as amateurs who could be approached for their photos or services, and Stock.xchng (www.sxc.hu) is a useful source of free imagery (as long as you respect the relevant copyright agreements).

Of course if you happen to be a professional photographer, what follows is simplistic in the extreme, so you might just want to skip over to some of the online resources below. For most of us, however, photography is an area where we can do a little preparation to make a big difference in our online image.

A basic set-up for product photography – such as items you're selling via your eBay store or Web pages – needn't be complex or expensive. Outdoor photography is simplest – estate agents do it all the time – but even so a short training course wouldn't be wasted[1]. For studio-based photography a reasonable digital camera, a tripod and a place like a table-top close to a window for plenty of natural light (north-facing to avoid harsh sunlight) is the least you need.

It's a good idea to have a neutral background which can simply be a large plain white or pale sheet hanging behind the subject and draped over the table itself. For small items, this could even be a large sheet of paper from the local art store. When you frame your shot, you should be able to exclude everything but the product and the plain background.

You can also take portraits in this situation, in which case you'll need a larger background. You can experiment with light or white sheets or darker cloth, rolls of which can be bought cheaply from market stalls. For portraits, it's often useful to have your subject close to a window and the background quite a way behind them so that it's not so in focus. Then try moving your subject at various angles to the light to get differing amounts of shadow across his or her face. This will affect the modelling of their features and change the mood of the shot. The camera is best at eye-level to the subject and a metre or so away from them.

You can adjust light by using a white or silver reflector on the opposite side of the main light source. This can be plain paper or card or even kitchen foil, and could simply be held there by an assistant. Shifting this around will affect how much light is filling in shadow areas.

It's always worth using a tripod to avoid motion-blurring, and if you have to take photos in lower light conditions it is essential (the camera takes longer to capture a photo when it's darker), and you could also

---

[1] For adult education courses in the UK, see http://tinyurl.com/6noxk3

probably look at one or more professional lights. Avoid using a flash, especially if it's attached to the camera, as it gives an unnaturally hard shadow and bleaches out colour and detail.

It is possible, with some experimentation and the right camera, to set up a domestic lamp or a worklight from an industrial suppliers or DIY store with something to diffuse the light; I've heard of photographers using a frame made out of plastic pipe and stretching parachute fabric over it. Be careful, because such lights can get very hot and your diffuser must be far enough away to avoid catching alight!

With a digital camera, you should take as many shots as you can to ensure you've got a usable picture. Even so, with additional lighting (in fact, with many shots under all kinds of conditions) you will often need to adjust the colour balance in the camera or on your PC.

Improving the picture

You will almost certainly also need some kind of photo retouching software to make your photos acceptable. If you're taking photos on location, then retouching will enable you to cut out unwanted background items or correct the colour. You can even make the sky above a holiday destination seem bluer, but be careful: unless you have consistency amongst your photographs, heavy retouching stands out as artificial. It's far easier (and more honest) to take advantage of good weather!

You can download and try, or even use free, a range of photo-related software by going to www.download.com and searching. Each program will have a brief description of what it does, and is rated by other users. If the producers of the software have a website, then check that out too for testimonials, samples and support.

One useful and inexpensive program is Serif's PhotoPlus (www.serif. com and look under the 'Products' tab). The latest version is X2, which at around £60 has many of the features of more expensive professional software. It takes some time to become a competent user, and there's no doubt it will work your PC hard – make sure you have more than enough processing power and memory – but it can product great results.

To try an earlier version completely free, visit www.freeserifsoftware. com and look for the download link for PhotoPlus version 6. You may find that this is more than adequate for your needs. There are also online photo retouching services at FotoFlexer (http://fotoflexer.com) and Phixr (www.phixr.com).

It's also worth noting that the companion products from Serif are also competitively priced. DrawPlus can produce highly finished graphics such as logos – at least when used by a suitably creative person!

Sharing photos

There are a number of sites that make the storage and sharing of photos easy. At its simplest, Flickr (www.flickr.com) is simply an online photo album. It's useful if you just want to share pictures with others, but comes into its own if you use these pictures in your blogs and websites where it may be more difficult to store a lot of pictures.

Once you have a free Flickr account, you are able to set up multiple albums and arrange your photos by subject or usage. You can link your photos to groups which may be joined by people with a particular interest – the sort of people who might want to look at your pictures . . . or use them in their blogs.

A pro account is about £13 a year and includes virtually unlimited uploading (100Mb a month) and storage. So if your business depends on showing a large inventory of products or you wanted to be able to call on a library of pictures, you could do so.

Of course such a library isn't necessarily just for 'artistic' photographs. You could, for example, keep a photo-journal of the progress of a large building job – perhaps to show a new technique or just how tidy your building site is kept!

If you want your photos to be used by others, tagging them is essential. Tags work like keywords in your blog postings or tags within Web pages. When someone searches for an image on a particular subject, or taken in a certain country or in a certain way, they'll use keywords.

Figure 1 *Flickr helps you keep track of your photos*

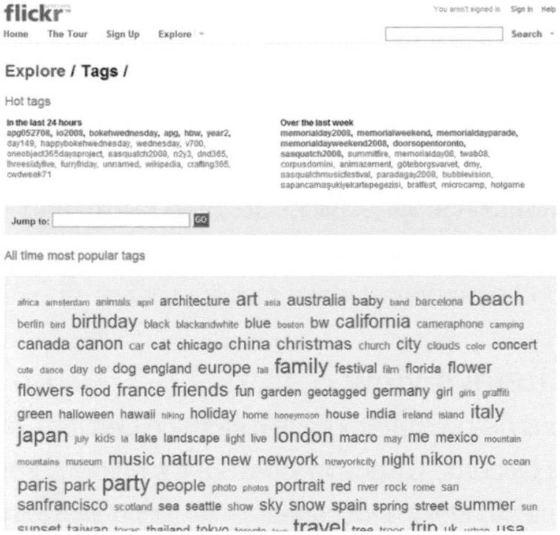

Figure 2 *Tagging photos in Flikr*

Other photo hosting sites include Photobucket (http://photobucket. com) and, of course, offerings from the major players such as Picasa from Google (http://picasa.google.com), which is also a download for organising photos on your PC. Many traditional camera and film manufacturers have their own version of this kind of software – often with some retouching facility.

Figure 3 *Foto offers more than just photo storage*

Others, such as Foto (www.foto.com and http://uk.foto.com), also offer similar kinds of services to Spreadshirt and CafePress in Chapter 11 so that you can put your photos on to mugs, mouse mats and more. Good promotional ideas, but not cheap.

A professional's view

Chris Rojas runs his own photographic studio in Denver, Colorado (www. cruxphotography.com). Given his location, it's hardly surprising that he produces some stunning landscapes.

However, his location might not be ideal for a photographer who is also capable of high-quality fashion and architectural photography too. After leaving college at the age of 18, Chris began to take photographs on climbing expeditions, and found his niche in snowboarding shoots in the mountains of the Pacific Northwest[2]. Starting Crux Photography in 2004, he found a few jobs through one website but quickly found that

---

[2] So clearly ideal for a link with Goose Loose!

putting high-resolution images online wasn't the best way of protecting his copyright.

Since then, Chris has used Flickr and MySpace as well as One Model Place (http://onemodelplace.com), where some of his fashion shoots appear. Jobs don't necessarily come direct through these sites, but they remain a permanently accessible portfolio.

He finds that there is a lot of clutter on sites like Flickr, precisely because they are free to sign up. While other sites may get more attention, Flickr users seem to have an older age profile and so may be more likely to be in a position to commission work.

Chris reckons he's still learning the tricks of getting noticed but says that joining groups and tagging photos carefully and extensively is important. He's also started to make slideshows on PhotoBucket which he can then post on to MySpace, and he had the inspired idea of shooting a behind-the-scenes video of a photoshoot for YouTube.

For Chris, the name of the game is to keep the commissions coming in. He's even used Craigslist and other similar sites, not only to advertise but to find photography jobs. Any opportunity to get noticed, cheaply, is worth considering. When he has time, he attends casting calls and does an impromptu photoshoot right after the audition to get the attention of new models, actors and actresses who might need to build their portfolio.

Creative 'guerrilla marketing' seems to work for Chris, who says 'I would much rather spend $2,000 on a new lens or studio equipment than on advertising that may or may not work. I may not be the biggest photographer in the Denver area, but at 23, I'm well on my way to running a successful business full-time.'

Can you use video?

Like photography, video is pretty much an expected part of the Web. Almost all social networking sites include the option to embed video, and it's often just a case of clicking a button within one site and navigating to another to specify the file you want.

Increasingly, sites depend on the moving image. For example, cartoonbrew (www.cartoonbrew.com) is a blog and website that simply wouldn't work without embedding video. The authors of the blog can simply pick up video and clips from the millions on YouTube and embed them on their site.

Video hosting sites like YouTube allow video files to be held on a server independent of the originator (saving bandwidth) and for them to be reviewed and then easily linked to or embedded elsewhere. The ease of this process encourages the viral spread of videos that people find entertaining or informative.

The technology of creating a video is well known to most people, although the quality can vary. A good digital camera with the facility to have a separate audio input is vital. Many of the comments above about still photography also apply. A separate microphone is useful for getting the sound you want, say from an on-screen presenter, and cutting out background noise; built-in microphones are just not up to the job.

Of course, if your video is simply a demonstration of a technique (like the plumbers and florist we've been mentioning), you might simply want the video footage and to overdub a soundtrack or commentary afterwards. We looked at very basic sound recording and the importance of listening to the quality in Chapter 3; background noise is the biggest enemy.

The comments about the use of copyrighted material apply here too – you can only use music and images that you have express permission to use or that are released for commercial use (usually with a clear acknowledgement and a link back to the originator).

The video-editing software MoviePlus from Serif, mentioned above, may suffice, and there is also a basic video-editing program called Movie Maker (for use with Windows XP) which is free to download from Microsoft (http://tinyurl.com/3fpo4). There are other alternatives at www. download.com.

There are also online video-editing sites such as JumpCut (http:// jumpcut.com) Eyespot (www.eyespot.com) and One True Media (www. onetruemedia.com).

Whatever you do, make sure you have your brand name and various Web addresses on show either throughout the video or at frequent intervals – that way even if the video is passed on through other sites or blogs, it's still clearly yours and potential customers can find you.

YouTube

YouTube has become the standard video hosting website. As more people have broadband and computers (and increasingly mobile devices) capable of running video, such sites allow sharing of ads and informational 'movies' around the world.

There are competitor sites. Of course Google has a platform (http://video.google.co.uk), as does Yahoo (http://video.yahoo.com), and both Flickr and Photobucket, mentioned above, allow for uploading of video.

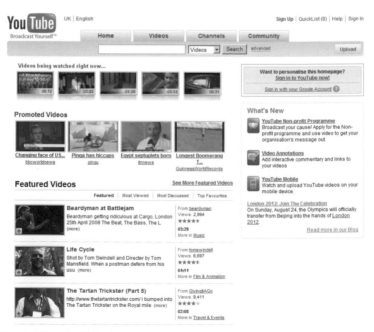

Figure 4 *The YouTube front page*

While YouTube is quite careful about not allowing overly sexual or violent videos, others like LiveLeak (www.liveleak.com) seem more liberal about the content – so you might not want to link through to it if you have a family audience. BlipTV (http://blip.tv), Blinx (www.blinkx.com), Imeem (www.imeem.com), MetaCafe (www.metacafe.com), and Vuze (www.vuze.com) all offer similar services, each with a slightly different feel and, I think, audience. Most have an element of social networking so that videos can be bookmarked or shared, or links sent to friends. The social element also allows for the reporting and filtering out of some content.

David Mullings' RealVibez.com (see Chapter 9) has produced video content to promote music performers on Vuze, YouTube and on more commercial channels such as MTV's Flux (www.mtv.co.uk/channel/flux), and there's no reason why you can't use video for any product or service.

Perhaps the best example of viral video for product or service demonstrations is 'Will it blend?', the brainchild of Tom Dickson at Blendtec (www.willitblend.com), who produce domestic and commercial blenders. In a perfect meeting of product and entertainment, each 'episode' released on YouTube features Tom placing an object into one of Blendtec's blenders – and then seeing the consequences. As the series has continued, viewers have requested ever more outlandish subjects for the experiments including drinks cans, brooms and video cameras – functioning at the time.

As a demonstration of the build quality of the product, there's no faulting the 'Will It Blend?' series and it has grown into a kind of soap opera, with every aspect of the production a subject for discussion online. The obliteration of one of Apple's newly launched iPhones in 2007 resulted in the remains being sold on eBay for nearly $1,000!

The same principles can be applied by smaller businesses and brands too, and, in some cases, create an opportunity for a whole new business.

Ina Stanley is an entrepreneur and also the Director of Durham Business & Networking, a professional alliance and business advocacy organisation,

Figure 5 *A Blendtec video – in this case, golf balls*

Figure 6 *The Virtual Sidekick home page, complete with embedded video*

in North Carolina in the US. Her latest venture is Virtual Sidekick (www. virtual-sidekick.com) which supports the marketing of homes for individuals and professional estate agents (or realtors, if you prefer). The virtual tours of houses that Ina puts together make it easy for potential purchasers to look around and decide which properties they should visit. Since they don't spend so much time travelling only to be disappointed, they are more likely to buy.

The great thing, I think, is that many of the avenues for distributing these video tours of houses are free. Of course making the video, editing it and posting it takes time, and the prices at Virtual Sidekick reflect that. However, for private vendors, these prices are still very attractive when compared to conventional estate agency fees.

Ina had already set up a home business which generated enough income to allow her to strike out on her own. According to Ina: 'While others have been spending hundreds, some even thousands, per month on PPC campaigns, guaranteed traffic packages and surveyed leads, I have probably spent less than $400 total in the past 11 months to advertise.'

'Because marketing though Web 2.0 has helped me to keep more of the money I've earned, we can launch our business with no debts, financing or monthly bills to pay for equipment.'

Ina is clearly an advocate of using video and viral marketing – she has posted her own advice at http://hubpages.com/hub/digitize_yourself. 'There is so much to be utilised online, and most of it is free. All it takes is knowledge of how things work, and how you can use them to your benefit.'

Video technology is so widely available that almost anyone can make a video, including your customers. If you have a look at the Doritos website in the UK (http://doritos.co.uk), you'll see that the results of its campaign to get customers involved with the brand – by getting them to make the ads – have a social-network angle.

The competition had to be well thought through, with strict rules covering acceptability and copyright, and had substantial prizes for the winner – not least their ad being shown on national television. Whilst you may not be able to create quite the same impact, or the flashy website, you can still invite participation and the recognition of other fans or members of your social network.

Doritos promoted the competition clearly on its packs, but there was a big viral element in the campaign. Most elements of the website – especially the ads themselves – could be sent to friends or embedded elsewhere. Much the same could be done on any of the social networking platforms in Chapters 8 and 9 – and free.

The Doritos campaign also used Facebook to bring together budding film-makers and help them with their project. Of course, the Facebook group itself also gained attention for the Doritos brand.

It's an approach that would suit Goose Loose very well, encouraging their customers to contribute videos of their travels and sports exploits, and perhaps even offering a small monthly prize.

Start thinking visually

There's no doubt that pictures and video add a dimension to your Web pages or blog. If you are in a business where it's difficult to imagine the use of video and where your competition seems to be using mainly text, then I'd say it's *essential* you start thinking visually.

If you're an engineer, a plumber, a florist, if you write wills or run a café, then you could include useful and interesting pictures and videos. They might showcase your work, give people step-by-step instructions, allow people to join in events they couldn't attend, or simply give your view on how to make the perfect cup of coffee.

At the very least, you should have useful product shots and photos of the people that your customers might want to meet or talk to – these all offer reassurance (remember those hygiene factors in Chapter 2?), but can encourage involvement too.

If you have something to say in your blog, then why not say it in person too with a video blog?

CHAPTER 11

FINDING VIRTUALLY FREE AND CHEAP SERVICES ONLINE

So far we've looked at getting your business online and communicating and working with colleagues and clients. Some of the services offered within major sites like eBay or Google are, of course, very valuable to your business, and many of the tools and platforms for delivering communication with clients and colleagues are freeware or open-source. But what happens if you need to source other products, if you need bespoke services or if there's some technical guidance you need?

You won't be surprised to know that there is no end of help available online for small businesses, much of it free, and some of it incredibly valuable. Don't ignore local authority and government-funded sources of advice such as Business Link (www.businesslink.gov.uk) and the Small Business Advice Service (www.smallbusinessadvice.org.uk).

To start with, any question you have is worth submitting directly to Google. No matter how badly phrased your query, you're likely to throw up some useful links. Try entering a question as you would ask it: 'How do I manage my cash flow for a small clothing shop?' generated 27,000 hits!

Rephrasing it can get a different set of results, and following up a few will lead to more ideas as well as some potential solutions. Remember the help pages of many websites, including Google itself, include forums of users and experts where your question may have been asked before and you can post further questions.

Crowdsourcing

Because, as we've seen, the cost of supplying information to one person online is pretty much the same as supplying it to a million, the Web is attractive to all kinds of experts. Just because some are easy to find (i.e. they're good at using Google AdWords) doesn't make them dependable, but on the other hand, there is genuine professional talent out there that is virtually free.

One site that employs the skills of a mass of Web users is Sitepoint (www.sitepoint.com) which holds a lot of free information on how to do most online things – especially designing and constructing websites and including some of the more complex areas like integrating pages with databases. Sitepoint also has a useful marketplace where you can buy anything from a short piece of 'script' (say, to make a logo move on your page) to complete Web-based businesses.

Advice on all aspects of Web design and online business can be found in the articles and forums on Sitepoint. Until recently it also hosted competitions for the design of websites, company and product names and logos and other marketing collateral. You can now find these at 99designs (http://99designs.com).

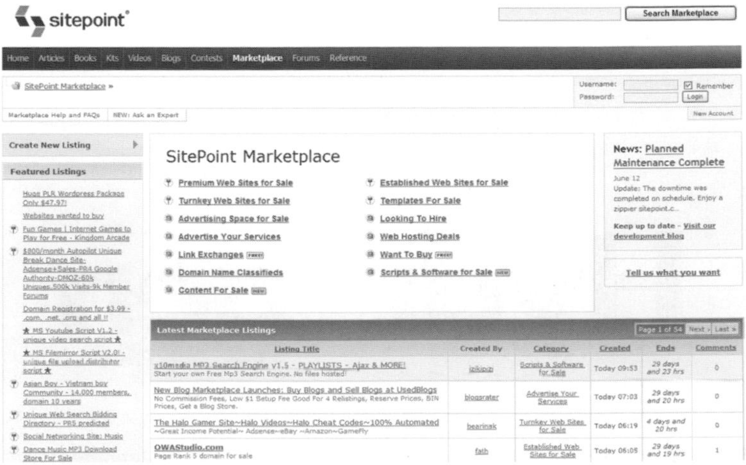

Figure 1 *Sitepoint's marketplace*

According to SitePoint, in 2007, 77 percent of its subscribers, customers and visitors claimed to be professional Web designers, and 22 percent of its visitors owned their own business. There are now over 5,000 registered designers on the 99designs website and eight different contest categories. You can brief them to design your logo, Web page, buttons, stationery, t-shirts, banners and Flash animation among other things.

Creating your own contest

If you'd like someone to design for you, you'll need to set up an account. Once on the home page you can go straight to 'Launch a contest' or you can look at other contests, current and past. It's a good idea to see how designers are briefed and the amount offered as a prize, and to get a feel for running a contest.

If you click on the link to launch a contest, you will need to register and agree to the terms and conditions. You'll decide on a screen name – one you're happy for people to see – and pay the initial fee ($40 at the time of writing) for opening the contest. You'll also decide on a prize – at least $100 – which you credit to your account. As you set up your contest, there is plenty of guidance online, and the Sitepoint forum may also be useful.

Figure 2 *One design submitted to 99designs.com for an environmentally-friendly bus company*

The success of your project depends largely on how clearly you explain your expectations. If you already have a pretty clear vision of how your logo should look, describe it in as much detail as possible. You can add links to show examples of styles you like, but if you're not sure what you're looking for, make the brief more general – don't over-direct the designers. In this way you will receive a range of very different ideas to choose from which will, in turn, give you new ideas about how you want to present your company.

Designers should have, at least, a description of your business and something about your company values (as in Chapter 2). You might suggest what feelings the logo should communicate, how a website needs to function, describe your targeted customer, and say how and where the resulting design will be used. It makes a significant difference if your logo is to be used on a website or printed – even the method of printing may make a difference – or if you are developing an e-commerce site. If in doubt, list all the possible applications and ask for advice and suggestions.

Likewise you will need your logo in 'vector' format files such as AI (Adobe Illustrator) and EPS. These formats enable to you to change the size of your logo without losing quality. Ask the winner to send your file in a format with 'editable layers and objects' so you can, if you need to, make further amendments to your logo. If you don't have relevant software to run AI or EPS files (see Chapter 10), ask the designer to provide you with other formats as well, such as TIFF, BMP, JPEG and GIF. You may need them for your website and for some print jobs.

Your logo should also have Pantone (PMS) colour numbers specified. These enable accurate reproduction of your logo time and again. And make sure that the fonts used in your designs are free for commercial use; not all are.

Feedback is crucial

Sitepoint and 99designs recommend that you give feedback on a daily basis. Under all entries there is a column discussion area everyone can view, and you can just click on a submitted image to give direct feedback.

Even if the given entry is far from what you are looking for in terms of the style, consider the quality of the project. The same artist, if properly encouraged, may come up with completely different ideas. However, don't over-commit yourself to one design; if you say 'I like this one' you'll quickly get designers submitting copies of that approach and kill the creativity you're looking for. If you don't find the ideal solution for your project straight away, you may extend the length of the contest.

Finalising your design

Once you have chosen your winner, it's your responsibility to check the designer's references. You can ask for any information you need about their work or previous experience; many will be experienced and highly-qualified designers using Sitepoint and 99designs to promote themselves.

You will have to sign a contract with the winner of your competition in order to assign copyright to you. Generic templates are available for download on SitePoint's forum, and you can modify them so that you are happy that the contract fully protects your rights.

Remember to be fastidious about copyright. Some designers use images which do not belong to them for the purposes of visualising their design, or they use royalty-free images of which you cannot have exclusive use. Make doubly sure that the designer has assigned all the rights to the design to you, and that they are entitled to do so, or you could have a shock in the future if someone else claims to own your corporate image![1]

There are alternative websites, including www.designcontest.net, www.logodesignguru.com, www.eelogo.com and www.mycorporatelogo. com. Some of these offer designs starting at $99, which sounds reasonable except that the choices are limited (you may be offered just a few alternative designs) and opportunities to give feedback to the

---

[1] For more on copyright, visit www.ipo.gov.uk/whatis/whatis-copy.htm

designers are restricted. Those that offer unlimited revisions include www.jet-web.co.uk and www.curtoons.com, but at much higher rates. To make contact with a freelance Web designer, try the global directory at Freelance Local Tech (www.freelancelocaltech.com).

Incidentally, if you do undertake your own design (and we've discussed some of the pitfalls elsewhere), there are sources of free imagery and free typefaces that may make your job easier. Check out Stock.Xchng (www.sxc.hu), FontFreak (www.fontfreak.com) and 1001 Free Fonts (www.1001freefonts.com) amongst others for typefaces. Bear in mind that you must read the terms and conditions of all these sites and that the licence may vary – some may not be for commercial use or for use in any product for re-sale. Even designers who offer completely open-source use understandably often want a credit and, if possible, a link back to their website, so play fair!

If you need creative work – graphic or Web design, photography, video and even more traditional services like tailoring – you might try tapping into the talent of students via www.studentgems.com. Typically students are training in the trades they offer, but not working full-time. They charge lower rates in the expectation of building up their experience and portfolio.

Branded products – no outlay

Once you have your logo, or any other image or information you want to distribute, whether to sell for to give away, there are a number of sites that will help you.

For clothing and other items frequently personalised you could try either CafePress (www.cafepress.com) or Spreadshirt (www.spreadshirt.net in the UK and .com elsewhere), both of which allow you to create designs and sell them without ever having to order products. In effect, your designs are created digitally as visuals that you can put on to your website or blog, and are only produced when ordered. Both sites handle the exchange and the fulfilment of the order. You can decide how much you charge over the base cost, and therefore your profit level.

Uploading graphics files can be slow, and both sites look closely at the quality of designs and tend to err on the side of caution with regards to the legality of the content. For example, Spreadshirt will not allow you to produce an item with a logo that you do not own.

Figure 3 *CafePress helps you create your own merchandise*

You will need to be competent with a graphics program in order to produce and amend graphics files and be confident that they will work. Unfortunately, there is no way of checking how good your design will turn out except by ordering the product yourself.

You can set up your own shops on these sites, and both offer free versions which are more restricted but perfectly adequate for most purposes. The more advanced stores allow more pages, better branding on the pages, and things like branded invoicing. Incidentally, a word of warning: look closely at the e-commerce part of your store as you set it up to make sure that it works in the right currency – your customers may be put off by dollar prices. Spreadshirt allows you to specify UK pounds or euros, but once decided, you can't change it.

Once you have a store with some designs for sale, you can generate the code for a widget (like those in your blog in Chapter 3 or from

Amazon in Chapter 6) to include your own products on your website. Products range from T-shirts to caps, mouse mats and even underwear. Your designs can be made available to others, and you can become an associate or affiliate in order to sell the designs of others.

One of the ways of promoting your expertise, as we've mentioned elsewhere, is to write a book! An e-book is fairly easy – it need only be a document but is often produced as an Adobe Acrobat file (with the suffix .pdf), which can be read but not edited by any purchaser. If your word processing software doesn't already allow you to export a file in this format, there are a number of free products that can, for example PrimoPDF (www.primopdf.com).

With the launch of Kindle, Amazon's e-book reader device (http://tinyurl.com/2j4bcl), formatting books to be read in this way may be worth investigating. Dennis Batchelder, an author, has experimented with distributing electronic copies of his novel and written about it on his blog (http://dennisbatchelder.com).

You can produce a printed book via CafePress above. An alternative is Lulu (www.lulu.com) which allows you to upload and market your book, calendar and even recordings online. Again your product is printed or produced on demand, so there is no cost until there is a purchaser, but you can also make your work available as an instant download.

As an example, Avand (www.avand.co.uk) promotes training courses in the UK – including in plumbing. Their training manuals are all made available through Lulu, making them globally accessible and relatively cheap to produce.

More business networking

You may already be using LinkedIn (Chapter 9) to find help, but there are plenty of other business networks that work in slightly different ways – some online. You should certainly look at sites like www.ryze. com, www.naymz.com and others, but be careful that they are not too small to give you enough contacts of the right sort (for example in your country or industry), or too big that you are lost. The Chemistry Club

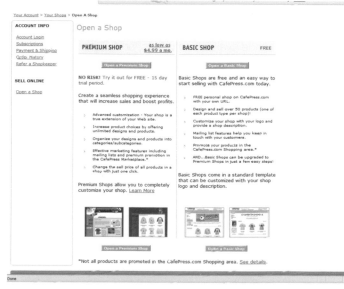

Figure 4 *Options for setting up a store in CafePress*

(www.thechemistry.com) for example is a strictly controlled group for the technology industry, and A Small World (www.asmallworld.net) is even more exclusive – you can't join, you must be invited – but its presumably wealthy and well-connected user base might be a good advertising audience.

It's difficult to strike a balance between a well-targeted community and one that has sufficient numbers, but e-mailing the people who run the site to ask about the profile of the users should elicit a useful response. If not, then they clearly don't need your subscription!

Ecademy (www.ecademy.com) is a well-established network set up to support online business and those existing in the real world too. Events are organised in an accessible calendar on the website so you can identify those local to you or of particular interest. Attendance at the events isn't just about learning; you can also promote yourself to clients who might then check you out on the Ecademy site. The network has various levels of membership – the basic is free, whereas the more advanced levels, costing up to £105 per month, include some selling tools and SEO for your profile. There's also a marketplace for all kinds of business services.

Another resource is Business Network International (www.bni-europe. com) which has a useful website but is probably even more useful in the real world for the 'speed-dating' approach to networking. Membership is controlled, so that you would be the only representative of your industry in your 'chapter', and you meet with other members regularly to give your two-minute pitch. It's an invaluable support forum for new businesses, with numerous examples of immediate, reciprocal, benefits for members in the newsletter, which you can see online.

www.guru.com and www.freelancers.net are both examples of sites that link freelancers with projects, but there are many more such as the FreelanceSwitch forum (http://freelanceswitch.com) which may be useful for getting you work or getting you help. Digital Eve (www.digitaleve. org) is exclusively for women in business. Like BNI, it is organised in chapters, including one in London (www.digitaleveuk.org).

Again, it's worth looking at several to see if they specialise in your industry or frequently feature the services you need or offer.

Some portal sites such as Women Republic (www.womenrepublic. co.uk) and listings or broker sites like Good Builder Guide (www. goodbuilderguide.co.uk), MyHammer (www.myhammer.co.uk), www. searchaccountants.co.uk and www.123getaquote.co.uk may be good sources for word-of-mouth recommendations for businesses like builders, engineers or accountants. As we've said elsewhere, the virtually free option is to get your satisfied clients to recommend you to these kinds of sites, and there's no reason why you couldn't make this a feature of an e-mail to clients or create a link on your website for this purpose, but you may find as much value in tracking down services *you* need.

Almost everything . . . online

I couldn't possibly include everything in this chapter that could be of use to you. By and large, using a search to find potential sources of help and information is the first step you can take. Then searching again for any reviews or comparisons of the various options you have found helps develop a short list.

Amongst the key words you should use is, of course, 'free'. You'll find free software (at sites such as www.download.com), often with reviews and ratings on the site, and you can find free website listings and directories (not surprisingly at www.thefreewebsitedirectory.co.uk but also at www.splut.com and others), and there is no shortage of advice and experience on forums and groups such as those on Yahoo (http://groups.yahoo.com) and Google. (http://groups.google.com).

Keep looking and keep exchanging information with others in business and in your industry and you'll keep coming across useful services. Martin Lewis's site www.moneysavingexpert.com is full of good advice that could help with day-to-day purchases, credit cards, insurance and phone deals. Who knows? Through online peer-to-peer finance websites like Prosper (www.prosper.com) and Zopa (www.zopa.com) you may even find funding for your business start-up!

OTHER WAYS OF
WORKING . . .

What we have seen so far is a mix of technologies. Some are decidedly Web 2.0 because they are collaborative; they alter the usual roles of producer and consumer. Others are less so, but seem to be moving in that direction. For the moment, however, I want to quickly touch on a few other tools that might help you collaborate with clients and colleagues. And reflect on what you can do *with* them and learn *from* them. The concept of 'virtually free' marketing goes beyond what you can get . . . to what you are able to give your customers.

As you may have gathered, the business model for Web 2.0 often involves getting users to commit to the product by giving it away free of charge. That means that products like GoogleDocs, Facebook, LinkedIn and Skype (below) become more like services than products. Unlike the old software companies, you don't buy version 1.0 then have to pay to upgrade to 1.1; customers come to rely on the products and expect it to be continuously improved.

Learning from experts

One pioneer in the new Web is 37signals (www.37signals.com), founded by Jason Fried and David Heinemeier Hansson[1]. They have been building online applications for about 10 years and have developed several useful tools for managing your work online.

We'll come on to their products in a moment, but there's more to 37signals than just a funky name and useful software. As a business

---

[1] Jason's blog is at the 37signals website and David's at www.loudthinking.com

they have captured a lot of what it takes to run a great small (creative) business. Aiming at small businesses where the purchaser is also the user, they have competed against larger companies by 'doing less'.

It may be counter-intuitive, but it's insightful. Knowing what a particular group of customers really wants and is prepared to pay for, and stripping out anything else, is a way of undermining bigger competitors (like Microsoft and Google). They have a very clear sense of purpose and strategic view of their world – it would fit easily into the Holden-Wilde matrix in Chapter 2.

Fortunately, I don't have to explain their approach at length: they've put their collected wisdom into a book called *Getting Real* which is available from their website. You can buy it or, in the spirit of the new Web, read it online completely free of charge – see http://gettingreal.37signals.com.

For 37signals and many Web 2.0 companies, the aim of the game is to get a critical mass of users, especially as many of the products are about communication *between* users. A network's value is measured by the number of connections. It's something worth thinking about for your community of users: your customers. What can you give them? How can you bring them together for their mutual benefit? Can you do it cheaply? What we've learned in this book would suggest you can.

To take this business model further, you might consider what you're able to give your customers or co-workers free, and then what additional services or products you might be able charge *some* of your customers for, once they are within your network.

Tools for sharing

Of course, as we've said, one of the themes of Web 2.0 is collaboration, and it may be that your business idea is no longer manageable by one person. Growing a small business is fraught with difficulties. Once again, the Web has offered a new solution to growing pains: don't grow.

Apart from some of the sites in Chapter 11 which enable you to share your expertise and pick the brains of others, there are thousands of individuals and companies like you and yours out there, willing to cooperate, and hundreds of tools to support this. Some of the affiliate schemes or add-ons (such as those from Amazon or Google) allow you to have a well-established name on your website and a rock-solid bit of programming doing some of the work for your business.

Expanding your company may instead be a case of finding partners – who can be anywhere in the world – and sharing documents and information with them. These partners (self-sufficient companies in their own right) become part of your 'value network' – contributors to the process of getting something of value to your customers[2].

Back to the office

So how can you start to collaborate? Back in Chapter 4 we mentioned Office Live from Microsoft and saw how it could be used to set up basic Web pages for our business. Now is the time to look at their Workspace product.

If you have an Office Live account (or a Windows Live login) you can re-enter this by clicking on the blue button to the top right. You may have set this up earlier; otherwise, you'll have to go through the same sign-up procedure set out in Chapter 4.

You'll be taken to the same dashboard screen we looked at previously, and you'll need to click on the 'Collaborate with customers and co-workers' link towards the top right. Again, Microsoft go for long titles (the Workspace name isn't used here for some reason, and in places they call the service Windows Sharepoint!).

The next screen sets out fairly clearly what Microsoft reckons the advantages are. If you already use Microsoft Office, Workspace is quite an easy product to use since it expects you to be working in Word, Outlook and Excel – and it's free.

---

[2] This, again, is a subject dealt with in *Marketing & PR*.

Figure 1 *The dashboard for Office Live Small Business*

As you enter your workspace, you'll see there is a pale yellow 'Help' at the top of the screen which is worth exploring. The shortcuts to your documents are below. In Figure 2, you can see these headed 'Documents'.

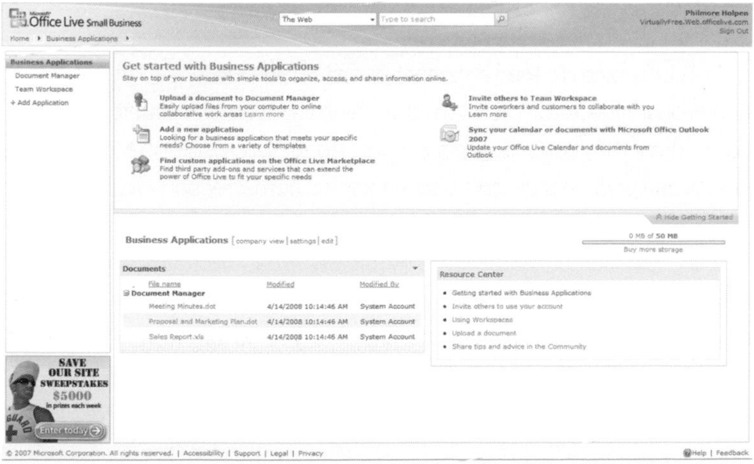

Figure 2 *Your desktop in Office Live*

The first stage is to try out transferring documents to your workspace. Any standard Office document can be shared, but you have a limit of 50 Mb on your free storage space. As soon as you click on the link, you are presented with a list of files already there, which may be any form of file such as a document, spreadsheet or picture. Clicking on any of these brings up a number of further options to view or edit the document in some way.

The 'Check Out' or 'Check In' options enable the system to keep track of what documents you are working on and you to add a brief description of what you've done. Changes are not visible to other users unless you check a document back in after editing – like putting them back in the filing cabinet.

To control users and/or to specify what they are able to access on your site, you can use the 'Sharing' menu on the right. You can also click on the 'Business Applications' link on your home page and look at or edit all users, and access a number of other options.

'Permissions' allows you to control which users can access or edit parts of your site or documents.

It's worth pointing out here that although your workspace has password protection, it isn't automatically encrypted. By clicking on the 'Enforce secure connections' link you can ensure that the site is using the SSL (Secure Sockets Layer) protocol. The reason this isn't standard is that it may slow down the response of the site, and some users with varying security set-ups on their PCs may experience other difficulties. However, if any of the information you are sharing is sensitive (and most is), you should start with this option selected.

By clicking on the menu in most views, you can set up new work groups and make them visible on the left menu of the screen. You can also track the usage of the various applications to see who is uploading, viewing or editing.

To go into the separate work groups you've set up, you simply need to click on the appropriate link on your left menu bar which will be visible every time you log in. Clearly, anyone else with access to your workspace

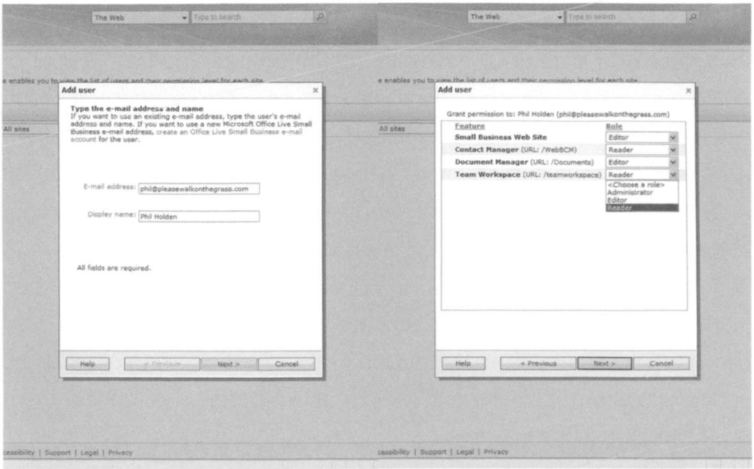

Figure 3 *Specify who you want to invite and assign them roles for each part of your workspace*

(because you invited them) and to each group (if you assigned them) will be able to see these options on their menu too. Across a group, you can share calendar information and synchronise with your locally-stored Outlook calendar.

Generally speaking, the menu you can see on the right of the screen will be there when you are actually inside a work group. Apart from allowing you to manage the access of other users you can, assuming you are the administrator, also manage other useful information that might come out of your working group. Look under the menu item 'Connect to Web Site' – this can help you manage the website you set up in Chapter 4, but could also link to several different websites.

Integrating your workspace and your website

Two clever things enabled by Office Live linking to your public website are the 'lists' and 'forms'.

Lists are, as the name suggests, ordered bits of information which could have value to your customers. So, for example, a list could be a number of documents such as service manuals available to customers, or it could be a regularly updated list of events or prices that your customers would want to know about.

Forms, on the other hand, are like real-world forms to be filled in with data – usually by visitors to your website – so they are great for handling enquiries and for customer research. These are set up to appear on your website itself, but the results of them being filled in are reported back to your workspace.

Remember, again, that data isn't automatically encrypted unless you use the SSL option. If you are using forms on Web pages hosted by another provider, they too must support this protocol.

As with most of these applications, the way to get to know it is to try it. Fortunately, Microsoft offers quite a lot of online help so, as you go through the set-up of your workspaces, you can also open a separate window showing the help pages at http://tinyurl.com/yaa8v8.

Whatever Microsoft can do Google (and Zoho) can too . . .

Don't forget, back in Chapter 5 we looked at some of the other services Google had to offer, including Google Docs. As it's free to sign up to all of these services, it's worth trying them before you commit yourself too far.

It can, however, be a bigger step to move across to Google (or its smaller rival Zoho – see http://zoho.com) because these do not necessarily use Microsoft Office tools. However, while Google Docs reads from and exports to popular file formats, Zoho has developed a plug-in for Microsoft Office which makes the two work together on- and offline.

These two sites offer serious rivals to locally-installed software such as Office, and may be preferable if your company has co-workers geographically spread out (though some applications have limited foreign language support) – especially if you don't want them to keep data locally, or if you simply don't want to pay for software and upgrades. All you need in order to use Google Docs or Zoho is a browser and a Web connection.

Zoho claims to be aimed more at business users than Google: all of its products are available as personal editions or for businesses. With Zoho Business, you can manage the access of co-workers (just like Office Live above) and personalise the whole work area with, for example, your own logo. It doesn't offer a way of setting up or managing Web pages (as with Microsoft or Google in Chapter 4), although it does offer a website monitoring product so that you could be alerted to any service issues, and a wiki and other tools (see Figure 4).

Zoho clearly offers some useful functionality, including the ability to prepare invoices and manage customer data, manage online chats, and conference.

All of Zoho's products are well explained and, once you've registered with the site, free for limited use or to try. Again, it's worth exploring the

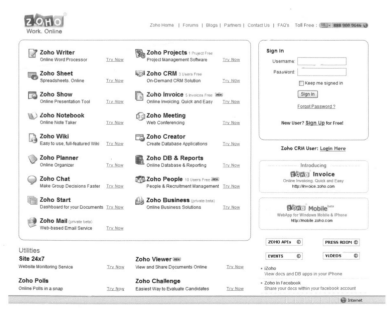

Figure 4 *Zoho offers many useful business applications*

functions before you commit too heavily; besides, Zoho charges a monthly fee once you move beyond three users, which can soon add up.

Specialised sharing platforms

From 37signals comes a whole set of online tools, all of which can be tried but which are also generally charged for on a monthly subscription basis. As I mentioned above, 37signals aims for lean products that do one job well. However, some of these jobs are complex and, you might feel, overlap. For example, you may want to keep a list of customers' details and attach sales records to them. If you also want to set up discussion areas with clients, you might want their details to be automatically available for that system too. It won't necessarily work that way.

The key to making a decision about any of these tools is to try them (free, of course) and then take some time to plan how you would use them and what benefit you might gain. Here's a quick rundown of the products.

Basecamp (www.basecamphq.com) is a project collaboration tool which allows you to share schedules, ideas and documents in a secure area. Tasks can be allocated and milestones set which are visible to everyone. In the free version, you can set up a single project and have an unlimited number of users, but you are not allocated storage space, so file-sharing is switched off. If you wanted to have three projects and 1Gb of storage the price goes up to around £6 a month. There are various subscription levels, up to 50Gb of storage and an unlimited number of projects costing around £75 a month. You can tour Basecamp at www.basecamphq.com/tour

For contact and customer relationship management, 37signals offers Highrise (www.highrisehq.com). It's useful if you depend on selling to a number of relatively large organisations or high-value customers, or if you need to keep track of agents, retailers or others. Highrise helps you keep track of who you talk to and what you talk about, and keeps a list of actions resulting.

If you're planning to grow beyond one person, then it's as well to start thinking about your contact database. Highrise is great if you have a geographically spread workforce – in effect, you can all work from home or, indeed, on the road. For data such as this, control is the key – see Figure 5.

For simply keeping track of contact details, wherever you are, you could use Soocial (www.soocial.com), which is in beta testing at the time of writing. It can link with Highrise and some other applications to make

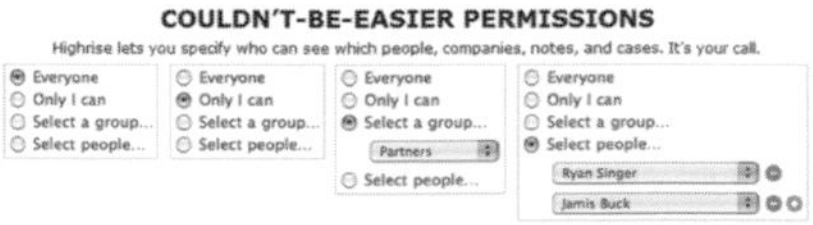

COULDN'T-BE-EASIER PERMISSIONS
Highrise lets you specify who can see which people, companies, notes, and cases. It's your call.

Figure 5 Setting access controls in Highrise

your centrally-updated contact list available to your PC, phone or even other applications such as Facebook.

Similar in some ways is Backpack (again 37signals – see www. backpackit.com), which is a kind of online notebook and diary. In it you gather notes, ideas, to-do lists, photos and files. You can use Backpack on your own (around £3.50 a month), but the 'intranet in 30 seconds' they offer costs more: up to six users around £12 a month. Backpack enables you to share calendars and can also remind you about appointments and other things in your various lists via your phone.

Finally, 37signals' Campfire (www.campfirenow.com) is a fairly simple 'group chat' application which offers real-time collaboration over the Internet. But it faces stiff competition from many other similar products. Some say that Google has copied Campfire with their new application HuddleChat but, just to confuse you, there is already a product called Huddle (www.huddle.net). For an alternative, try Vyew (www.vyew.com), another collaborative workspace which is free to sign up, allowing up to 20 users at a time.

Campfire allows 10Mb of storage and up to four users in its free version, while Huddle allows three workspaces and unlimited users plus 1Gb of storage in its free version. Huddle is also completely free for charities – 50 workspaces and 25Gb.

Among the interesting developments of Huddle is the ability to integrate with Facebook (http://tinyurl.com/5osxor) to create a private meeting space for your Facebook contacts.

The plethora of alternatives poses problems. One of the complaints that even regular users of Backpack, Campfire, Basecamp and Highrise have is that they don't all integrate. For example a to-do list in one can't necessarily be used in another, nor can all contact details in Highrise be automatically updated in, say, Basecamp. Nevertheless, the applications all have their fans and seem to be particularly useful for small businesses where a specific group of functions is needed.

It's certainly worth exploring all of 37signals' products, since they are mostly free to sign up and try. You will also see existing users contributing experiences and ideas on the respective website discussion areas, which may give you ideas of how to use them and forewarn you of potential difficulties.

Call me . . .

If instant messaging and real-time chat isn't appropriate for your business or customers, try the phone. There's no doubt that many people still like to be able to pick up the phone (especially to get rapid service), so being able to offer free, or virtually free, telephone calls is attractive.

The Internet is playing havoc with the telephone. All the main phone, cable and satellite TV companies and Internet service providers (ISPs) seem to be offering deals. Of particular interest to small businesses, however, is VoIP, voice over Internet protocol. Rather than sharing your phone line with your broadband connection, you can now use your broadband to carry your calls. Confused?

In Chapter 3 we touched on integrating the telephone with your blog. At the time of writing, the Google product, GrandCentral, is yet to be fully launched, but promises much. In the meantime, there are other alternatives that give many of the benefits of conventional telecoms carriers, without quite the same costs.

. . . or Skype me!

The point of VoIP is that the voice call itself is supposed to use spare bandwidth on the relevant networks and so incurs virtually no cost. However, calls often, and seamlessly, use public networks (run by large telecoms providers) and so attract charges.

Skype is, perhaps, the best known, having recently been bought by eBay for $2.6 billion, a price even they now admit might have been over the top. The last time I looked, however, there were over 12 million users online, and the program itself had been downloaded some 99 million times! There may be disappointment at eBay, but there are many committed Skype users – hardly surprising since it enables you to make calls without any of the variable costs usually associated with the big telecoms carriers. Although there are alternatives, Skype seems to be the most popular and visible, and still the potential for integration with eBay trading activities seems promising. If Skype maintains its position – and there's every reason to suppose it will – then eBay users, and many others, will see Skype as an essential part of their business.

Setting up a Skype account couldn't be much easier. Downloading the software (www.skype.com) takes you through the set-up. You'll need a microphone and headphones (though you might have a microphone and speakers built into your PC), which can cost as little as a couple of pounds. Telephone handsets that plug into a USB port specifically designed for such VoIP calls are also available, but these cost rather more. Skype also sells suitable handsets and headphones, so you don't even have to leave your Skype set-up to buy them. See http://tinyurl. com/6ypj3a for Skype products generally and http://tinyurl.com/3ypofr for handsets.

There is very immediate help on all Skype screens, so it's easy to get things installed on your PC. A note of caution, however: the help usually directs you to a Web page and often defaults to the US site, so you might find yourself looking at dollar prices or references to 'local cellphone calls' which may not apply in your country.

Once installed, the program appears as a small control panel, somewhat less than a quarter of your screen size but it also resides on your toolbar (usually down at the bottom right of your screen recognisable by the 'green tick' logo) and runs in the background every time you switch on.

You can set up a free account at first, and this is enough to enable you to make and receive calls between Skype users. As soon as you complete the set-up, you are invited to make a test call (free) to Skype itself, and this tells you if all your sound equipment is working.

Skype will offer you the option of gathering contact information from your e-mail program and will insert any phone numbers it finds; you can then also search for any of these or other contacts in Skype's own database.

If you have colleagues who also work from home, or indeed from offices, and they have a Web connection, you can now all chat free of

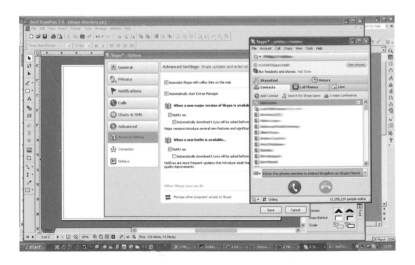

Figure 6 *On the right, your contacts in Skype; on the left, some of the options*

charge. It's a simple matter of clicking on a contact and then the green call button. All the people you know who also have Skype will appear at the top of your contacts list with the green logo by their name.

Skype also usefully tells you if they are online or if they are unavailable. You can set this feature to tell other people your status by clicking on the green tick logo right at the bottom left of the main Skype control panel.

But Skype isn't just a free phone. As you set it up, you'll notice a number of options. For example, you can integrate Skype with your Web browser so that any telephone number is replaced by a clickable button – you just click on the number on the screen and the call is initiated. This could be invaluable for researching supplier and customer prospects online, saving you keying numbers over and over again. You can see this option at the top of the left-hand screen in Figure 9 above.

Skype also allows you to use instant messaging and to make video and conference calls – the free version allows you to conference with nine people. These are simply accessed from the Skype panel (shown on the right of Figure 6).

To make calls to non-Skype numbers, however, you need to purchase call credit from Skype. To receive calls from non-Skype users, you will need a 'SkypeIn' number which is around £35 (€50) for a year, but this offers a number of advantages for a small business, including the ability to access your calls anywhere you are online. A Skype subscription from around £2 a month may well save money on some of the chargeable extras and includes unlimited calls within a country or region (see http://tinyurl.com/3opdgf).

Given what we've considered in Chapter 7, you'll want to give customers as many ways of contacting you as possible. Adding a Skype button (http://tinyurl.com/38jlry) to your website or e-mail signature gives another alternative that is instantly accessible the world over: with a SkypeIn number you can be accessible from any phone, anywhere, but it also gives Skype users the opportunity

Figure 7 *A simple Skype button you can put onto your site*

to call you free of charge – for them it's like a freephone number. If you also have a SkypeIn number, then you have an easy way of enabling enquiries from potential customers.

As Skype belongs to eBay, new ways of integrating the two will be added in the coming months, perhaps to allow online bidders to request and receive more information (including live video) of a product.

Other Skype extras

There are plenty of extras with Skype already, and many are free. You can easily add these on to your Skype account by clicking on the 'Tools' menu item, then on 'Do more', where you will see some of the built-in applications (mostly games) and an option to add more. You can always get a little more information within Skype, but you should visit the Skype website at www.skype.com and https://extras.skype.com and the websites for the specific products before you install, to make sure you know what you are getting. Some are reluctant to explain in great detail what is included in the free version and some have user feedback which is less than complimentary. Nevertheless, some offer potentially useful functions.

Skylook (www.skylook.biz) is one of a handful of extras certified by Skype, and it integrates the phone application with Microsoft Outlook so you continue to use that software to manage your contacts. Skylook adds a new toolbar into Outlook enabling you to use Skype features, including dialling direct from your address book. The fully-featured version includes an answering/voicemail option, and you can also record some or all of your calls as MP3 files and keep track of SMS and chat messages.

Another interesting free extra is Tumara XS (http://xs.tumara.com), which potentially gives you the ability to access your Skype telephone system from your mobile, from another computer (via the Tumara website) or from another phone while you are out and about. You can then pick up messages and return calls – even internationally – often much more cheaply than normal since you are using your Skype account.

Tumara allows you to receive SMS notifications of messages and even to set up different voices for the automated part of the service. There are still bugs with the program – call quality and reliability rely on the mobile network *and* your Web-access speed – so it can be frustrating. The basic download is free, however, and it's a good idea to test the system before you go on to buy the pro version.

HypeCall (www.hypecall.net) also makes calls possible from your mobile, but in a very different way – by sending and receiving an SMS. The cost of calls, however, compares favourably with conventional mobiles and some landline tariffs.

Others Skype extras give you call-centre type facilities, including Sky-click (www.sky-click.com) a product from Ads-Click (www.ads-click.com) which enables you to manage a number of call-centre workers and their handling of incoming calls. Sky-click automates the inclusion of call-back requests (via Skype) on Web pages, directing them to the in-house Skype users you specify and queuing them until they are dealt with. The details of managing inbound or outbound telemarketing are way outside the scope of this book, but potentially tools like Sky-click allow a number of dispersed home workers (even in different countries and using different languages) to act as a combined sales force.

You could have, for example, a number of technical experts around the world who only respond to certain queries. They needn't be in your office, nor do they need to be employed full-time. An engineering company might offer advice on the installation or maintenance of a wide range of projects and construction materials by linking certain call requests to suitably qualified co-workers – and pay them per call. You could easily combine this with one of the other collaborative tools mentioned earlier.

The Sky-Click website offers some good user guides, so it's easy to see how the full versions of these products are set up and used. You can see a useful demonstration of Sky-click at www.sky-click.com/pages/demo.htm. The same company offers a customer relationship management program (www.salesforce.com) which could be worth investigating since it integrates completely with Sky-Click. It's ideal for a larger company needing to manage its customer contacts as they grow in number, as it enables anyone in the company to view customer details during a phone call, online chat or video conference (compare with Highrise and others above).

Unyte from WebDialogs (www.webdialogs.com) is available as a standalone product and as a Skype extra. It enables people connected by Skype to securely view or share documents or applications and desktops with each other. You can use Unyte from within different programs, whether chatting or messaging or just with contacts in your Skype contacts list, just by using the 'Do more' menu.

Alternatives to Skype

There are several alternative providers of VoIP products. Some appear to be more like conventional telecoms companies, for example, www.vonage.co.uk which is big in the US. There are free alternatives – open-source and for different operating systems – including Gizmo and Twinkle (for the Linux operating system) – each offering various levels of usability and various ways of charging for elements of the service.

Twinkle is, for example, open-source and so comes free, but also without any kind of warranty. You'd also have to spend some considerable time setting it up. Vonage, on the other hand, looks and feels exactly like a big telecoms company – with the charging structures to match.

It is important you look closely at the kind of deal you get in the free package and to try the service out. Like the mobile phone companies, some VoIP companies seem to delight in making their various tariffs complicated. It's also worth noting that VoIP doesn't work in all countries, is blocked in some places and networks and, in others, is illegal! As I say, read the service agreement carefully. The site www.voipuser.org is a good place to investigate what is happing in the marketplace, and you can find a list of providers at http://gizmoproject.com.

The drawbacks to VoIP in general include the fact that free calls are generally only available between two people on the same network (customers of the same provider, such as Skype) The main drawback,

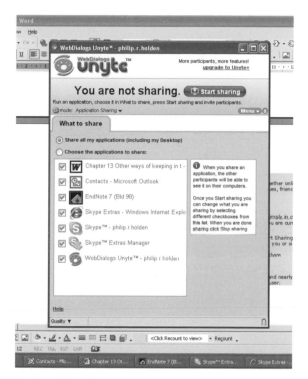

Figure 8 *Unyte enables Skype users to share items on their PCs*

until recently, was that in order to make a call you had to be near your PC and plugged in.

Having said all that, making free calls is pretty attractive. If you have a few clients that you speak to on a regular basis then signing up and, crucially, getting them to sign up for Skype may save you money. Even being able to make cheap calls whilst you are, say, managing your auctions on eBay may be enough of an advantage for you.

The mobile phone company 3 has been offering a Skype account as part of one if its tariffs and, no doubt, others will follow. For a fairly low-cost monthly payment you could have a mobile phone for your own use along with some free Skype calls and even Internet access.

Wikis and DIY communities

One very accessible and relatively low-tech option for communicating between colleagues or with clients is a forum: Informe (www.informe. com) was mentioned in Chapter 9 as one free provider. You will also have seen Yahoo and Google groups in earlier chapters.

Forums are essentially lists of messages posted under particular headings – so it's relatively easy for a visitor to find out if their question has already been answered. An alternative is to set up a wiki.

The definitive wiki is, of course, Wikipedia (http://en.wikipedia.org), the online, collaborative encyclopedia. Wikis are open to almost anyone to edit, and demand a certain level of community spirit to avoid abuse. Generally speaking, you would ask people to register in order to edit pages, and you would lock certain pages to prevent essential information being altered.

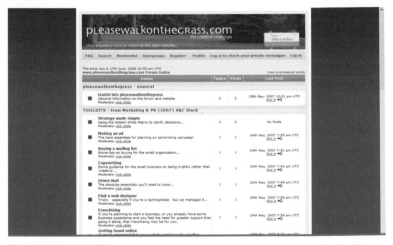

Figure 9 *A typical forum page*

Wikis have a clear strength in building up a body of shared knowledge – they are increasingly used within organisations to ensure that everyone has access to the same information – and they can be used to share expertise with customers as well. As we've noted before, this kind of resource can position you as an expert in your field.

These kind of forums and wikis are commonly used for support. Instead of simply having a static page of frequently asked questions (FAQ), you could have a live discussion group in which both you and customers could answer queries and share experiences. For nonprofits, these kinds of forum enable a small group to have a global reach with help and advice. You could also check out MeetUp (www.meetup.com) which combines online communication with real-life meetings for sports, arts hobbies and other interests – a great avenue for promotion.

Wikia (www.wikia.com) and ScribbleWiki (www.scribblewiki.com) are both free wiki-hosting services, but there are many others, some of which have a free service. You can also see a comparison of alternatives at http://tinyurl.com/ykarmx.

Figure 10 *A typical wiki page*

As you will see if you look at any of the help forums for Google, Yahoo, MSN, Facebook or Skype (indeed all the other programs and platforms in this book), once you have a forum, your company is open for criticism as well as praise. However, if you host your own discussion or help group you have, at least, the opportunity to see complaints and, as important, to respond visibly.

Key questions, rules of the forum and further contact details should be displayed prominently in all message areas. There is usually a facility to post 'sticky' messages that will always stay at the top of a list of questions and answers, or to lock descriptive text under a topic heading.

A free forum or wiki, wherever it is hosted, can simply be linked to your main website and given an explanatory title. After that it's simply a matter of responding promptly to questions and complaints – as well as compliments.

Be clear about what you want to achieve

The marketing potential of some of these tools isn't always clear. Pretty much all applications hinge on the ability to communicate, so have another look at who you communicate with and what sort of communication is necessary or desirable. By and large, none of the applications replace traditional forms of communication, but they may enhance them.

In summary, many of these tools can help with collaboration on research or product design. The can also give you a private channel of communication with clients – especially useful for premium services or consultancy. The application of the Holden-Wilde matrix in Chapter 2 might help you make sense of this: if you can't possibly communicate individually with all your clients, which ones should you focus on, and could a broader communication channel such as those in Chapters 8 and 9 help?

In short, free or cheap online tools can make a difference. The important thing is to use them not because they are toys, but because they do something that impacts on customers and so contribute to your objectives. So think about customer benefits:

- *a helpline or order line that runs on Skype (with an inbound number for customers) may be easier for you to manage from your home or office. It may save you money and be more attractive to other Skype users.*
- *an online collaboration space may enable you to keep in touch with distant partners in your business and to have more productive meetings electronically.*

- *a real-time, online meeting room always open to your clients may enable you to get frequent feedback on a project and avoid expensive mistakes.*
- *a help zone – a forum or wiki – could pick up on customer problems before they get serious, and give you some insight into your clients' needs.*

All these are of marketing value if they enable you to:

a) *get more customers – for example, by responding more efficiently to enquirers*

b) *get more business from your existing customers – perhaps offering them enhanced levels of service*

or both a) *and* b) – for example, by creating an online centre of knowledge about your product area and positioning yourself as the expert.

TOMORROW'S WEB – THE WEIRD AND THE WONDERFUL

Of course, 'tomorrow' never comes.

Which is why it's easy for business writers to go on endlessly about what companies should prepare for. It's also easy for those in business to get a little tired of the warnings and opportunities of the future. Seemingly, very few writers tell you what to do right now.

I hope this book is (has been) different. If it has worked, then you will have spent quite a bit of time slaving over a hot keyboard, surfing and making things happen online and off. But nevertheless, here is my comparatively short forecast for the future online world. It won't be online. The future, you see, doesn't exist in the future; you can see the telltales here and now.

No more PCs, no more wires, no more waiting

Your mobile phone contains more computing power than put a man on the moon, and it also communicates more rapidly and more widely than any technology before. Before too long, your phone will connect seamlessly with the broadband, ubiquitous, wireless Web – some already do.

TV won't consist of broadcast channels but content, some of which will be high-definition TV quality and some of which won't even be video but Web-type pages. If the developments of CERN's 'grid' and experiments in universities around the world pay dividends, the daughter of the World Wide Web will be a thousand times faster. The capacity in fibre-optic networks is already there.

You, or your children, will no longer see the difference between a TV set and a computer, or maybe even the almost paper-like screens being developed by Sony (http://tinyurl.com/5mefl7). You'll be able to browse and contribute to the Web from any such device, anywhere – again, you can see from the interconnections of some of the sites and tools we've looked at that some people already do. There is already a comedy show (http://230milesoflove.com) designed specifically for downloading to your car's satellite navigation system!

In time, consumers won't even need to own a PC or pay for access. Connectivity will be a utility like electricity which, in some cases, will be provided free. Wireless access is already going this way. So going online could be a bit like picking up a free newspaper.

Virtual real estate

The representation of data, people and places in cyberspace will become more intuitive with far better 3D rendering effects, not simply for entertainment but for usability, along with near-instantaneous video and convergence with geographical data. You will be able to see your relatives (or customers) in Australia and introduce them to others in Nova Scotia and see how they get on. At the same time you will be able to give them access to complex data and models (like plans for your holiday, your new house, product specs and mock-ups) to manipulate.

Remote, real-time delivery of services is imminent. Why can't a car's engine, mostly regulated by computer chips, be checked over by someone a thousand miles away?

Immersive games like SecondLife (www.secondlife.com) have already made virtual millionaires of people like Ailin Graef (www.anshechung. com) who builds and sells (un)real estate within this artificial world.

It sounds odd, but there are many virtual worlds in which money changes hands and in which there is a market opportunity. You can see a summary of just a few that are based in the English-speaking world at Robin Good's influential website (http://tinyurl.com/39wbzb). The Croquet Consortium (www.opencroquet.org) is an open-source (and therefore free) virtual environment that allows sharing of documents and even video feed within seemingly limitless 'rooms' you can build yourself. What is it for? Well, that's up to you and your marketing objectives.

So is everything going to be online?

The future is simply: increasingly powerful devices + pervasive access + convergence of technology. And that is what is happening now: anything that can be digitised will be. This, always-on, always-there, rapid and totally converged 'megalonet' will change every business in some way.

You customers will naturally – perhaps unknowingly – turn to the megalonet to find out that you live around the corner, charge £15 an hour and are free on Thursday afternoon. And after they've met you, they will go back to their favoured device to tell others how they rate your service.

There will still be coffee, theatre, flower stalls, childminding, window-cleaning, plumbers, MOTs, childbirth, carnivals, counselling, fruit and vegetables to squeeze, churches and temples, trips to the DIY store on a Sunday and a whole host of things that will never be completely online. Thank God.

So, no, not everything is going to be online. But every piece of information about everything is. So the fact is, if you want keep your head above the water tomorrow, you'll have to learn to swim. And for that, you'll have to dip your toe in the water today.

But be quick

Incidentally, writing this book I thought I had a pretty good grasp of what was going on. I've blogged, twittered, stumbled and set up accounts with nearly all the sites mentioned in this book. Some I use frequently, some I don't. Some seem to have great potential for my business, some are difficult to understand.

So when I invented the word 'megalonet' to describe the future of communications technology (*megalo* from the Greek meaning 'very large' or 'exaggerated' and *net* meaning, well . . . 'net') I thought I'd summed up the power of the convergence and transparency mention above – with a little of the hype that goes with Web 2.0.

Then I found out that there is a fictional company called *Megalo* (within a Korean immersive 3D online game called *Trickster*) which has a product called a *Megalonet 5000* (www.ntreev.com). I might have known.

Your business is changing rapidly. If you haven't already jumped in at the deep end, return to the beginning of this book and get paddling.

APPENDIX

WHAT YOU WILL NEED . . .

If you're really starting from scratch, here's a quick rundown of the hardware and software you'll need.

It's probably stating the obvious, but you'll need a computer (PC or Mac, though some of the tools in the later chapters are designed primarily for PCs), probably a printer, and you'll need an Internet connection. Whatever else you can get free, these are generally not.

I'd also say that you need to sign up to a reputable Internet service provider (ISP) and have a POP3 e-mail account (one that you generally pick up at home or work through your own Internet connection using something like Microsoft Explorer). These are usually provided by your ISP and differ from the online services such as Hotmail and Googlemail which may, indeed, be useful but are generally less well trusted by some of the service providers you may use, such as eBay.

One of the things we recommend is that you set up at least one Hotmail or similar e-mail account. All online services require an e-mail address from you. Sometimes you will want this to be an e-mail address for, say, raising queries or even ordering products, but initially you just want to get access to the site and get accustomed to the way it works. In most cases, you can change your e-mail address or even add alternatives at a later date.

When you register for Web 2.0 sites they seem, inevitably, to ask for decisions about your site that you may want to change later, but with free resources you shouldn't worry: just sign up again later. Sometimes you may want to be fairly anonymous when you're surfing, and with an e-mail address set aside for testing, you can avoid cluttering up your main e-mail account. It's also useful when you want to look at a service from a customer's point of view.

You'll need a set of tools like Microsoft Office. I say 'like' because there are alternatives, some of which are free and, if you don't already have such basic software, could be a good place to start. Have a look for Open Office (www.openoffice.org) and also at Mozilla (www.mozilla.org).

Open Office (not to be confused with Microsoft's Office or Office Live, which we looked at in Chapters 4 and 5) is a suite of programs that allow you to write documents, edit pictures and make presentations just like Microsoft . . . but it's free. Just visiting the website gives you an indication of the way such open-source projects work: by inviting collaboration from users.

Similarly, Mozilla (and the related products such as Firefox) is open-source and offers tools ideally suited for online small businesses that need to handle e-mail and browsing, but also help you to create Web pages and other online marketing 'assets'. It's worth spending a little while playing with the various Mozilla-related tools to see what they can do; for example, many of the sites and applications described in this book can be incorporated into Mozilla's SeaMonkey browser as easily as they can into Internet Explorer from Microsoft by the use of small add-on programs. Your browser can then become more like a 'dashboard' for your online activities.

Practising setting up small Web pages is useful because it will introduce you to some of the basics of HTML. You won't need to know much, but occasionally you will want to tweak things online – by using switches like <b> for bold type (followed by </b> to switch it off) – and to cut and paste larger chunks of code into templates.

It all sounds a bit tricky and technical, and it can be, so a little preparation is usually rewarded. However, there is plenty of help available online, and I have tried to point you in the right direction in the relevant chapters.

Apart from being free, these open-source versions of browsers and other programs have another advantage: they are usually less susceptible to viruses and hacking. Because they have fewer users, there is less of an incentive for hackers and spammers. In addition, however, to protect your PC anyway you should look to install several defensive products.

Two free ones that protect you against spyware and adware and are frequently updated are Spybot Search & Destroy (www.safer-networking. org) and Adaware (www.lavasoft.com). It's also worth paying for a full version of an anti-virus program, such as those from Symantec (www. symantec.com). It's also worth considering the wide range of programs available free from Google – simply go to http://pack.google.com. Again, we considered some of these in Chapter 5.

For most people (certainly in the UK), broadband access is now the standard. Dial-up accounts can be used, but they are clumsy and tie up your phone line. If you're in business, you may well want to use your computer for hours at a time *and* be able to speak to customers, suppliers . . . even friends and family, as you do so. There are so many new broadband packages springing up each day so simply shop around, but take into account other people's recommendations. And, given the number of things you could be doing simultaneously online, you need the bandwidth. You can find recommendations at www. ispreview.co.uk.

There are a couple of other things you could look at. If you're out of the office all the time (or indeed you prefer to work in Starbucks and save on office rental), a BlackBerry®-style phone is a big help. It doesn't have to be that particular brand, of course: you can now find several phone packages that will push e-mail out to your phone, and plenty of phones that will enable you to read and respond. One of my favourites was the recent offer from 3 (the UK 3G provider, www.three.co.uk) which bundled an Internet connection with a low-price monthly rental and included a Skype account. See Chapter 12 for other add-ons that might help you manage your business.

Portable data storage is becoming cheaper week by week, and it's possible to get 20 to 40 gigabytes of storage no bigger than a pack of cards. Online, this kind of pocket hard disk drive (HDD) can cost as less than £30. Larger, less portable storage, vital for backing up all your records and transactions, is more expensive, but around £100 (for 250GB) is a smallish price to pay to keep your business going.

A free version of SyncBack (version 3.2.18.0 is at www.2brightsparks. com) will help you with regular back-ups; you can set this to copy certain files every night, others weekly and so on. It can also help you keep copies on a remote server, which would be useful if your house burnt down with computer and back-up drive inside! Some of the tools in Chapter 5 will also help with keeping your data secure and yet accessible.

If you have a small, portable drive – even a reasonably-sized USB pen – and you add to this a product like Dmailer (www.dmailer.com; free to try but selling at about $40), it's possible to take your virtual office with you, especially useful if you find yourself using clients' computers or Internet cafés. Dmailer copies all your e-mail and Internet settings, along with any other files you think are vital, on to any portable device. It can be just a few megabytes (if you're careful) and once done, plugging the device into almost any other PC will enable you to use it as if it is your own – e-mailing, browsing, updating documents – without leaving a trace on the host machine. When you return home, Dmailer will synchronise any files you have used.

Another really useful bit of software is one that keeps track of the numerous passwords you will be using as you move between websites and services. One such is PasswordSafe (http://passwordsafe.sourceforge. net) which is free and enables you to use complex unguessable passwords and to automatically paste them into the relevant sites as you access them.

Apart from those things, you'll need the usual notepaper and business cards . . . although you might want to just print them when you need to, adding various contact details as they change (and they will) and you want to engage in real-world promotion (see Chapter 7). Some online tools automate the production of invoices or even help with keeping your accounts, so investigate them before splashing out on printing.

Finally, you'll need some confidence. That is, you need to be prepared to try things and see what happens. With almost every 'virtually free' tool, program or website in this book you are able to go back and edit and update profiles, pages, images and settings and you will . . . oh, you will. So don't worry that you don't get your online marketing quite right first time: no one does. But if it's virtually free, that's okay.

INDEX

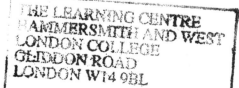